West

FIRESIDE TREASURY OF

GREAT HUMOR

EDITED BY AL SARRANTONIO

A FIRESIDE BOOK · PUBLISHED BY SIMON & SCHUSTER, INC. · NEW YORK

A Fireside Book
Published by Simon and Schuster, Inc.
Simon & Schuster Building
Rockefeller Center
1230 Avenue of the Americas
New York, New York 10020
FIRESIDE and colophon are registered trademarks of
Simon & Schuster, Inc.

Designed by Martin D. Berman

Manufactured in the United States of America

1   3   5   7   9   10   8   6   4   2

Library of Congress Cataloging-in-Publication Data

Fireside treasury of great humor.

"A Fireside book"—T.p. verso.
1. American wit and humor.   2. English wit and humor.
I. Sarrantonio, Al.   II. Title: Great humor.
PN6162.F48   1987   814'.008   87-7524
ISBN: 0-671-63283-3

The author is grateful for permission to reprint the following:
"Cloudland Revisited: Roll On, Thou Deep and Dark Scenario, Roll" from *The Most of S. J. Perelman* by S. J. Perelman, copyright © 1930, 1931, 1932, 1933, 1935, 1936–1953, 1955, 1956, 1958 by S. J. Perelman. Reprinted by permission of Simon & Schuster, Inc.
"A Real Nice Clambake" copyright © 1978 by Calvin Trillin. Originally appeared in *The New Yorker*.

(continued at back of book)

My thanks to Lora Porter and Ellen Smith of the Putnam Valley Library for their help, and to Carol Christiansen for her patient explanations of the Byzantine ways of copyright law.

And special thanks to Tim McGinnis, editor, humorist, for his many excellent suggestions.

For my
grandfather,
who knew how to laugh.

CONTENTS

INTRODUCTION
BY AL SARRANTONIO

In an oft-quoted line, E. B. White once suggested that we shouldn't try to figure out what humor is. "Humor can be dissected, as a frog can," he wrote, "but the thing dies in the process." Despite his words of caution, though, it seems everyone else *except* E. B. White has tried to define humor. James Thurber called it "emotional chaos remembered in tranquility," and Romain Gary, in *Promise at Dawn*, considered it "an affirmation of dignity, a declaration of man's superiority to all that befalls him." The closest Robert Benchley came to defining humor was to say that a joke is funny only if the jokester and his audience agree on its funniness— something on which Benchley and his audience rarely disagreed. And Stephen Leacock, in *The Saving Grace of Humor*, thought of it as a sort of survival mechanism:

> . . . *we must take adversity with a smile or a joke. Tell any man that he has lost his job, and his "reaction," as they say in college, will be to make some kind of joke about having lots of time now for golf.*

Thomas Hobbes, not famous for his stand-up comedy, saw humor in his discourse on human nature as stemming from a sense of superiority. "The passion of laughter," he wrote, "is nothing else but sudden glory arising from some sudden con-

ception of some eminency in ourselves by comparison with
the infirmity of others, or with our own formerly. . . ."

And then there's Freud. In *Jokes and Their Relation to the
Unconscious,* he admitted the difficulties inherent in the
study of humor. "It is only with misgivings," he wrote, "that I
venture to approach the problem of the comic itself." The
closest he came to finding the roots of humor was to state,
"The comic arises in the first instance as an unintended discovery derived from human social relations." He says that
what is spontaneously funny is rooted in surprise or in an unintended or unnatural ordering of things. He goes on:

> *It is found in people—in their movements, forms, ac-
> tions and traits of character. . . . By means of a very
> common sort of personification, animals become comic
> too, and inanimate objects. At the same time, the comic
> is capable of being detached from people. . . . In this way
> the comic situation comes about. . . .*

Maybe he was thinking of situation comedies with that last
comment? He went on to speculate that once the individual
discovers the techniques of producing the comical, he can
use these techniques for hostile and aggressive purposes.
"But even if such an intention habitually underlies making
people comic," he concluded, "this need not be the meaning
of what is comic spontaneously."

One of the best attempted definitions of humor was Joseph
Addison's. In *The Spectator,* Number 35, he saw humor in an
allegorical sense, explaining its genealogy and disposition:

> *Truth was the founder of the family, and the father of
> Good Sense. Good Sense was the father of Wit, who mar-
> ried a lady of a collateral line called Mirth, by whom he
> had issued Humour. Humour therefore being the youn-
> gest of this illustrious family, and descended from par-
> ents of such different dispositions, is very various and
> unequal in his temper; sometimes you see him putting on
> grave looks and a solemn habit, sometimes airy in his*

behaviour, and fantastic in his dress: insomuch that at different times he appears as serious as a judge, and as jocular as a merry-andrew. But as he has a great deal of the mother in his constitution, whatever mood he is in, he never fails to make his company laugh.

Which brings me to my own definition of humor. Which is, simply, the thirty-five pieces that follow this introduction. They were painstakingly assembled with your good humor in mind, in the hope that they make you laugh.

That, as Joseph Addison so wisely recognized, is what humor is all about, no matter what it's root cause or psychological basis. And, therefore, I think that Mark Twain, S. J. Perelman, H. L. Mencken, Hunter S. Thompson (in my opinion Mencken's natural and culminating heir in political humor), Alan Coren, Jean Shepherd and, yes, E. B. White, along with the other twenty-eight extremely funny authors in this book, make my definition of humor as good as any.

FIRESIDE TREASURY OF
GREAT
HUMOR

CLOUDLAND REVISITED: ROLL ON, THOU DEEP AND DARK SCENARIO, ROLL

One August morning during the third summer of the First World War, Manuel Da Costa, a Portuguese eel fisherman at Bullock's Cove, near Narragansett Bay, was calking a dory drawn up beside his shack when he witnessed a remarkable exploit. From around a nearby boathouse appeared a bumpkin named Piggy Westervelt, with a head indistinguishable from an Edam cheese, lugging a bicycle pump and a coil of rubber hose. Behind him, with dragging footsteps, because of the quantities of scrap iron stuffed into his boots, came another stripling, indistinguishable from the present writer at the age of twelve, encased in a diving helmet that was improvised from a metal lard pail. As Da Costa watched with fascinated attention, Piggy ceremoniously conducted me to the water's edge, helped me kneel, and started securing the hose to my casque.

"Can you breathe in there all right?" he called out anxiously. There was some basis for his concern, since, in the zeal of creation, we had neglected to supply a hinge for my visor, and between lack of oxygen and the reek of hot lard my eyes were beginning to extrude like muscat grapes. I signaled Piggy to hurry up and start pumping, but he became unaccountably angry. "How many hands do you think I got?" he bawled. "If you don't like the way I'm doing it, get somebody else!" Realizing my life hung on a lunatic's caprice, I adopted the only rational attitude, that of the sacrificial ox, and shallowed my breathing. Finally, just as the old mitral valve was about to close forever, a few puffs of fetid air straggled through the tube and I shakily prepared to submerge. My objective was an ancient weedy hull thirty feet offshore, where the infamous Edward Teach, popularly known as Blackbeard, was reputed to have foundered with a cargo of bullion and plate. Neither of us had the remotest idea what bullion and plate were, but they sounded eminently useful. I was also to keep a sharp lookout for ambergris, lumps of which were constantly being picked up by wide-awake boys and found to be worth forty thousand dollars. The prospects, viewed from whatever angle, were pretty rosy.

They began to dim the second I disappeared below the surface. By that time, the hose had sprung half a dozen leaks, and Piggy, in a frenzy of misdirected co-operation, had pumped my helmet full of water. Had I not been awash in the pail, I might have been able to squirm out of my boots, but as it was, I was firmly anchored in the ooze and a definite candidate for Davy Jones's locker when an unexpected savior turned up in the person of Manuel Da Costa. Quickly sculling overhead, he captured the hose with a boat hook, dragged me inboard, and pounded the water out of my lungs. The first sight I saw, as I lay gasping in the scuppers, was Manuel towering over me like the Colossus of Rhodes, arms compressed and lips akimbo. His salutation finished me forever as an undersea explorer. "Who the hell do you think you are?" he demanded, outraged. "Captain Nemo?"

That a Rhode Island fisherman should invoke anyone so recherché as the hero of Jules Verne's submarine saga may seem extraordinary, but actually there was every justification for it. All through the preceding fortnight, a movie version of *Twenty Thousand Leagues Under the Sea* had been playing to packed houses at a local peepshow, engendering almost as much excitement as the Black Tom explosion. Everyone who saw it was dumfounded—less, I suspect, by its subaqueous marvels than by its hallucinatory plot and characters—but nobody besides Piggy and me, fortunately, was barmy enough to emulate it. In general, I experienced no untoward effects from my adventure. It did, however, prejudice me unreasonably against salt water, and for years I never mentioned the ocean floor save with a sneer.

Some weeks ago, rummaging through the film library of the Museum of Modern Art, I discovered among its goodies a print of the very production of *Twenty Thousand Leagues* that had mesmerized me in 1916, and, by ceaseless nagging, bedeviled the indulgent custodians into screening it for me. Within twenty minutes, I realized that I was watching one of the really great cinema nightmares, a *cauchemar* beside which *King Kong, The Tiger Man,* and *The Cat People* were as staid as so many quilting bees. True, it did not have the sublime irrelevance of *The Sex Maniac,* a masterpiece of Krafft-Ebing symbolism I saw in Los Angeles whose laboratory monkeyshines climaxed in a scene where two Picassoesque giantesses, armed with baseball bats, beat each other to pulp in a cellar. On the other hand, it more than equaled the all-time stowage record set by D. W. Griffith's *Intolerance,* managing to combine in one picture three unrelated plots— *Twenty Thousand Leagues, The Mysterious Island,* and *Five Weeks in a Balloon*—and a sanguinary tale of betrayal and murder in a native Indian state that must have fallen into the developing fluid by mistake. To make the whole thing even more perplexing, not one member of the cast was identified—much as if all the actors in the picture had been slain on its completion and all references to them expunged. I daresay that if Stuart Paton, its director, were functioning today, the votaries of the Surrealist film who sibilate around the Little Carnegie and the Fifth Avenue Playhouse would be weaving garlands for his hair. That man could make a cryptogram out of Mother Goose.

The premise of *Twenty Thousand Leagues,* in a series of quick nutshells, is that the Navy, dismayed by reports of a gigantic sea serpent preying on our merchant marine, dispatches an expedition to exterminate it. Included in the party are Professor Aronnax, a French scientist with luxuriant crepe hair and heavy eye make-up who looks like a phrenologist out of the funny papers; his daughter, a kittenish ingénue all corkscrew curls and maidenly simpers; and the latter's heartbeat, a broth of a boy identified as Ned Land, Prince of Harpooners. Their quarry proves, of course, to be the submarine *Nautilus,* commanded by the redoubtable Captain Nemo, which sinks their vessel and takes them prisoner. Nemo is Melville's Captain Ahab with French dressing, as bizarre a mariner as ever trod on a weevil. He has a profile like Garibaldi's, set off by a white goatee; wears a Santa Claus suit and a turban made out of a huck towel; and smokes a church-warden pipe. Most submarine commanders, as a rule, busy themselves checking gauges and twiddling the periscope, but Nemo spends all his time smiting his forehead and vowing revenge, though on whom it is not made clear. The décor of the *Nautilus,* obviously inspired by a Turkish cozy corner, is pure early Matisse; Oriental rugs, hassocks, and mother-of-pearl taborets abound, and in one shot I thought I detected a parlor floor lamp with a fringed shade, which must have been a problem in dirty weather. In all justice, however, Paton's conception of a submarine interior was no more florid than Jules Verne's. Among the ship's accouterments, I find on consulting the great romancer, he lists a library containing twelve thousand volumes, a dining room with oak sideboards, and a thirty-foot drawing room full of Old Masters, tapestry, and sculpture.

Apparently, the front office figured that so straightforward a narrative would never be credible, because complications now really begin piling up. "About this time," a subtitle announces, "Lieutenant Bond and four Union Army scouts, frustrated in an attempt to destroy their balloon, are carried out to sea." A long and murkey sequence full of lightning, falling sandbags, and disheveled character actors occupies the next few minutes, the upshot being that the cloud-borne quintet is stranded on a remote key called Mysterious Island. One of its more mysterious apsects is an unchaperoned young person in a leopardskin sarong, who dwells in the trees and mutters gibberish to herself. The castaways find this tropical Ophelia in a pit they have dug to ward off prowling beasts, and Leutenant Bond, who obviously has been out of touch with women since he was weaned, loses his heart to her. To achieve greater obscurity, the foregoing is intercut with limitless footage of Captain Nemo and his hostages goggling at the wonders of the deep through a window in the side of the submarine. What they see is approximately what anybody might who has quaffed too much sacramental wine and is peering into a home aquarium, but, after all, tedium is a relative matter. When you come right down to it, a closeup of scup feeding around a coral arch is no more static than one of Robert Taylor.

At this juncture, a completely new element enters the plot to further befuddle it, in the form of one Charles Denver, "a retired ocean trader in a distant land." Twelve years earlier, a flashback reveals, Denver had got a skinful of lager and tried to ravish an Indian maharani called Princess Daaker. The lady had thereupon plunged a dagger into her thorax, and Denver, possibly finding the furniture too heavy, had stolen her eight-year-old daughter. We see him now in a mood of remorse approaching that of Macbeth, drunkenly clawing his collar and reviling the phantoms who plague him—one of them, by the way, a rather engaging Mephistopheles of the sort depicted in advertisements for quick-drying varnish. To avoid losing his mind, the trader boards his yacht and sets off for Mysterious Island, a very peculiar choice indeed, for if ever there was a convocation of loonies anywhere, it is there. Captain Nemo is fluthering around in the lagoon, wrestling with an inflated rubber octopus; Lieutenant Bond and the leopard girl (who, it presently emerges, is Princess Daaker's daughter, left there to die) are spooning on the cliffs; and, just to enliven things, one of Bond's scouts is planning to supplant him as leader and abduct the maiden.

Arriving at the island, Denver puts on a pippin of a costume, consisting of a deerstalker cap, a Prince Albert coat, and hip boots, and goes ashore to seek the girl he marooned. He has just vanished into the saw grass, declaiming away like Dion Boucicault, when the screen suddenly blacks out, or at least it did the day I saw the picture. I sprang up buoyantly, hoping that perhaps the film had caught fire and provided a solution for everybody's dilemma, but it had merely slipped off the sprocket. By the time it was readjusted, I, too, had slipped off, consumed a flagon or two, and was back in my chair waiting alertly for the payoff. I soon realized my blunder. I should have stayed in the rathskeller and had the projectionist phone it to me.

Denver becomes lost in the jungle very shortly, and when he fails to return to the yacht, two of the crew go in search of him. They meet Lieutenant Bond's scout, who has meanwhile made indecent overtures to the leopard girl and been declared a pariah by his fellows. The trio rescue Denver, but, for reasons that defy analysis, get plastered and plot to seize the yacht and sail away with the girl.

During all this katzenjammer, divers from the *Nautilus* have been reconnoitering around the craft to learn the identity of its owner, which presumably is emblazoned on its keel, inasmuch as one of them hastens to Nemo at top speed to announce with a flourish, "I have the honor to report that the yacht is owned by Charles Denver." The Captain forthwith stages a display of vindictive triumph that would have left Boris Thomashefsky, the great Yiddish tragedian, sick with envy; Denver, he apprises his companions, is the man against whom he has sworn undying vengeance. In the meantime (everything in *Twenty Thousand Leagues* happens in the meantime; the characters don't even sneeze consecutively), the villains kidnap the girl, are pursued to the yacht by Bond, and engage him in a fight to the death. At the psychological moment, a torpedo from the *Nautilus* blows up the whole shebang, extraneous characters are eliminated, and as the couple are hauled aboard the submarine, the big dramatic twist unfolds: Nemo is Prince Daaker and the girl his daughter. Any moviemaker with elementary decency would have recognized this as the saturation point and quit, but not the producer of *Twenty Thousand Leagues*. The picture bumbles on into a fantastically long-winded flashback of Nemo reviewing the whole Indian episode and relentlessly chewing the scenery to bits, and culminates with his demise and a strong suspicion in the onlooker that he has talked himself to death. His undersea burial, it must be admitted, has an authentic grisly charm. The efforts of the funeral party, clad in sober diving habit, to dig a grave in the ocean bed finally meet with defeat, and, pettishly tossing the coffin into a clump of sea anemones, they stagger off. It seemed to me a bit disrespectful not to blow "Taps" over the deceased, but I suppose nobody had a watertight bugle.

An hour after quitting the Museum, I was convalescing on a bench in Central Park when a brandy-nosed individual approached me with a remarkable tale of woe. He was, he declared, a by-blow of Prince Felix Youssoupoff, the assassin of Rasputin, and had been reared by Transylvanian gypsies. Successively a circus aerialist, a mosaic worker, a diamond cutter, and a gigolo, he had fought (or at least argued) with Wingate's Raiders, crossed Outer Mongolia on foot, spent two years in a Buddhist monastery, helped organize the Indonesian resistance, and become one of the financial titans of Lombard Street. A woman, he confided huskily, had been his undoing—a woman so illustrious that the mere mention of her name made Cabinets totter. His present financial embarrassment, however, was a purely temporary phase. Seversky had imported him to the States to design a new helicopter, and if I could advance him a dime to phone the designer that he had arrived, I would be amply reimbursed. As he vanished into oblivion cheerily jingling my two nickels, the old lady sharing my bench put down her knitting with a snort.

"Tommyrot!" she snapped. "Hunh, you must be a simpleton. That's the most preposterous balderdash I ever heard of."

"I *am* a simpleton, Madam," I returned with dignity, "but you don't know beans about balderdash. Let me tell you a movie I just saw." No sooner had I started to recapitulate it than her face turned ashen, and without a word of explanation she bolted into the shrubbery. An old screwbox, obviously. Oh, well, you can't account for anything nowadays. Some of the stuff that goes on, it's right out of a novel by Jules Verne.

A REAL NICE CLAMBAKE

I think it's only prudent to be wary about accepting an invitation to attend a clambake at a gentlemen's club. I have always thought of a clambake as a long picnic whose atmosphere is somewhere between informal and roistering— the sort of event that ends late in the evening with bad sunburns and worse singing and a demand by the big fellow who has had too much beer that everyone help him display his strength by forming a pyramid on his stomach. Wouldn't a gentlemen's-club version of that event result in a lot of sand getting down into the leather armchairs? My suspicion that a gentlemen's club might be an unusually formal setting for a clambake was confirmed by the person who had in fact phoned to invite me to a clambake at the Squantum club, in Providence—Donald Breed, a reporter for the Providence *Journal.* As a new member of the club, Breed showed up for his first clambake not long ago wearing a sport coat but no tie, and was drawn aside by the steward, who reminded him, in a kindly sort of way, that he was not properly dressed for the occasion. As it happens, I would be wary about accepting an invitation to eat anything at a gentlemen's club. Some years ago, in the course of attending a round of weddings just after college graduation, I stumbled across a simple truth about clubs in America: the tastelessness of the food varies in direct proportion to the exclusiveness of the club. The discovery came to me during a wedding reception on the North Shore of

Long Island, about the time I finished a canapé that I had an-
alyzed as a small section of Kraft pre-sliced American cheese
resting on a quarter of a piece of middle-aged Wonder bread.
After many years of trying to figure out why fancy clubs have
such awful food, I have finally arrived at an explanation that
seems logical: the food in such places is so tasteless because
the members associate spices and garlic with just the sort of
people they're trying to keep out.

When I spoke to Breed on the telephone, I got the impression that the Squantum club is, as men's clubs go, fairly flexible about bloodlines—although not to the point of retaining a
chef who goes heavy on the oregano and schmalz. Breed told
me that the Squantum had actually been founded, in the
mid-nineteenth century, by people who were drawn together
by a strong interest in eating seafood—it is built on a point
that juts into Narragansett Bay—and that it had never strayed
from the values of its founders to the extent of installing anything like a golf course or a sauna bath. Breed said that the
Squantum bake could provide a sort of warmup for the first
public bake of the season at Francis Farm a few days later—
Francis Farm, in Rehoboth, Massachusetts, not far from Providence, being a place that stages clambakes of the sort that
last all day and include horseshoe pitching and may even fea-
ture, now and then, a big fellow who wants everyone to form a
pyramid on his stomach. I told Breed I would be pleased to
join him at the Squantum, and he asked me—in the discreet
way people ask these days, when anybody might show up anywhere wearing anything—if I happened to own a necktie.

Like a lot of serious shellfish eaters I have encountered
over the years, Breed had a landlocked childhood—in north-
western Illinois, near the Wisconsin state line. He was fortunate enough to come to roost in a section of the Northeast
where the custom of clambakes remains strong. People all
over New England, of course, have always baked clams on the
beach—built a fire of hardwood over stones that will retain
the heat, then piled on four or five inches of rockweed that
pops and sizzles as it steams—but the custom seems particu-

larly institutionalized around Providence. Elderly people in the area speak of going by horse and buggy earlier in the century to annual clambakes that are still being held—the Hornbine Church Bake, for instance, or the Moosup Valley Grange Bake. There are said to be old-timers around Providence who can tell from the taste of a clam not just where it came from but whether it was baked over oak or cherry.

Around Narragansett Bay, in fact, the tradition of clambakes seems to have outlasted the clams. Although there are still enough quahogs in the bay for chowder, the clams that are actually baked on a clambake tend to be soft-shell clams trucked in from Maine. The Narragansett clam supply has been cut by pollution, of course. According to some work being done at the University of Rhode Island, though, an equally serious threat to the supply of clams and flounder and cod and tuna and the other seafoods traditionally eaten in this country is the rigidity of American notions about which fish is and which fish is not fit to eat. A project at U.R.I. has been doing what it can do for the popularity of such "underutilized species" as the ocean pout, a fish that looks almost as bad as it sounds, and the dogfish, which the Rhode Island specialists prefer to call the grayfish. One of the people involved, Spiros Constantinides, told me that the strain on the clam supply could be eased if people simply utilized the available mussels and whelks as well. If the University of Rhode Island folks had their way, high-school productions of "Carousel" would probably include a song entitled "This Was a Real Nice Whelk Bake."

I like mussels myself, and I think that over the years I have done my share to see that they are not underutilized. But I also like clams. I like steamed clams and clams on the half shell—although the first time I saw one of those, when I was fresh from my own landlocked childhood, I thought it was some sort of mistake. I love fried clams. I suppose my favorite clam dish is something called Soft Clam Belly Broil, a specialty of Gage & Tollner, in Brooklyn, and I might as well admit that my pleasure in downing an order used to be en-

hanced rather than diminished by imagining that some un-
wary traveller on some lonely turnpike was, at that very moment, eating necks that had been cut off my clam bellies and
buried in batter. (I eventually learned that turnpike fried
clams are made not with discarded clam necks but with strips
cut from an ocean clam—a creature of the size to produce the
sort of ashtrays favored by chain smokers.) I like clam chowder so much that I have occasionally been willing to listen to
Boston and New York fanciers argue about whether its base
should be tomatoes or cream—the East Coast equivalent of
the even drearier Southwestern argument about what belongs in chili—as long as I had a bowl of one type or the other
in front of me during the discussion. In fact, almost as soon as
I sat down for dinner at the Squantum—in a huge outbuild-
ing called a bakehouse, which the members had the good
sense to build on a patch of ground that people lacking their
historical perspective might have used for a tennis court—I
realized how the chowder theorists might symbolize the identity problems facing Providence as the large Northeastern
coastal city that is neither Boston nor New York: some places
around Providence, including the Squantum, make clam
chowder with both cream and tomatoes, so that the bitter argument between red and white is avoided with an ambivalent
pink.

The chowder had been preceded by clams on the half
shell—served at the main clubhouse, a spectacular turn-of-
the-century pile overlooking the bay—and clam broth and
clam fritters. After some sausage and sweet potato and the
baked clams themselves, the waitress brought around a dish
of ice cream. I told Breed that the Squantum bake was a
pretty good feed—considering that it was run by a gentlemen's club fancy enough to line up five forks at each place
setting, and that many of those in attendance seemed of an
age to exercise some moderation about what they ate in the
six or eight hours before bedtime. Breed told me that we were
being served ice cream merely to cleanse the palate for the
rest of the meal. Although I didn't remember any palate

cleansing at the "Carousel" clambake, I followed the example of my host—and then followed it again as he downed some shad and a dish of coleslaw and more potatoes and a small lobster and some Indian pudding. The assembled club members consumed all this with routine dignity, as if they were eating prime ribs of beef au jus with potatoes au gratin and choice of one vegetable.

Breed was already talking about the bake to be held at Francis Farm a few days later. "Go easy on the clam cakes out there," he warned me.

"Aren't they any good?" I asked.

"Delicious," he said. "Small and very crisp. But they'll fill you up for the clams. You have to pace yourself."

"The chowder makes them expand in your stomach," one of the regulars at the Francis Farm public bake explained to me the following Sunday. He was warning me about the clam cakes, and he was popping some of them into his mouth as he gave the warning. Like the Squantum club, Francis Farm has been putting on clambakes for about a century, but, unlike the Squantum club, where only the clams are actually baked over the traditional wood coals and seaweed, Francis Farm is militantly anti-stove. Except for the substitution of iron ingots for large stones, the bake at Francis Farm is done the way it has always been done—starting with a four-foot-high hardwood fire. As the fire burns down, a troupe of college boys appears, like travelogue natives who have always known their role in the ritual. The coals and ingots are raked smooth, bags of rockweed are piled on, a screen is placed over the rockweed, just about everything anybody intends to eat is placed on the screen, and the entire pile is covered with canvases until the college boys return an hour later to "pull the bake." Francis Farm uses the traditional fire to bake clams, lobsters, sausage, potatoes, filet of pollack, onions, and even stuffing. George Taylor—who, along with his father-in-law, Frank Miller, bought the clambake operation from the Francis family twenty years ago—likes to say that everything is done "on the bake" except the chowder and the clam cakes, the watermelon, the coffee, and the condiments.

Most of the clambakes staged at Francis Farm are private—for a lodge gathering, say, or a company picnic or a high-school reunion. The grounds are arranged like back-to-back summer camps—summer camps where everyone is well fed and not homesick and allowed to drink beer without worrying about the counsellors—and there are two clambakes a day every day of the summer. A lot of organizations come back the same day every year; the Red Men Lodge has thrown a clambake at Francis Farm on the first Saturday in August for the past fifty-seven years. A true joiner, of course, can manage several cracks at the clams every summer. Tom Brady, for instance, a vice-president of the Old Colony Coöperative Bank of Providence, comes once a summer with the Rhode Island Commandery of the Military Order of Foreign Wars, once with the Sons of Irish Kings, and once for his bank's annual picnic. He apparently is still not able to get his fill: I met him at a public bake.

Francis Farm holds nine or ten public clambakes a summer—building up to a crowd of seven or eight hundred people by August—and even those bakes seem dominated by regulars. The man sitting across from me—Dick Lundgren, a sales engineer who works in Providence and lives in Seekonk, Massachusetts—has been going to bakes at Francis Farm on and off for forty years, ever since, as a child, he accompanied his father to the annual bake of the Seekonk Volunteer Fire Department. He attends most of the public bakes, and he always sits at the same table with Len Estes, who ran boiler rooms for one enterprise or another before he retired in Newport, and Ed Gardner, a grounds keeper for the University of Rhode Island, in Kingston. The regulars call each other by their last names—perhaps because last names are written in marking pen on the paper tablecloth in front of each place—and what they say tends to be something like "Pass the melted butter, Gardner" or "Are there any more clams over there, Estes?"

I was hungry, and I was feeling particularly virtuous, having dined the previous evening on broiled scup—a fish that sounds bad enough to be an underutilized species, although it happens to taste very good. Still, I tried to pace myself to leave room for the dishes Breed had recommended highly—the clams and the onions and the pollack. The regulars next to me continued to hand out their own pacing advice, ignoring it all the while. Down the table, Breed seemed to be eating everything indiscriminately. Next to him, Tom Brady was eating in his own clambake style—pouring melted butter into a coffee cup and then tossing everything into it, like a Chinese eater constantly adding to a bowl of rice. ("Not everything," Brady told me later, in the tone of someone accused of using the wrong fork. "I never put in the stuffing.")

When I commented on the steady eating, I was informed by the regulars that the most serious eater among them, a Boston maintenance man named Vastow, had not shown up. At the final bake of last season, Vastow had apparently mentioned that he would be changing jobs, and some of the regulars surmised that he was no longer able to get away on Sundays. It sounded as if Vastow needed all of a Sunday to make it to the clambake, since he was said to take a train to Providence, a bus to Rehoboth, and, unless someone stopped to pick him up, a hike of two or three miles from Route 44 to the farm. "He's very skinny," Lundgren told me, "but he always has four bowls of chowder."

"He always heaps the last bowl high and covers it with a plate so it stays warm while he starts in on the clam cakes," one of the regulars said. "Then he takes a little walk, and comes back and finishes it off."

We were on the baked clams ourselves at the time. The waitress returned regularly to fill the platters, and Estes complained regularly about finding too many broken shells without clams. I was finding Breed's recommendations well considered. A clambake clam tastes like a steamer enhanced by a slight smoky flavor—and the same flavor works particularly well with fish and onions. "He's more than six feet tall," Estes said, talking of Vastow again.

"Completely bald," Lundgren added as he reached for more clams. "Doesn't drive a car."

"Mostly shells here," Estes said, picking around at the bowl of clams. "This must be the bottom of the barrel."

The waitress brought more clams and more onions and more brown bread and more sweet potatoes and more white potatoes. "Yes, sir," someone said. "He can eat four bowls of chowder, then go to the bar for a beer."

"He's six foot six and thin as a rail," Estes said. "He must be about a foot wide." Estes turned to Gardner. "Wouldn't you say about a foot wide?"

"Yeah, about a foot," Gardner said between bites of pollack.

The regulars were still talking about Vastow as they finished off their watermelon. Suddenly, the meal was over, and they disappeared. A private clambake at Francis Farm usually lasts most of the day—there is ordinarily a break of a few hours for recreation between the clam-cake-and-chowder course and the time the bake is pulled—but some regulars at a public bake just show up to eat. I went to compliment George Taylor on the meal and to ask him if there really is a storied eater named Vastow.

"Oh, yeah—he looks like Silas Marner," said Taylor, who used to be a high-school teacher. "I don't know what became of him today."

I still think about Vastow, particularly when I'm hungry for clams. I can see him rising early in the morning in Boston, carefully straightening his small room, and silently setting out for the long journey to Rehoboth. "It's Vastow," one of his neighbors says to another. "Off again—wherever he goes." At South Station, he digs an old-fashioned coin purse out of his pocket and buys a round-trip ticket to Providence. He stares out of the window on the train, thinking of clam cakes. At the bus station in Providence, the ticket agent just nods, and punches out a round trip to Rehoboth. *"Bon appétit,"* the agent says. Vastow nods silently. He walks in from route 44 toward Francis Farm—a steady pace, surprisingly graceful for a man who is six feet six inches tall and only a foot wide.

Someone picks him up for the last mile or so—a fan, who says, "Four bowls today, Vastow?" Vastow smiles. Then they are at Francis Farm. The bake has been on for half an hour. Puffs of smoke escaping from under the canvas carry the smell of clams and onions. It is time for the chowder. Vastow sits down to eat.

HOW TO WRITE GOOD

"If I could not earn a penny from my writing, I would earn my livelihood at something else and continue to write at night."

—Irving Wallace

"Financial success is not the only reward of good writing. It brings to the writer rich inner satisfactions as well."

—Elliot Foster
Director of Admissions
Famous Writers School

INTRODUCTION

A long time ago, when I was just starting out, I had the good fortune to meet the great Willa Cather. With all the audacity of youth, I asked her what advice she would give the would-be-writer and she replied:

"My advice to the would-be-writer is that he start slowly, writing short un-demanding things, things such as telegrams, flip-books, crank letters, signature scarves, spot quizzes, capsule summaries, fortune cookies and errata. Then, when he feels he's ready, move up to the more challenging items such as mandates, objective correlatives, passion plays, pointless diatribes, minor classics, *manifestos, mezzotints, oxymora, exposés, broadsides and papal bulls.*

And above all, never forget that the pen is mightier than the plowshare. By this I mean that writing, all in all, is a hell of a lot more fun than farming. For one thing, writers seldom, if ever, have to get up at five o'clock in the morning and shovel manure. As far as I'm concerned, that gives them the edge right there."

She went on to tell me many things, both wonderful and wise, probing the secrets of her craft, showing how to weave a net of words and capture the fleeting stuff of life. Unfortunately, I've forgotten every bit of it.

I do recall, however, her answer when I asked "If you could only give me one rule to follow, what would it be?" She paused, looked down for a moment, and finally said, "Never wear brown shoes with a blue suit."

There's very little I could add to that except to say "Go to it and good luck!"

LESSON 1 · THE GRABBER

The "grabber" is the initial sentence of a novel or short story designed to jolt the reader out of his complacency and arouse his curiosity, forcing him to press onward. For example:

"It's no good, Alex," she rejoined, "Even if I did love you, my father would never let me marry an alligator."

The reader is immediately bombarded with questions, questions such as: "Why won't her father let her marry an alligator?" "How come she doesn't love him?" and "Can she learn to love him in time?" The reader's interest has been "grabbed"!

Just so there'll be no misunderstanding about grabbers, I've listed a few more below:

"I'm afraid you're too late," sneered Zoltan. "The fireplace has already flown south for the winter!"

Sylvia lay sick among the silverware . . .

"Chinese vegetables mean more to me than you do, my dear," Charles remarked to his wife, adding injury to insult by lodging a grapefruit knife in her neck.

One morning Egor Samba awoke from uneasy dreams to find himself transformed into a gigantic Volkswagen.

"I have in my hands," Professor Willowbee exclaimed, clutching a sheaf of papers in his trembling fingers and pacing in circles about the carpet while I stood at the window, barely able to make out the Capitol dome through the thick, churning fog that rolled in off the Potomac, wondering to myself what matter could possibly be so urgent as to bring the distinguished historian bursting into my State Department office at this unseemly hour, "definitive proof that Abraham Lincoln was a homo!"

These are just a handful of the possible grabbers. Needless to say, there are thousands of others, but if you fail to think of them, feel free to use any or all of these.

LESSON 2 · THE ENDING

All too often, the budding author finds that his tale has run its course and yet he sees no way to satisfactorily end it, or, in literary parlance, "wrap it up." Observe how easily I resolve this problem:

Suddenly, everyone was run over by a truck.
—THE END—

If the story happens to be set in England, use the same ending, slightly modified:

Suddenly, everyone was run over by a lorry.
—THE END—

If set in France:

Soudainement, tout le monde était écrasé par un camion.
—FINIS—

You'll be surprised at how many different settings and situations this ending applies to. For instance, if you were writing a story about ants, it would end "Suddenly, everyone was run over by a centipede." In fact, this is the only ending you ever need use.*

> *WARNING—*If you are writing a story about trucks, do* not *have the trucks run over by a truck.* Have the trucks run over by a *mammoth truck.*

LESSON 3 · CHOOSING A TITLE

A friend of mine recently had a bunch of articles rejected by the *Reader's Digest* and, unable to understand why, he turned to me for advice. I spotted the problem at a glance. His titles were all wrong. By calling his pieces such things as "Unwed Mothers—A Head Start on Life," "Cancer—The Incurable Disease," "A Leading Psychologist Explains Why There Should Be More Violence on Television," "Dognappers I Have Known and Loved," "My Baby Was Born Dead and I Couldn't Care Less" and "Pleasantville—Last of the Wide-Open Towns," he had seriously misjudged his market. To steer him straight, I drew up this list of all-purpose, surefire titles:

> ———*at the Crossroads*
> *The Case for*———
> *The Role of*———
> *Coping with Changing*———
> *A Realistic Look at*———
> *The*———*Experience*
> *Bridging the*———*Gap*
> *A*———*for All Seasons*

Simply fill in the blanks with the topic of your choice and, if that doesn't work, you can always resort to the one title that never fails:

South America, the Sleeping Giant on Our Doorstep

LESSON 4 · EXPOSITION

Perhaps the most difficult technique for the fledgling writer to master is the proper treatment of exposition. Yet watch the sly, subtle way I "set the scene" of my smash play, *The Last to Know*, with a minimum of words and effort.

(The curtain opens on a tastefully appointed dining room, the table ringed by men in tuxedos and women in costly gowns. There is a knock at the door.)

Lord Overbrooke:

Oh, come in Lydia. Allow me to introduce my dinner guests to you.

This is Cheryl Heatherton, the madcap soybean heiress whose zany antics actually mask a heart broken by her inability to meaningfully communicate with her father, E. J. Heatherton, seated to her left, who is too caught up in the heady world of high finance to sit down and have a quiet chat with his own daughter, unwanted to begin with, disposing of his paternal obligations by giving her everything, everything but love, that is.

Next to them sits Geoffrey Drake, a seemingly successful merchant banker trapped in an unfortunate marriage with a woman half his age, who wistfully looks back upon his days as the raffish Group Captain of an R.A.F. bomber squadron that flew eighty-one missions over Berlin, his tortured psyche refusing to admit, despite frequent nightmares in which, dripping with sweat, he wakes screaming, "Pull it up! Pull it up, I say! I can't hold her any longer! We're losing altitude! We're going down! Jerry at three o'clock! Aaaaaaaaaaaaaaaggh!", that his cowardice and his cowardice alone was responsible for the loss of his crew and "Digger," the little Manchester terrier who was their mascot.

The empty chair to his right was vacated just five minutes ago by Geoffrey's stunning wife, twenty-three-year-old, golden-tressed Edwina Drake, who, claiming a severe migraine, begged to be excused that she might return home and rest, whereas, in reality, she is, at this moment, speeding to the arms of another man, convinced that if she can steal a little happiness now, it doesn't matter who she hurts later on.

The elderly servant preparing the Caviar en Socle is Andrew who's been with my family for over forty years although he hasn't received a salary for the last two, even going so far as to loan me his life's savings to cover my spiraling gambling debts but it's only a matter of time before I am exposed as a penniless fraud and high society turns its back on me.

The dark woman opposite me is Yvonne de Zenobia, the fading Mexican film star, who speaks of her last movie as though it was shot only yesterday, unwilling to face the fact that she hasn't been before the cameras in nearly fifteen years; unwilling to confess that her life has been little more than a tarnished dream.

As for her companion, Desmond Trelawney, he is an unmitigated scoundrel about whom the less said, the better.

And of course, you know your father, the ruthless war profiteer, and your hopelessly alcoholic mother, who never quite escaped her checkered past, realizing, all too late, that despite her jewels and limousines, she was still just a taxi-dancer who belonged to any man for a drink and a few cigarettes.

Please take a seat. We were just talking about you.

This example demonstrates everything you'll ever need to know about exposition. Study it carefully.

LESSON 5 · FINDING THE RAW MATERIAL

As any professional writer will tell you, the richest source of material is one's relatives, one's neighbors and, more often than not, total strangers. A day doesn't go by without at least one person, upon learning that I'm a professional writer, offering me some terrific idea for a story. And I'm sure it will come as no shock when I say that most of the ideas are pretty damn good!

Only last week, a pipe-fitter of my acquaintance came up with a surprise ending guaranteed to unnerve the most jaded reader. What you do is tell this really weird story that keeps on getting weirder and weirder until, just when the reader is muttering, "How in the heck is he going to get himself out of this one? He's really painted himself into a corner!" you spring the "mind-blower": "But then he woke up. It had all been a dream!" (which I, professional writer that I am, honed down to: "But then the alarm clock rang. It had all been a dream!") And this came from a common, run-of-the-mill pipe-fitter! For free!

Cabdrivers, another great wealth of material, will often remark, "Boy, lemme tell ya! Some of the characters I get in this cab would fill a book! Real kooks, ya know what I mean?" And then, without my having to coax even the slightest, they tell me about them, and they *would* fill a book. Perhaps two or three books. In addition, if you're at all interested in social science, cabdrivers are able to provide countless examples of the failures of the welfare state.

To illustrate just how valid these unsolicited suggestions can be, I shall print a few lines from a newly completed play inspired by my aunt, who had the idea as far back as when she was attending grade school. It's called *If an Old House Could Talk, What Tales It Would Tell:*

The Floor: *Do you remember the time the middle-aged lady who always wore the stiletto heels tripped over an extension cord while running to answer the phone and spilled the Ovaltine all over me and they spent the next 20 minutes mopping it up?*
The Wall: *No.*

Of course, I can't print too much here because I don't want to spoil the ending (although I will give you a hint: it involves a truck . . .), I just wanted to show you how much the world would have missed had I rejected my aunt's suggestion out of hand simply because she is not a professional writer like myself.

LESSON 6 · QUOTING OTHER AUTHORS

If placed in a situation where you must quote another author, always write " [sic] " after any word that may be misspelled or looks the least bit questionable in any way. If there are no misspellings or curious words, toss in a few " [sic] "s just to break up the flow. By doing this, you will appear to be knowledgeable and "on your toes," while the one quoted will seem suspect and vaguely discredited. Two examples will suffice:

"O Sleepless as the river under thee,
Vaulting the sea, the prairies' dreaming sod,
Unto us lowiest sometime sweep, descend
And of the curveship [sic] lend a myth to God."
                                        —*Hart Crane*

"Beauty is but a flowre [sic],
Which wrinckles [sic] will devoure [sic],
Brightnesse [sic] falls from the ayre [sic],
Queenes [sic] have died yong [sic] and faire [sic],
Dust hath closde [sic] Helens [sic] eye [sic].
I am sick [sic], I must dye [sic]:
    Lord, have mercy on us."
                                        —*Thomas Nashe*

Note how only one small " [sic] " makes Crane's entire stanza seem trivial and worthless, which, in his case, takes less doing than most. Nashe, on the other hand, has been rendered virtually unreadable. Anyone having to choose between you and Nashe would pick you every time! And, when it's all said and done, isn't that the name of the game?

LESSON 7 · MAKING THE READER FEEL INADEQUATE

Without question, the surest way to make a reader feel inadequate is through casual erudition, and there is no better way to achieve casual erudition than by putting the punchline of an anecdote in a little-spoken foreign language. Here's a sample:

One crisp October morning, while taking my usual stroll down the Kurfürsten-strasse, I spied my old friend Casimir Malevitch, the renowned Suprematist painter, sitting on a bench. Noting that he had a banana in his ear, I said to him, "Excuse me, Casimir, but I believe you have a banana in your ear."

"What?" he asked.

Moving closer and speaking quite distinctly, I repeated my previous observation, saying, "I said 'You have a banana in your ear!'"

"What's that you say?" came the reply.

By now I was a trifle piqued at this awkward situation and, seeking to make myself plain, once and for all, I fairly screamed, "I SAID THAT YOU HAVE A BANANA IN YOUR EAR, YOU DOLT!!!"

Imagine my chagrin when Casimir looked at me blankly and quipped,

"১৯০২ বেড়েই চম্মো এবর পররাজ্ঞাহা প্রোসডেন্ট রজে ১৯০৭) কিংগ, বাতে."

Oh, what a laugh we had over that one.

With one stroke, the reader has been made to feel not only that his education was second-rate, but that you are getting far more out of life than he. This is precisely why this device is best used in memoirs, whose sole purpose is to make the reader feel that you have lived life to the fullest, while his existence, in comparison, has been meaningless and shabby. . . .

LESSON 8 · COVERING THE NEWS

Have you ever wondered how reporters are able to turn out a dozen or so news articles day after day, year after year, and still keep their copy so fresh, so vital, so alive? It's because they know The Ten Magic Phrases of Journalism, key constructions with which one can express *every known human emotion!* As one might suppose, The Phrases, discovered only after centuries of trial and error, are a closely guarded secret, available to no one but accredited members of the press. However, at the risk of being cashiered from the Newspaper Guild, I am now going to reveal them to you:

The Ten Magic Phrases of Journalism
  1· "VIOLENCE FLARED"
  2· "LIMPED INTO PORT"
  3· "ACCORDING TO INFORMED SOURCES"
  4· "WHOLESALE DESTRUCTION"
  5· "NO IMMEDIATE COMMENT"
  6· "STUDENT UNREST"
  7· "RIOT-TORN"
  8· "FLATLY DENIED"
  9· "GUTTED BY FIRE"
  10· "ROVING BANDS OF NEGRO YOUTHS"

Let's try putting The Phrases to work in a sample news story:

> *NEWARK, N.J., Aug. 22 (UPI)*—Violence flared *yesterday when* roving bands of Negro youths *broke windows and looted shops in* riot-torn *Newark. Mayor Kenneth Gibson had* no immediate comment *but,* according to informed sources, *he* flatly denied *saying that* student unrest *was behind the* wholesale destruction *that resulted in scores of buildings being* gutted by fire, *and added, "If this city were a Liberian freighter,* we just may have* limped into port."

Proof positive that The Ten Magic Phrases of journalism can express every known human emotion *and then some!*

LESSON 9 · TRICKS OF THE TRADE
  Just as homemakers have their hints (e.g. a ball of cotton, dipped in vanilla extract and placed in the refrigerator, will absorb food odors), writers have their own bag of tricks, a bag

* Whenever needed, "Norwegian tanker" can always be substituted for "Liberian freighter." Consider them interchangeable.

of tricks, I might hasten to point out, you won't learn at any Bread Loaf Conference. Most writers, ivory tower idealists that they are, prefer to play up the mystique of their "art" (visitations from the Muse, *l'ecriture automatique*, talking in tongues, et cetera, et cetera), and sweep the hard-nosed practicalities under the rug. Keeping in mind, however, that a good workman doesn't curse his tools, I am now going to make public these long suppressed tricks of the trade.

Suppose you've written a dreadful chapter (we'll dub it Chapter Six for our purposes here), utterly without merit, tedious and boring beyond belief, and you just can't find the energy to re-write it. Since it's obvious that the reader, once he realizes how dull and shoddy Chapter Six really is, will refuse to read any further, you must provide some strong ulterior motive for completing the chapter. I've always found lust effective:

> *Artfully concealed with the next chapter is the astounding secret of an ancient Bhutanese love cult that will increase your sexual satisfaction by at least 60% and* possibly more—
>
> (*Print Chapter Six.*)

Pretty wild, huh? Bet you can hardly wait to try it! And don't forget to show your appreciation by reading Chapter Seven! *

Fear also works:

DEAR READER, THIS MESSAGE IS PRINTED ON CHINESE POISON PAPER WHICH IS MADE FROM DEADLY HERBS THAT ARE INSTANTLY ABSORBED BY THE FINGERTIPS SO IT WON'T DO ANY GOOD TO WASH YOUR HANDS BECAUSE YOU WILL DIE A HORRIBLE AND LINGERING DEATH IN ABOUT AN HOUR UNLESS YOU TAKE THE SPECIAL ANTIDOTE WHICH IS REVEALED IN CHAPTER SIX AND YOU'LL BE SAVED.

> SINCERELY,
> (Your Name)

---

*This insures that the reader reads Chapter Six not once but several times. Possibly, he may even read Chapter Seven.

Or even:

> *DEAR READER,*
>
> *YOU ARE OBVIOUSLY ONE OF THOSE RARE PEOPLE WHO ARE IM-*
> *MUNE TO CHINESE POISON PAPER SO THIS MESSAGE IS PRINTED*
> *ON BAVARIAN POISON PAPER WHICH IS ABOUT A HUNDRED*
> *THOUSAND TIMES MORE POWERFUL AND EVEN IF YOU'RE WEAR-*
> *ING GLOVES YOU'RE DEAD FOR SURE UNLESS YOU READ CHAP-*
> *TER SIX VERY CAREFULLY AND FIND THE SPECIAL ANTIDOTE.*
>
>   *SINCERELY,*
>
>   (Your Name)

Appealing to vanity, greed, sloth and whatever, you can keep this up, chapter by chapter, until they finish the book. In fact, the number of appeals is limited only by human frailty itself. . . .

LESSON 10 · MORE WRITING HINTS

There are many more writing hints I could share with you, but suddenly I am run over by a truck.

                     ——THE END——

BARE ESSENTIALS

London Edition

THE CELEBRITY BULLETIN
10, Dover Street, London, WIX 3PH

London · Paris · Rome · New York · Hollywood

(499·9511 Established 1902)

WEEK OF TUESDAY, 28th SEPTEMBER
— MONDAY 4th OCTOBER, 1976

WHAT THEY ARE DOING THIS WEEK	HERE
MICHAEL PENNINGTON and CHERIE LUNCHI	will open on Tuesday in "DESTINY" at the Other Place, Stratford-upon-Avon.
ALAN COREN and EUGENE IONESCO	will open at the Phoenix Theater on Thursday, in "CARTE BLANCHE"
STAN KENTON and	will appear in concert at the Fairfield

If you ring the number listed above, and if you ask how it comes about that Alan Coren and Eugene Ionesco should be appearing in Mr Tynan's latest flesh-mortifying erotorama, a very nice lady will—as far as it is possible to do so over the telephone—blush, and tell you that it is all a terrible mistake for which they have already apologised to an incensed Mr Coren, whose relatives have been jumping out of high windows rather than face the opprobrium attendant upon the scion of their ancient line running round in public with his clothes off.

Yet despite her fulsomely apologetic denials, may there not still be some unkind souls out there who, when they see smoke, shout 'Fire!'? Is it not possible, I hear some of you say, that literati eke out their paltry livings by leading such devious double lives?

Should I, in short, come clean?

How strange that history is almost invariably made in inauspicious places! To think that the revolution which was to change not just the theatre but the whole tone and temper of modern convention should have undergone its birth pangs at that lowly environ, the Alhambra, Bradford!

We had been engaged to open the second half on that chill February Monday, just a few short years ago: IONESCO & AL, A JOKE, A SONG, A SMILE. We were in our bleak little bedsitter in Mrs Compton-Burnett's Theatrical Boarding House, wiring our revolving bow-ties to the batteries in our hats and polishing the climax of our act (*Ionesco: 'My dog's got no nose.' Me: 'Your dog's got no nose? How does he smell?' Ionesco: 'Awful!'*) when there was the most fearful thumping and barking from the floor above.

'Stone me!' cried Ionesco, snatching off his rubber conk in justifiable irritation. 'How do they expect us to rehearse with all that bleeding racket going on? Are we artistes or are we not?' He hopped to the door on his giant shoes, and wrenched it open. 'IVY!' he roared.

Mrs Compton-Burnett came heavily up the creaking stairs. She pushed a wisp of ginger hair under her mob-cap with a dripping soup-ladle.

'Madame,' said Ionesco, hand on hip, left profile tilted to the bulblight, 'us acolytes of bleeding Thespis are at pains to . . .'

'It's T. S. Eliot,' said Mrs Compton-Burnett, 'he's got that bloody seal upstairs with him again. I don't know how many

times I've told him.' She leaned into the stairwell. 'YOU BRING
'IM DOWN OUT OF THERE, MR ELIOT!' she shrieked. 'I GOT
ENOUGH TROUBLE WITHOUT CODS' HEADS IN THE S-BEND!'

An upstairs door opened, and T. S. Eliot's top-hatted head
appeared over the banister.

'Boris is an artiste,' he shouted. 'You cannot expect him to
spend his days juggling jam-jars on his hooter and his nights
in a bloody toolshed! A seal has his pride, too.'

'Well, some of us is trying to synchronise revolving bows
and funny walks down here,' Ionesco shouted back. 'Don't
bloody mind us, mate!'

'TENANTS OF THE HOUSE!' yelled Eliot. 'THOUGHTS OF A DRY
BRAIN IN A DRY SEASON!'

He slammed the door again.

'Patter!' snapped Ionesco. 'That's all he is, bloody patter.
First house Monday night at Bradford, who gives a toss
whether he should have been a pair of ragged claws scuttling
across the floors of silent seas? Get the seal on, get your plates
up on your sticks, tell 'em the one about the one-legged un-
dertaker, and get off. Never mind your bleeding patter!'

The door across the landing opened, and two fat men in
fright wigs emerged. Between them stood a balding midget.

'I don't think you've met Evelyn Waugh's Harmonica
Fools,' said Mrs Compton-Burnett. 'Evelyn, Alec, and little
Auberon.'

We all shook hands.

'Only trying to rehearse the bloody *Thunder And Lightning
Polka*, weren't we?' said Evelyn, testily. 'Got into the middle
twelve and going like the bloody clappers, suddenly there's all
this shouting, Morris the Musical Dog bites Alec in the leg,
little Auberon falls off his shoulders, bang!'

Mrs Compton-Burnett stroked the midget's pate.

'Did he hurt himself, then?' she murmured.

The midget opened its mouth, and a strange discordant
wheeze came out.

'Only swallowed his wossname, hasn't he?' snapped Evelyn. 'His organ.'

'What will you do?' I said.

'I'll have a heart attack, that's what I'll do,' said Evelyn. 'I'll bang my head on the wall. Better ideas you got?'

'We should never have left Poland,' said Alec.

They went back inside.

'Come on,' said Ionesco, 'we're on in half an hour, and J. B. Priestley's borrowed my bloody monocycle, we'll have to take the short cut across the allotments.'

A far door opened.

'Across the allotments?' cried a voice. 'Why, as you wend your way 'twixt elm and privet, who is this bounding up to you? "Arf, arf!" it goes. "Why, it is Rover the dog!" you cry, "and who is this with him?" "Baa, baa!" "Goodness me!" you exclaim, taken somewhat aback, "what is this little lamb doing so near the pig-sty?" "Oink, oink!" the pigs inform us, their little . . . '

We went back to our own room, and shut the door.

'C. P. Snow,' explained Ionesco. 'A professional to his fingertips. Ever heard his starling?'

I shook my head.

'A masterpiece,' said Ionesco. 'I seen him do it riding bareback at Bertram Mills' one Christmas, I'll never forget it. 'Course, I'm going back a bit now. It was when he was with Compton Mackenzie's Elephant Ensemble.'

'They were great days, I understand,' I said.

'The best, son,' said Ionesco, his eyes moistening. 'Remember Graham Greene & His Krazy Kar? That was one of the Queen Mother's favourites, you know. She used to send Graham a pound of cobnuts from the Sandringham estates every Guy Fawkes' Night. We go back a long way, him and me. I knew him when he was Brian Breene.'

'I didn't know he'd changed his name,' I said.

'Had to,' said Ionesco. 'Started out as a ventriloquist. The dummy used to introduce him, and afterwards people'd come up to him in the street and say "I know you, you're Grian Greene" so he decided to make life easier for himself.'

We packed our props and stage suits in our hold-alls, went downstairs through the reek of cabbage and dove-droppings, and walked briskly through the sleet to the theatre.

Stone-faced matrons thronged the foyer, and bronchitic British Legionnaires, and drunks with Brasso bottles in their hip-pockets, and malevolent small boys a-gleam with bright acne. There was a smell of rainsoaked dandruff.

'Bloody hell!' said Ionesco, the seams lengthening in his sad Rumanian face. 'I'd rather be opening the first half, son, before they've had a chance to get their eye in. It'll be like the bloody Somme after the interval.'

We crept past them, and down the back stairs to the mean little dressing-room we shared with Angus Wilson. He was sitting slumped in the corner, in his horse's head. There was despair written all over the little white legs poking out beneath the dappled torso.

'What's up, then, Angus?' said Ionesco.

The head turned, very slowly, towards us. Its glass eyes rolled.

'Me hindquarters,' it said, 'have gone down with sciatica. I just heard.'

'No!' cried Ionesco, 'old Betjeman not turned up?'

'Crippled,' muttered the horse. 'Lying there like Gregor bleeding Samsa. What am I going to do?'

'*We're* not on till the second half!' I cried, in true showbiz tradition. 'Why don't I do the back legs for you? It's the easy bit, no singing or juggling involved, just the tap-dance at the end.'

'It's very nice of him, Eugene,' said the horse, 'but he doesn't understand, does he?'

'You don't understand,' said Ionesco, to me. 'Angus can't get in a horse with any Tom, Dick or Harry, no offence meant. It's a very intimate relationship. It's got to be built up over the wossname, years.'

'It wouldn't feel right,' said the horse.

'Look,' said Ionesco. 'Suppose we both got in?'

'Don't talk bloody daft,' said the horse. 'Six legs hanging down? We'd look like a giant ant. I'm not billed as ANGUS THE WONDER INSECT, am I?'

'I didn't mean that,' said Ionesco. 'You go off home, me and him'll do your act. The management'll never know.'

'Would you really?' cried the horse.

'Say no more!' replied Ionesco.

We went on fourth, after H. E. BATES, WIZARD OF THE XYLO-PHONE, and we managed well enough, despite some personal embarrassment during the somersault, but when we returned to our dressing-room, we found ourselves to be so sweat-wrung that there was nothing for it but to take off the underwear in which we had performed the act and hang it in front of the electric fire to dry. After which we turned to our mirrors in order to make up for our own act. So intent was I upon this, that I did not notice the smell until Ionesco suddenly turned from his dressing-table and said:

'What's burning?'

'Burning?' I said, 'I don't . . . '

'FIRE!' shrieked Ionesco, and I looked round, and our underwear had not only ignited, but had also set fire to the curtains! As the flames licked the pelmets, Ionesco and I rushed, naked, for the door.

The corridor was packed. C. P. Snow was mooing expertly to himself, The Singing Pakenhams were combing one another's coifs, Cyril Connolly and Doris were shoving cards up one another's sleeves—the exit was completely blocked!

'Come on!' cried Ionesco, and we took off in the opposite direction, not knowing, in our panic, where we were going, until, suddenly, we burst through a door and found ourselves in the middle of the spotlit stage, from which the previous act (W. H. AUDEN, HE FILLS THE STAGE WITH FLAGS) had just made his exit.

The audience roared!

The audience shrieked!

The audience cheered!

'Come on!' I hissed, grabbing his bare arm. 'Let's get off!'

'*Get off*?' cried Ionesco. 'GET OFF? Laddie, we'll never get a reception like this again!' He threw an arm around my naked shoulder. 'I say, I say, I say!' he shouted.; "What's got nine legs, three ears, and walks like my Uncle Bert?'

It was still not too late for me to run, but the applause of the crowd filled my ears, and the smell of the greasepaint, and the blaze of the lights, and all those wonderful things ravished my senses, and . . .

'I don't know,' I replied, 'what *has* got nine . . .'

And after that, we never looked back.

UPON ABANDONING SHIP

Sea disasters have a way of happening in the most unsuitable weather. And it could be for this reason that crews made nervous by the high waves behave in a singularly disconcerting manner, especially those of nationalities without a great seafaring tradition to uphold. Some of these ruffians have been known to come on deck after rifling first class staterooms to commandeer the lifeboats exclusively for themselves. And don't be surprised if you see kitchen hands mounting the davits stretching your good woman's diamond bracelets over their wrists while waving a magnum of crystal brut champagne in one fist and gnawing on a chunk of smoked salmon held in the other.

It is quite understandable that no matter who you are, when a ship is sinking, folk want off with a degree of speed commonly referred to as in a hurry. Adding to this distress is the lack of the ship's company's diligence to the usual protocol and courtesy shown first class passengers. Especially now when this is most needed in the face of cabin and tourist type voyagers invading precincts reserved strictly for first class. So do please be prepared for these previous people to behave just as if their lives were absolutely as important as those travelling in the top privileged condition. It is further quite disconcerting when you remonstrate with those clearly elevated up from the bowels of the ship and making merry free in one's luxurious preserves when they answer you with:

"It's everyman for himself, squire."

However, in such emergency, the casual if not boorish regard paid to you from the more plebeian members of the vessel's passenger list, although it often leaves much to be desired, should under no circumstances be the cause of your losing your perspective in providing for your own survival and that of your loved ones. And you may even venture to employ the otherwise forbidden behaviour of rudeness expected is to be rudeness given and simply shoulder these clodhoppers out of the way.

Nevertheless make it a habit as you leave your stateroom to always take with you a few fistfuls of your more excitingly enticeful valuables. These are awful handy up on deck in the milling and melee when it may be necessary to bargain your way into a lifeboat past a bunch of vintage wine consuming seaport hardened cut throats. It is no joke that a small pouch of uncut diamonds cuts the most ice for this purpose. Especially as you can whisper a description of the contents to your adversary and it won't make you look as crass as the whole slew of folk tendering outright handfuls of vulgar ready cash which even at that moment may be being critically devalued on some international bourse. With the ill luck attendant at such times this whole scene is bound to be during dinner and if so, your evening clothes and natural silk shirt will help vouch for the genuineness of the pouch's contents. And it is a wise precaution to be continually splendidly attired at sea.

Some of the most wretched and heartrending moments of human trial however, have taken place in the wee hours of the morning following the alarm to abandon ship. Again it must be stressed that your clothing should at all times give immediate recognition to your haughty particularity. Your choice of bed wear therefore, must be most meticulous. Attiring yourself in a half arsed manner when you think you are out of sight simply will not do. You will of course see others in slipshod sleeping garments revealing their true and perhaps humbler status than the superior one they were pretending while playing bridge. And to you this display of tattiness should not matter. For as a person of finer feelings there is no doubt as to where your duty lies and social distinctions should not be imposed where children, mothers and other ladies' lives are concerned. Should you suffer any momentary hesitation in this respect, forcefully remind yourself that it is simply not on to save your own neck while ignoring the desperate pleas and cries of help from those weaker and beseeching the safety of the lifeboats. If a ruffian is barring the way use strong words.

> *"Remove yourself you bounder, before I strike you."*
> *"Take it easy on the apoplexy pops and you won't get hurt."*

Under no circumstances let this kind of riposte deter you. It is understandable that only a minute or two previous, you may have been relaxing in the clubby atmosphere of the captain's quarters following dinner on the veranda deck and now over port and cigars you are enthralling a specially selected group of your fellow first class travelling mates with a rollicking yarn over which the ship's chief engineer is hammering his knees in helpless laughter. At that moment back there all the world was yours. Precipitated, savoured and enjoyed as only a vessel underway on the high seas can make it. And now rushing in a fuss in your life jacket which the captain himself chucked to you, you confront at nearly every turn of the corridor some son of a bitch escaped up out of steerage with a bottle of Napoleon brandy to his lips having a whale of a time as he sinks his unsavoury lunch hooks into the elegance of other people's property. This is only the beginning of the heinousness so steel yourself.

If you have no knowledge of seafaring ways the ship's officers especially those of the higher ranks must be looked to at this time for guidance. They will issue you with instructions and if necessary assign you appropriate duties befitting any well known responsibilities you may have held in your terra firma station in life. But don't think because of this, that you know it all. As the ship lists you may start directing your upper class passengers to run appropriately to the highest side and there enjoy this privileged area. It is in this blind pursuit of elite supremacy that many of your patrician folks drown. Plus you look pretty stupid and sheepish with the bunch of your exalted gullibles marooned standing suspended high on a forlorn bulge of hull. Which at its present angle of elevation will make a head busting distance for you all to dive from.

Be mindful also in encountering embarrassment in having to take on your authoritative position. People with whom you have established a passing recognition if not a friendship of happy equality over quoits and backgammon may take it upon themselves to absolutely ignore your commands and rush past lifebelted and clutching their emeralds as if they had never seen you before. Don't hesitate to take action.

> *"Madam. Stop."*
> *"Who the hell are you suddenly telling me to stop."*
> *"Madam I have for the benefit of passengers' safety been put in authority by the executive officer and there also happens to be a celebrity gold star next to my name on the passenger list."*
> *"Well the purser has put me in possession of this famous make of pistol from my safety deposit box and I hope there'll be a rest in peace next to your name after I shoot you."*

Such unthoroughbred behaviour is deeply troubling but should not be taken personally. Not everyone is able in times of stress to adhere to the simple niceties. Especially ocean voyaging dowagers with vast private incomes. In any case ladies carrying pistols do not need your assistance as a firearm is a great aid in securing a place in a lifeboat. And the one this lady is about to board you would do well to keep out of.

EDITHA'S CHRISTMAS BURGLAR

It was the night before Christmas, and Editha was all agog. It was all so exciting, so exciting! From her little bed up in the nursery she could hear Mumsey and Daddy downstairs putting the things on the tree and jamming her stocking full of broken candy and oranges.

"Hush!" Daddy was speaking. "Eva," he was saying to Mumsey, "it seems kind of silly to put this ten-dollar gold-piece that Aunt Issac sent to Editha into her stocking. She is too young to know the value of money. It would just be a bauble to her. How about putting it in with the household money for this month? Editha would then get some of the food that was bought with it and we would be ten dollars in."

Dear old Daddy! Always thinking of someone else! Editha wanted to jump out of bed right then and there and run down and throw her arms about his neck, perhaps shutting off his wind.

"You are right, as usual, Hal," said Mumsey. "Give me the gold-piece and I will put it in with the house funds."

"In a pig's eye I will give you the gold-piece," replied Daddy. "You would nest it away somewhere until after Christmas and then go out and buy yourself a muff with it. I know you, you old grafter." And from the sound which followed, Editha knew that Mumsey was kissing Daddy. Did ever a little girl have two such darling parents? And, hugging her Teddy-bear close to her, Editha rolled over and went to sleep.

She awoke suddenly with the feeling that someone was downstairs. It was quite dark and the radiolite traveling-clock which stood by her bedside said eight o'clock, but, as the radiolite traveling-clock hadn't been running since Easter, she knew that that couldn't be the right time. She knew that it must be somewhere between three and four in the morning, however, because the blanket had slipped off her bed, and the blanket always slipped off her bed between three and four in the morning.

And now to take up the question of who it was downstairs. At first she thought it might be Daddy. Often Daddy sat up very late working on a case of Scotch and at such times she would hear him down-stairs counting to himself. But whoever was there now was being very quiet. It was only when he jammed against the china-cabinet or joggled the dinner-gong that she could tell that anyone was there at all. It was evidently a stranger.

Of course, it might be that the old folks had been right all along and that there really was a Santa Claus after all, but Editha dismissed this supposition at once. The old folks had never been right before and what chance was there of their starting in to be right now, at their age? None at all. It couldn't be Santa, the jolly old soul!

It must be a burglar then! Why, to be sure! Burglars always come around on Christmas Eve and little yellow-haired girls always get up and go down in their nighties and convert them. Of course! How silly of Editha not to have thought of it before!

With a bound the child was out on the cold floor, and with another bound she was back in bed again. It was too cold to be fooling around without slippers on. Reaching down by the bedside, she pulled in her little fur foot-pieces which Cousin Mabel had left behind by mistake the last time she visited Editha, and drew them on her tiny feet. Then out she got and started on tip-toe for the stairway.

She did hope that he would be a good-looking burglar and easily converted, because it was pretty gosh-darned cold, even with slippers on, and she wished to save time.

As she reached the head of the stairs, she could look down into the living-room where the shadow of the tree stood out black against the gray light outside. In the doorway leading into the dining room stood a man's figure, silhouetted against the glare of an old-fashioned burglar's lantern which was on the floor. He was rattling silverware. Very quietly, Editha descended the stairs until she stood quite close to him.

"Hello, Mr. Man!" she said.

The burglar looked up quickly and reached for his gun.

"Who the hell do you think you are?" he asked.

"I'se Editha," replied the little girl in the sweetest voice she could summon, which wasn't particularly sweet at that as Editha hadn't a very pretty voice.

"You's Editha, is youse?" replied the burglar. "Well, come on down here. Grandpa wants to speak to you."

"Youse is not my Drandpa," said the tot getting her baby and tough talk slightly mixed. "Youse is a dreat, bid burglar."

"All right, kiddy," replied the man. "Have it your own way. But come on down. I want ter show yer how yer kin make smoke come outer yer eyes. It's a Christmas game."

"This guy is as good as converted already," thought Editha to herself. "Right away he starts wanting to teach me games. Next he'll be telling me I remind him of his little girl at home."

So with a light heart she came the rest of the way downstairs, and stood facing the burly stranger.

"Sit down, Editha," he said, and gave her a hearty push which sent her down heavily on the floor. "And stay there, or I'll mash you one on that baby nose of yours."

This was not in the schedule as Editha had read it in the books, but it doubtless was this particular burglar's way of having a little fun. He *did* have nice eyes, too.

"Dat's naughty to do," she said, scoldingly.

"Yeah?" said the burglar, and sent her spinning against the wall. "I guess you need attention, kid. You can't be trusted." Whereupon he slapped the little girl. Then he took a piece of rope out of his bag and tied her up good and tight, with a nice bright bandana handkerchief around her mouth, and trussed her up on the chandelier.

"Now hang there," he said, "and make believe you're a Christmas present, and if you open yer yap, I'll set fire to yer."

Then, filling his bag with the silverware and Daddy's imitation sherry, Editha's burglar tip-toed out by the door. As he left, he turned and smiled. "A Merry Christmas to all and to all a Good Night," he whispered, and was gone.

And when Mumsey and Daddy came down in the morning, there was Editha up on the chandelier, sore as a crab. So they took her down and spanked her for getting out of bed without permission.

ADVENTURES OF A Y.M.C.A. LAD

When I reach the shades at last it will no doubt astonish Satan to discover, on thumbing my *dossier,* that I was once a member of the Y.M.C.A. Yet, a fact is a fact. What is more remarkable, I was not recruited by a missionary to the heathen, but joined at the suggestion of my father, who enjoyed and deserved the name of an infidel. I was then a little beyond fourteen years old, and a new neighborhood branch of the Y, housed in a nobby pressed-brick building, had just been opened in West Baltimore, only a few blocks from our home in Hollins street. The whole upper floor was given over to a gymnasium, and it was this bait, I gathered, that fetched my father, for I was already a bookworm and beginning to be a bit round-shouldered, and he often exhorted me to throw back my shoulders and stick out my chest.

Apparently he was convinced that exercise on the wooden horse and flying rings would cure my scholarly stoop, and make a kind of grenadier of me. If so, he was in error, for I remain more or less Bible-backed to this day, and am often mistaken for a Talmudist. All that the Y.M.C.A.'s horse and rings really accomplished was to fill me with an ineradicable distaste, not only for Christian endeavor in all its forms, but also for every variety of callisthenics, so that I still begrudge the trifling exertion needed to climb in and out of a bathtub, and hate all sports as rabidly as a person who likes sports hates common sense. If I had my way no man guilty of golf would be eligible to any office of trust or profit under the United States, and all female athletes would be shipped to the white-slave corrals of the Argentine.

Indeed, I disliked that gymnasium so earnestly that I never got beyond its baby-class, which was devoted to teaching freshmen how to hang their clothes in the lockers, get into their work-suits, and run around the track. I was in those days a fast runner and could do the 100 yards, with a fair wind, in something better than fourteen seconds, but how anyone could run on a quadrangular track with sides no more than fifty feet long was quite beyond me. The first time I tried it I slipped and slid at all four corners, and the second time I came down with a thump that somehow contrived to skin both my shins. The man in charge of the establishment—the boys all called him Professor—thereupon put me to the punching-bag, but at my fourth or fifth wallop it struck back, and I was floored again. After that I tried all the other insane apparatus in the place, including the horizontal bars, but I always got into trouble very quickly and never made enough progress to hurt myself seriously, which might have been some comfort, at least on the psychological side. There were other boys who fell from the highest trapezes, and had to be sent home in hacks, and yet others who broke their arms or legs and were heroic figures about the building for months afterward, but the best I ever managed was a bloody nose, and that was caused, not by my own enterprise, but by another boy falling on me from somewhere near the roof. If he had landed six inches farther inshore he might have fractured my skull or broken my neck, but all he achieved was to scrape my nose. It hurt a-plenty, I can tell you, and it hurt still worse when the Professor doused it with arnica, and splashed a couple of drops into each of my eyes.

Looking back over the years, I see that that ghastly gymnasium, if I had continued to frequent it, might have given me an inferiority complex, and bred me up a foe of privilege. I was saved, fortunately, by a congenital complacency that has been a godsend to me, more than once, in other and graver situations. Within a few weeks I was classifying all the boys in the place in the inverse order of their diligence and prowess, and that classification, as I have intimated, I adhere to at the present moment. The youngsters who could leap from bar to bar without slipping and were facile on the trapeze I equated with simians of the genus *Hylobates,* and convinced myself that I was surprised when they showed a capacity for articulate speech. As for the weight-lifters, chinners, somersaulters, leapers and other such virtuosi of striated muscle, I dismissed them as *Anthropoidea* far inferior, in all situations calling for taste or judgment, to schoolteachers or mules.

I should add that my low view of these prizemen was unaccompanied by personal venom; on the contrary, I got on with them very well, and even had a kind of liking for some of them—that is, in their private capacities. Very few, I discovered, were professing Christians, though the Y.M.C.A., in those days even more than now, was a furnace of Protestant divinity. They swore when they stubbed their toes, and the older of them entertained us youngsters in the locker-room with their adventures in amour. The chief free-and-easy trysting-place in West Baltimore, at the time, was a Baptist church specializing in what was called "young people's work." It put on gaudy entertainments, predominantly secular in character, on Sunday nights, and scores of the poor working girls of the section dropped in to help with the singing and lasso beaux. I gathered from the locker-room talk that some of those beaux demanded dreadful prices for their consent to the lassoing. Whether this boasting was true or not I did not know, for I never attended the Sabbath evening orgies myself, but at all events it showed that those who did so were of an antinomian tendency, and far from ideal Y.M.C.A. fodder. When the secretaries came to the gymnasium to drum up customers for prayer-meetings downstairs the Lotharios always sounded razzberries and cleared out.

On one point all hands were agreed, and that was on the point that the Professor was what, in those days, was called a pain in the neck. When he mounted a bench and yelled "Fellows!" my own blood always ran cold, and his subsequent remarks gave me a touch of homicidal mania. Not until many years afterward, when a certain eminent politician in Washington took to radio crooning, did I ever hear a more offensive voice. There were tones in it like the sound of molasses dripping from a barrel. It was not at all effeminate, but simply saccharine. Had I been older in worldly wisdom it would have suggested to me a suburban curate gargling over the carcass of a usurer who had just left the parish its richest and stupidest widow. As I was, an innocent boy, I could only compare it to the official chirping of a Sunday-school superintendent. What the Professor had to say was usually sensible enough, and I don't recall him ever mentioning either Heaven or Hell; it was simply his tone and manner that offended me. He is now dead, I take it, for many years, and I only hope that he has had good luck *post mortem,* but while he lived his harangues to his students gave me a great deal of unnecessary pain, and definitely slanted my mind against the Y.M.C.A. Even when, many years later, I discovered as a newspaper correspondent that the Berlin outpost thereof, under the name of the *christliche Verein junger Männer,* was so enlightened that it served beer in its lamissary, I declined to change my attitude.

But I was driven out of the Y.M.C.A. at last, not by the Professor nor even by his pupils in the odoriferous gymnasium— what a foul smell, indeed, a gymnasium has! how it suggests a mixture of Salvation Army, elephant house, and county jail!—but by a young member who, so far as I observed, never entered the Professor's domain at all. He was a pimply, officious fellow of seventeen or eighteen, and to me, of course, he seemed virtually a grown man. The scene of his operations was the reading-room, whither I often resorted in self-defense when the Professor let go with "Fellows!" and began one of his hortations. It was quiet there, and though most of the literature on tap was pietistic I enjoyed going through it, for my long interest in the sacred sciences had already begun. One evening, while engaged upon a pamphlet detailing devices for catching boys and girls who knocked down part of their Sunday-school money, I became aware of the pimply one, and presently saw him go to a bookcase and select a book. Dropping into a chair, he turned its pages feverishly, and presently he found what he seemed to be looking for, and cleared his throat to attract attention. The four or five of us at the long table all looked up.

"See here, fellows," he began—again that ghastly "fellows!"—"let me have your ears for just a moment. Here is a book"—holding it up—"that is worth all the other books ever written by mortal man. There is nothing like it on earth except the One Book that our Heavenly Father Himself gave us. It is pure gold, pure meat. There is not a wasted word in it. Every syllable is a perfect gem. For example, listen to this—"

What it was he read I don't recall precisely, but I remember that it was some thumping and appalling platitude or other—something on the order of "Honesty is the best policy," "A guilty conscience needs no accuser," or "It is never too late to mend." I guessed at first that he was trying to be ironical, but it quickly appeared that he was quite serious, and before his audience managed to escape he had read forty or fifty such specimens of otiose rubbish, and following nearly every one of them he indulged himself in a little homily, pointing up its loveliness and rubbing in its lesson. The poor ass, it appeared, was actually enchanted, and wanted to spread his joy. It was easy to recognize in him the anti-social animus of a born evangelist, but there was also something else—a kind of voluptuous delight in the shabby and preposterous, a perverted aestheticism like that of a latter-day movie or radio fan, a wild will to roll in and snuffle balderdash as a cat rolls in and snuffles catnip. I was, as I have said, less than fifteen years old, but I had already got an overdose of such blah in the McGuffey Readers and penmanship copybooks of the time, so I withdrew as quickly as possible, unhappily aware that even the Professor was easier to take than this jitney Dwight L. Moody. I got home all tuckered out, and told my father (who was sitting up reading for the tenth or twentieth time a newspaper account of the hanging of two labor leaders) that the Y.M.C.A. fell a good deal short of what it was cracked up to be.

He bade me go back the next evening and try again, and I did so in filial duty. Indeed, I did so a dozen or more nights running, omitting Sundays, when the place was given over to spiritual exercises exclusively. But each and every night that imbecile was in the reading-room, and each and every night he read from that revolting book to all within ear-shot. I gathered gradually that it was having a great run in devotional circles, and was, in fact, a sort of moral best-seller. The author, it appeared, was a Methodist bishop, and a great hand at inculcating righteousness. He not only knew by heart all the immemorial platitudes, stretching back to the days of Gog and Magog; he had also invented many more or less new ones, and it was these novelties that especially aroused the enthusiasm of his disciple. I wish I could recall some of them, but my memory has always had a humane faculty for obliterating the intolerable, and so I can't. But you may take my word for it that nothing in the subsequent writings of Dr. Orison Swett Marden or Dr. Frank Crane was worse.

In a little while my deliverance was at hand, for though my father had shown only irritation when I described to him the pulpit manner of the Professor, he was immediately sympathetic when I told him about the bishop's book, and the papuliferous exegete's laboring of it. "You had better quit," he said, "before you hit him with a spittoon, or go crazy. There ought to be a law against such roosters." *Rooster* was then his counter-word, and might signify anything from the most high-toned and elegant Shriner, bank cashier or bartender to the most scurvy and abandoned Socialist. This time he used it in its most opprobrious sense, and so my career in the Y.M.C.A. came to an end. I carried away from it, not only an indelible distrust of every sort of athlete, but also a loathing of Methodist bishops, and it was many years afterward before I could bring myself to admit any such right rev. father in God to my friendship. I have since learned that some of them are very pleasant and amusing fellows, despite their professional enmity to the human race, but the one who wrote that book was certainly nothing of the sort. If, at his decease, he escaped Hell, the moral theology is as full of false alarms as secular law.

THE COCKROACH WHO HAD BEEN TO HELL

listen to me i have
been mobbed almost
there s an old simp cockroach
here who thinks he has
been to hell and all
the young cockroaches make a
hero out of him and admire
him he sits and runs his front
feet through his long white
beard and tells the story one
day he says he crawled into a yawning
cavern and suddenly came on a
vast abyss full of whirling
smoke there was a light
at the bottom billows
and billows of yellow smoke
swirled up at him and
through the horrid gloom he
saw things with wings flying
and dropping and dying they veered
and fluttered like damned
spirits through that sulphurous mist

listen i says to him
old man you ve never been to hell

at all there isn t any hell
transmigration is the game i
used to be a human vers libre
poet and i died and went
into a cockroach s body if
there was a hell i d know
it wouldn t i you re
irreligious says the old simp
combing his whiskers excitedly

ancient one i says to him
while all those other
cockroaches gathered into a
ring around us what you
beheld was not hell all that
was natural some one was fumigating
a room and you blundered
into it through a crack
in the wall atheist he cries
and all those young
cockroaches cried atheist
and made for me if it
had not been for freddy
the rat i would now be
on my way once more i mean
killed as a cockroach and transmigrating
into something else well
that old whitebearded devil is
laying for me with his
gang he is jealous
because i took his glory away
from him don t ever tell me
insects are any more liberal
than humans

                          archy

TRUTH IN ADVERTISING

Acting in a spirit of new-found militancy, the Federal Trade Commission recently stiffened its regulations covering advertising to require advertisers to refrain from making claims, demonstrations, dramatizations, broad comparisons, or statistical statements involving their products which they are not prepared to instantly substantiate when requested to do so by the commission. The possibility that the new FTC rules will actually convince advertisers to tell the truth is so unsettling that we are offering, as a public service, three examples of what an honest commercial might be like, to prevent the inevitable onset of mass hysteria should one ever appear.

(*A kitchen. It could be anywhere, but is, in fact, in the studio of a major network. In the sink, on either side of the drain, lurk two stains the size of veal cutlets. The doorbell rings and a comely homemaker admits a well-known female plumber.*)

JOSEPHINE: Hi, there, Mrs. Waxwell. Say, that sinks looks like the scuppers of a frigate. Where did those stains come from, anyway?
MRS. WAXWELL: Oh, the man from the advertising agency put them there. Actually, they're just poster paint. But they *are* identical—he used a micrometer.
JOSEPHINE: Well, this looks like a job for new, improved Cos-

mic, which differs from old Cosmic in that its frankly decep-
tive container is made from aluminum, whereas its predeces-
sor was composed of cheesy old steel.

MRS. WAXWELL: Cosmic? Why not this can of ordinary rock
salt which one of the stagehands has labeled "Another Household Cleanser"?

JOSEPHINE: I'll tell you why! Because only Cosmic contains
Chloraxo, a Beaver Bros. trade name for certain coal tar glob-
ules added chiefly for bulk. Tell you what, let's try your
cleanser against new Cosmic, to which, for purposes of this
demonstration, lye, potassium, formic acid, and iron filings
have been added. You put yours on that stain, and I'll put
Cosmic on this one.

MRS. WAXELL: Due to an arthritic condition, I will be unable to
muster much more scrubbing force than that of a healthy fly.

JOSEPHINE: That's all right, just sort of swish it around while I
grind in Cosmic with the powerful right hand I developed
pitching horseshoes and juggling sash weights. There! Now
let's rinse and see which cleanser did better.

MRS. WAXWELL: Gosh, Cosmic even pitted the porcelain, while
my disappointing, slug-a-bed cleanser just sat there and
fizzed! If in my real life I ever got closer to a kitchen than the
Mariner 7 space probe did to Mars, to wit, five thousand nau-
tical miles, I'd switch to Cosmic in a trice!

JOSEPHINE: Though not in reality a licensed plumber, I must
say that such a move would seem to be indicated!

*(A pair of children, one each of the two leading sexes, are
poised around a pet's dish, into which Mom is pouring something that looks a lot like shrapnel.)*

JUNIOR: Gee, Ma, I sure hope Muffin likes these Kitty-
Krunchies. He hasn't eaten anything for days!

MOM: And no wonder, considering his incarceration in a prop
trunk backstage.

SIS: Say, why do cats crave Kitty-Krunchies? Is it due to the
thin coating of a habit-forming drug which overrides the animal's natural revulsion to these otherwise tasteless nuggets of
pressed cellulose and fly ash, or could it be the powerful feline

hormones added to each and every pellet by the manufacturer to unhinge their instincts?

JUNIOR: Maybe it's their eatability. After all, these bite-size chunks pass right through kitty's digestive system without even stopping for breath, then emerge as an easily disposable, odorless slime that keeps kitty's box as fresh and sweet-smelling as a track shoe!

MOM: Yes, and unlike other cat foods which contain chalky cereals and lumps of unhealthy meat, Kitty-Krunchies are laced with common gravel, which gives cats the weight and stability they need to stay in one place. And what's more, when submitted to a panel of distingushed veterinarians, Kitty-Krunchies were preferred two-to-one over an alternate diet consisting of a leading spot remover and ground glass.

SIS: Here comes Muffin now! Wow, look at him pack away those Kitty-Krunchies!

JUNIOR: Golly, Ma, let's get all the great Kitty-Krunchie gourmet dinners! There are more than eight to choose from, and although the taste-tempting treat illustrated in full color on the outside of the box bears no relation whatsoever to its contents, each one is doused liberally with a different colored lead-based paint to perk up puss's flagging interest!

MOM: That's right, and Kitty-Krunchies cost only pennies a serving, or, if you have no pennies, two quarters and a dime. Get Kitty-Krunchies today!

(A teenager's room. Plenty of penants, five guitars, and a toss pillow imprinted with a road sign. Bob is in a funk as Ted enters.)

TED: Going to the dance on Saturday night, Bob? All the gang will be there.

BOB: Aw, I can't, Ted. As these daubs of red stage paint on my face are intended to indicate, I've broken out in hundreds of sickening pimples. I just can't let the gang see me like this.

TED: Well, Bob, doctors know that the prime cause of acne is enlarged pores, and, say, yours look big enough to plant shrubs in. What you need is Dermathex, the inert jellylike substance that separates the men from the boils and makes carbuncles cry "uncle." Here, I just happen to have a tube of the aforementioned preparation in my chinos.

BOB: How does it work?

TED: Frankly, Bob, a scientific study conducted recently at a major university showed that it doesn't, but then, who trusts a bunch of ivory-tower longhairs, anyway? After all, what do eggheads know about blackheads?

BOB: But isn't it just another coverup cream?

TED: Of course, but why not give it a try? All you have to do is rub it into affected regions. Then, as soon as Dermathex strikes your skin, your facial lymph glands—your body's first line of defense—will slam shut your pores rather than permit the many impurities Dermathex contains to penetrate any deeper. With any luck, once you've managed to remove the tough screen Dermathex provides, your pimples will have packed their bags.

BOB: Hell, I'll try anything.

(That Saturday.)

TED: Hey, Bob, how about that dance?

BOB: You bet! Since my entire face is now as raw as a flank steak, I can say I just fell asleep under the sun lamp. The gang will never know the difference!

TED: Dermathex, it's better than nothing!

THE STORY-TELLER

It was a hot afternoon, and the railway carriage was correspondingly sultry, and the next stop was at Temple-combe, nearly an hour ahead. The occupants of the carriage were a small girl, and a smaller girl, and a small boy. An aunt belonging to the children occupied one corner seat, and the further corner seat on the opposite side was occupied by a bachelor who was a stranger to their party, but the small girls and the small boy emphatically occupied the compartment. Both the aunt and the children were conversational in a limited, persistent way, reminding one of the attentions of a housefly that refused to be discouraged. Most of the aunt's remarks seemed to begin with "Don't," and nearly all of the children's remarks began with "Why?" The bachelor said nothing out loud.

"Don't, Cyril, don't," exclaimed the aunt, as the small boy began smacking the cushions of the seat, producing a cloud of dust at each blow.

"Come and look out of the window," she added.

The child moved reluctantly to the window. "Why are those sheep being driven out of that field?" he asked.

"I expect they are being driven to another field where there is more grass," said the aunt weakly.

"But there is lots of grass in that field," protested the boy; "there's nothing else but grass there. Aunt, there's lot of grass in that field."

"Perhaps the grass in the other field is better," suggested the aunt fatuously.

"Why is it better?" came the swift, inevitable question.

"Oh, look at those cows!" exclaimed the aunt. Nearly every field along the line had contained cows or bullocks, but she spoke as though she were drawing attention to a rarity.

"Why is the grass in the other field better?" persisted Cyril.

The frown on the bachelor's face was deepening to a scowl. He was a hard, unsympathetic man, the aunt decided in her mind. She was utterly unable to come to any satisfactory decision about the grass in the other field.

The smaller girl created a diversion by beginning to recite "On the Road to Mandalay." She only knew the first line, but she put her limited knowledge to the fullest possible use. She repeated the line over and over again in a dreamy but resolute and very audible voice; it seemed to the bachelor as though some one had had a bet with her that she could not repeat the line aloud two thousand times without stopping. Whoever it was who had made the wager was likely to lose his bet.

"Come over here and listen to a story," said the aunt, when the bachelor had looked twice at her and once at the communication cord.

The children moved listlessly towards the aunt's end of the carriage. Evidently her reputation as a story-teller did not rank high in their estimation.

In a low, confidential voice, interrupted at frequent intervals by loud, petulant questions from her listeners, she began an unenterprising and deplorably uninteresting story about a little girl who was good, and made friends with every one on account of her goodness, and was finally saved from a mad bull by a number of rescuers who admired her moral character.

"Wouldn't they have saved her if she hadn't been good?" demanded the bigger of the small girls. It was exactly the question that the bachelor had wanted to ask.

"Well, yes," admitted the aunt lamely, "but I don't think they would have run quite so fast to her help if they had not liked her so much."

"It's the stupidest story I've ever heard," said the bigger of the small girls, with immense conviction.

"I didn't listen after the first bit, it was so stupid," said Cyril.

The smaller girl made no actual comment on the story, but she had long ago recommended a murmured repetition of her favourite line.

"You don't seem to be a success as a story-teller," said the bachelor suddenly from his corner.

The aunt bristled in instant defence at this unexpected attack.

"It's a very difficult thing to tell stories that children can both understand and appreciate," she said stiffly.

"I don't agree with you," said the bachelor.

"Perhaps *you* would like to tell them a story," was the aunt's retort.

"Tell us a story," demanded the bigger of the small girls.

"Once upon a time," began the bachelor, "there was a little girl called Bertha, who was extraordinarily good."

The children's momentarily-aroused interest began at once to flicker; all stories seemed dreadfully alike, no matter who told them.

"She did all that she was told, she was always truthful, she kept her clothes clean, ate milk puddings as though they were jam tarts, learned her lessons perfectly, and was polite in her manners."

"Was she pretty?" asked the bigger of the small girls.

"Not as pretty as any of you," said the bachelor, "but she was horribly good."

There was a wave of reaction in favour of the story; the word horrible in connection with goodness was a novelty that commended itself. It seemed to introduce a ring of truth that was absent from the aunt's tales of infant life.

"She was so good," continued the bachelor, "that she won several medals for goodness, which she always wore, pinned on to her dress. There was a medal for obedience, another medal for punctuality, and a third for good behaviour. They were large metal medals and they clicked against one another as she walked. No other child in the town where she lived had as many as three medals, so everybody knew that she must be an extra good child."

"Horribly good," quoted Cyril.

"Everybody talked about her goodness, and the Prince of the country got to hear about it, and he said that as she was so very good she might be allowed once a week to walk in his park, which was just outside the town. It was a beautiful park, and no children were ever allowed in it, so it was a great honour for Bertha to be allowed to go there."

"Were there any sheep in the park?" demanded Cyril.

"No," said the bachelor, "there were no sheep."

"Why weren't there any sheep?" came the inevitable question arising out of that answer.

The aunt permitted herself a smile, which might almost have been described as a grin.

"There were no sheep in the park," said the bachelor, "because the Prince's mother had once had a dream that her son would either be killed by a sheep or else by a clock falling on him. For that reason the Prince never kept a sheep in his park or a clock in his palace."

The aunt suppressed a gasp of admiration.

"Was the Prince killed by a sheep or by a clock?" asked Cyril.

"He is still alive, so we can't tell whether the dream will come true," said the bachelor unconcernedly; "anyway, there were no sheep in the park, but there were lots of little pigs running all over the place."

"What colour were they?"

"Black with white faces, white with black spots, black all over, grey with white patches, and some were white all over."

The story-teller paused to let a full idea of the park's treasures sink into the children's imaginations; then he resumed:

"Bertha was rather sorry to find that there were no flowers in the park. She had promised her aunts, with tears in her eyes, that she would not pick any of the kind Prince's flowers, and she had meant to keep her promise, so of course it made her feel silly to find that there were no flowers to pick."

"Why weren't there any flowers?"

"Because the pigs had eaten them all," said the bachelor promptly. "The gardeners had told the Prince that you couldn't have pigs and flowers, so he decided to have pigs and no flowers."

There was a murmur of approval at the excellence of the Prince's decision; so many people would have decided the other way.

"There were lots of other delightful things in the park. There were ponds with gold and blue and green fish in them, and trees with beautiful parrots that said clever things at a moment's notice, and humming birds that hummed all the popular tunes of the day. Bertha walked up and down and enjoyed herself immensely, and thought to herself: 'If I were not so extraordinarily good I should not have been allowed to come into this beautiful park and enjoy all that there is to be seen in it,' and her three medals clinked against one another as she walked and helped to remind her how very good she really was. Just then an enormous wolf came prowling into the park to see if it could catch a fat little pig for its supper."

"What colour was it?" asked the children, amid an immediate quickening of interest.

"Mud-colour all over, with a black tongue and pale grey eyes that gleamed with unspeakable ferocity. The first thing that it saw in the park was Bertha; her pinafore was so spotlessly white and clean that it could be seen from a great distance. Bertha saw the wolf and saw that it was stealing towards her, and she began to wish that she had never been allowed to come into the park. She ran as hard as she could, and the wolf came after her with huge leaps and bounds. She managed to reach a shrubbery of myrtle bushes and she hid herself in one of the thickest of the bushes. The wolf came sniffing among the branches, its black tongue lolling out of its mouth and its pale grey eyes glaring with rage. Bertha was terribly frightened, and thought to herself: 'If I had not been so extraordinarily good I should have been safe in the town at this moment.' However, the scent of the myrtle was so strong that the wolf could not sniff out where Bertha was hiding, and the bushes were so thick that he might have hunted about in them for a long time without catching sight of her, so he thought he might as well go off and catch a little pig instead. Bertha was trembling very much at having the wolf prowling and sniffing so near her, and as she trembled the medal for obedience clinked against the medals for good conduct and punctuality. The wolf was just moving away when he heard the sound of the medals clinking and stopped to listen; they clinked again in a bush quite near him. He dashed into the bush, his pale grey eyes gleaming with ferocity and triumph and dragged Bertha out and devoured her to the last morsel. All that was left of her was her shoes, bits of clothing, and the three medals for goodness."

"Were any of the little pigs killed?"

"No, they all escaped."

"The story began badly," said the smaller of the small girls, "but it had a beautiful ending."

"It is the most beautiful story that I ever heard," said the bigger of the small girls, with immense decision.

"It is the *only* beautiful story I have ever heard," said Cyril.

A dissentient opinion came from the aunt.

"A most improper story to tell to young children! You have undermined the effect of years of careful teaching."

"At any rate," said the bachelor, collecting his belongings preparatory to leaving the carriage, "I kept them quiet for ten minutes, which was more than you were able to do."

"Unhappy woman!" he observed to himself as he walked down the platform of Templecombe station; "for the next six months or so those children will assail her in public with demands for an improper story!"

THE END OF BOB'S BOB HOUSE

In the thirties, it was in the basement of the old Vanderbob Towers Hotel. In the forties, it moved into the first floor of the Youbob Building on Fifty-second Street. In the late fifties, it settled in what was to become its final home, the plush revolving lounge on the top of the BobCo Building. No matter where they found it through the years, patrons of Bob's Bob House (and there were many who were much more than patrons—devotees might be a better word) knew that any place old Bob Bobson, God love him, was hanging out there was sure to be excitement, fun, and big thick steaks nearby. I'll never forget back in '54, I'd just been fired by Bill Veeck for alcoholism, and I walked into the Bob House with a face about a mile long. Bob took one look at me and hollered, "Christ, you're *sober,* Doc!" (He always called me Doc. Of course, I didn't have a medical degree, but I did have my own stapling gun. He called me Doc ever since the war, over in Korea.) "Anything you want, it's on me." My God, I drank the place dry that night, and then I had a good solid piece of American grain-fed beef and got in my car and ran over a claims adjuster and ended up in Matteawan State Hospital for the Criminally Insane. That's the kind of guy Bob was.

If you were a friend of Bob's, there was nothing he wouldn't do for you, even to the point of making soup out of your underwear and drinking the broth, as he once did for longtime crony and companion Maria Montessori, the Italian educator. But if you fell among the unfortunate few who Bob considered enemies, then look out: he might refuse to give you a good table or, looking serious, say he was going to put your dog through the bologna slicer. I'll never forget, it was June of '58 and my first ex-wife had just won a thousand dollars a month alimony so she could go and shack up with that big Mennonite buck she used to run with, plus custody of my little son and daughter. I told the judge, "God damn it, she's got the boy sleeping in a basket of fish heads—now, I don't think that's right. She's making my daughter lick dead bugs off the car radiator grille. You think that's the behavior of a fit mother?" Well, hell, she got custody anyway. The judge gave her custody. I suppose he knows better than me.

The only friend I had left in the world in those days was old Bob. I spent most of my time at the Bob House. "Mother of God, Highpockets," he'd say. (Always called me Highpockets. Course, I was only five-eight, but I did have my own cattle prod.) "Highpockets, buddy, let me tell you what happened to my luggage"—and off he'd go on a long involved rigamarole that never failed to make me feel white again.

It was through Bob, of course, that I first met Senator Robert Mebob. This was back before all the controversy surrounding the Committee to Re-Bob Mebob, as we all called it, which Bob got tangled up in with that crazy prank where he and someone on the Senator's staff put a Saltine in a cup of warm tea (an allegation that was never proved, by the way). At any rate, Bob took me over to the Senator's table at the Bob House one night. "Curly," he said to me. (He always called me Curly. Course, I didn't have any hair of my own, but I did have my own meat thermometer.) "Curly," he says, "I want you to meet the Honorable Robert Youbob Mebob—I call him Bob, buddy of mine—he's the greatest guy, he's a helluva guy. God, I love him. I'll bet you didn't know that this guy right here, Senator Bob Mebob, he's the father of my oldest boy, Bobby." Then he grinned and grabbed the Senator in a big bear hug and his eyes filled with tears, and I have to admit I was surprised, even though I knew that Bob's wife, who used to wait tables at the Bob House, was a great and beautiful lady and a fine help-meet and a terrific gal who shacked up with any damned guy she felt like, and a terrific mother who loved to drink and drive. Later, when the Senator got indicted, Bob never forgot him, and once sent him five dozen red roses with a note asking if he was still in love with Otis Sistrunk, of the Oakland Raiders. That's the way it was if you were friends with Bob—you were in love with Otis Sistrunk, although probably you weren't.

Now, after forty years and who knows how many stomachs pumped, they're closing down the old Bob House, where so many of us had such great times and blacked out so many times over the years, and we're sure going to miss it. Of course, Bob has slowed down a lot, and he can't threaten people as well as he used to when he was younger, and that, along with the incident last fall where a bunch of kids broke in after hours and taped live ferrets to the salad bar, has taken a lot of the fun out of the Bob House for him. Bob is moving to Jersey, where he plans to just take it easy and collect moving violations and rifle the desks of guys who know him and trust him, and we wish him the best. I know I speak for everybody else who has known Bob and his Bob House when I say that we love him and think he's the greatest guy and the cutest guy and has done a terrific job not only for the restaurant business but also for the city as a whole.

ITALIAN WITHOUT A MASTER

It is almost a fortnight now that I am domiciled in a medieval villa in the country, a mile or two from Florence. I cannot speak the language; I am too old now to learn how, also too busy when I am busy, and too indolent when I am not; wherefore some will imagine that I am having a dull time of it. But it is not so. The "help" are all natives; they talk Italian to me, I answer in English; I do not understand them, they do not understand me, consequently no harm is done, and everybody is satisfied. In order to be just and fair, I throw in an Italian word when I have one, and this has a good influence. I get the word out of the morning paper. I have to use it while it is fresh, for I find that Italian words do not keep in this climate. They fade toward night, and next morning they are gone. But it is no matter; I get a new one out of the paper before breakfast, and thrill the domestics with it while it lasts. I have no dictionary, and I do not want one; I can select my words by the sound, or by orthographic aspect. Many of them have a French or German or English look, and these are the ones I enslave for the day's service. That is, as a rule. Not always. If I find a learnable phrase that has an imposing look and warbles musically along I do not care to know the meaning of it; I pay it out to the first applicant, knowing that if I pronounce it carefully *he* will understand it, and that's enough.

Yesterday's word was *avanti*. It sounds Shakespearian, and

probably means Avaunt and quit my sight. To-day I have a whole phrase: *sono dispiacentissimo.* I do not know what it means, but it seems to fit in everywhere and give satisfaction. Although as a rule my words and phrases are good for one day and train only, I have several that stay by me all the time, for some unknown reason, and these come very handy when I get into a long conversation and need things to fire up with in monotonous stretches. One of the best ones is *Dov' è il gatto.* It nearly always produces a pleasant surprise, therefore I save it up for places where I want to express applause or admiration. The fourth word has a French sound, and I think the phrase means "that takes the cake."

During my first week in the deep and dreamy stillness of this woodsy and flowery place I was without news of the outside world, and was well content without it. It had been four weeks since I had seen a newspaper, and this lack seemed to give life a new charm and grace, and to saturate it with a feeling verging upon actual delight. Then came a change that was to be expected: the appetite for news began to rise again, after this invigorating rest. I had to feed it, but I was not willing to let it make me its helpless slave again; I determined to put it on a diet, and a strict and limited one. So I examined an Italian paper, with the idea of feeding it on that, and on that exclusively. On that exclusively, and without help of a dictionary. In this way I should surely be well protected against overloading and indigestion.

A glance at the telegraphic page filled me with encouragement. There were no scare-heads. That was good—supremely good. But there were headings—one-liners and two-liners— and that was good too; for without these, one must do as one does with a German paper—pay our precious time in finding out what an article is about, only to discover, in many cases, that there is nothing in it of interest to you. The head-line is a valuable thing.

Necessarily we are all fond of murders, scandals, swindles, robberies, explosions, collisions, and all such things, when we know the people, and when they are neighbors and friends, but when they are strangers we do not get any great pleasure out of them, as a rule. Now the trouble with an American paper is that it has no discrimination; it rakes the whole earth for blood and garbage, and the result is that you are daily overfed and suffer a surfeit. By habit you stow this muck every day, but you come by and by to take no vital interest in it—indeed, you almost get tired of it. As a rule, forty-nine-fiftieths of it concerns strangers only—people away off yonder, a thousand miles, two thousand miles, ten thousand miles from where you are. Why, when you come to think of it, who cares what becomes of those people? I would not give the assassination of one personal friend for a whole massacre of those others. And, to my mind, one relative or neighbor mixed up in a scandal is more interesting than a whole Sodom and Gomorrah of outlanders gone rotten. Give me the home product every time.

Very well. I saw at a glance that the Florentine paper would suit me: five out of six of its scandals and tragedies were local; they were adventures of one's very neighbors, one might almost say one's friends. In the matter of world news there was not too much, but just about enough. I subscribed. I have had no occasion to regret it. Every morning I get all the news I need for the day; sometimes from the headlines, sometimes from the text. I have never had to call for a dictionary yet. I read the paper with ease. Often I do not quite understand, often some of the details escape me, but no matter, I get the idea. I will cut out a passage or two, then you will see how limpid the language is:

IL RITORNO, DEI REALI D'ITALIA
ELARGIZIONE DEL RE ALL' OSPEDALE ITALIANO

The first line means that the Italian sovereigns are coming back—they have been to England. The second line seems to mean that they enlarged the King at the Italian hospital. With a banquet, I suppose. An English banquet has that effect. Further:

IL RITORNO DEI SOVRANI
A ROMA
ROMA, 24 ore 22,50.-I Sovrani e le
Principessine Reali si attendono a Roma domani alle ore
15,51.

Return of the sovereigns to Rome, you see. Date of the telegram, Rome, November 24, ten minutes before twenty-three o'clock. The telegram seems to say, "The Sovereigns and the Royal Children expect themselves at Rome to-morrow at fifty-one minutes after fifteen o'clock."

I do not know about Italian time, but I judge it begins at midnight and runs through the twenty-four hours without breaking bulk. In the following ad. the theaters open at half-past twenty. If these are not matinées, 20,30 must mean 8:30 P.M., by my reckoning.

SPETTACOLL DEL DI 25
TEATRO DELLA PERGOLA—(Ore 20,30)—Opera: Bohème.
TEATRO ALFIERI—Compagnia drammatica Drago—(Ore 20,30)—La Legge.
ALHAMBRA—(Ore 20,30)—Spettacolo variato.
SALA EDISON—Grandioso spettacolo Cinematografico: Quo-Vadis?—Inaugurazione della Chiesa Russa—In coda al Direttissimo—Vedute di Firenze con gran movimento—America: Trasporto tronchi giganteschi—I ladri in casa del Diavolo—Scene comiche.
CINEMATOGRAFO—Via Brunelleschi n. 4.—Programma straordinario, Don Chisciotte—Prezzi popolari.

The whole of that is intelligible to me—and sane and rational, too—except the remark about the Inauguration of a Russian Cheese. That one oversizes my hand. Gimme five cards.

This is a four-page paper; and as it is set in long primer leaded and has a page of advertisements, there is no room for the crimes, disasters, and general sweepings of the outside world—thanks be! To-day I find only a single importation of the off-color sort:

UNA PRINCIPESSA
CHE FUGGE CON UN COCCHIERE

PARIGI, 24.—*Il* Matin *ha da Berlino che la principessa Schovenbsre-Waldenbura scomparve il 9 novembre. Sarebbe partita col suo cocchiere.*

La Principessa ha 27 anni.

Twenty-seven years old, and scomparve—scampered—on the 9th November. You see by the added detail that she departed with her coachman. I hope Sarebbe has not made a mistake, but I am afraid the chances are that she has. *Sono dispiacentissimo.*

There are several fires: also a couple of accidents. This is one of them:

GRAVE DISGRAZIA SUL PONTE VECCHIO

Stamattina, circa le 7,30 mentre Giuseppe Sciatti, di anni 55, di Casellina e Torri, passava dal-Ponte Vecchio, stando seduto sopra un barroccio carico di verdura, perse l' equilibrio e cadde al suolo, rimanendo con la gamba destra sotto una ruota del veicolo.

Lo Sciatti fu subito raccolto da alcuni cittadini, che, per mezzo della pubblica vettura n. 365, lo trasportarono a San Giovanni di Dio.

Ivi il medico di guardia gli riscontrò la frattura della gamba destra e alcune lievi escoriazioni giudicandolo guaribile in 50 giorni salvo complicazioni.

What it seems to say is this: "Serious Disgrace on the Old Old Bridge. This morning about 7:30, Mr. Joseph Sciatti, aged 55, of Casellina and Torri, while standing up in a sitting posture on top of a carico barrow of verdure (foliage? hay? vegetables?), lost his equilibrium and fell on himself, arriving with his left leg under one of the wheels of the vehicle.

"Said Sciatti was suddenly harvested (gathered in?) by several citizens, who by means of public cab No. 365 transported him to St. John of God."

Paragraph No. 3 is a little obscure, but I think it says that the medico set the broken left leg—right enough, since there was nothing the matter with the other one—and that several are encouraged to hope that fifty days will fetch him around in quite giudicandolo-guaribile way, if no complications intervene.

I am sure I hope so myself.

There is a great and peculiar charm about reading news-scraps in a language which you are not acquainted with—the charm that always goes with the mysterious and the uncertain. You can never be absolutely sure of the meaning of anything you read in such circumstances; you are chasing an alert and gamy riddle all the time, and the baffling turns and dodges of the prey make the life of the hunt. A dictionary would spoil it. Sometimes a single word of doubtful purport will cast a veil of dreamy and golden uncertainty over a whole paragraph of cold and practical certainties, and leave steeped in a haunting and adorable mystery an incident which had been vulgar and commonplace but for that benefaction. Would you be wise to draw a dictionary on that gracious word? would you be properly grateful?

After a couple of days' rest I now come back to my subject and seek a case in point. I find it without trouble, in the morning paper; a cablegram from Chicago and Indiana by way of Paris. All the words save one are guessable by a person ignorant of Italian:

REVOLVERATE IN TEATRO

PARIGI, 27. - *La* Patrie *ha da Chicago:*

Il guardiano del teatro dell'opera di Wallace (Indiana), avendo voluto espellere uno spettatore che continuava a fumare malgrado il divieto, questo spalleggiato dai suoi amici tiro diversi colpi di rivoltella. Il guardiano rispose. Nacque una scarica generale. Grande panico tra-gli spettatori. Nessun ferito.

Translation.—"REVOLVERATION IN THEATER. *Paris, 27th. La Patrie* has from Chicago: The cop of the theater of the opera of Wallace, Indiana, had willed to expel a spectator which continued to smoke in spite of the prohibition, who, spalleggiato by his friends, tirò (Fr. *tiré,* Anglice *pulled*) manifold revolver-shots. The cop responded. Result, a general scare; great panic among the spectators. Nobody hurt."

It is bettable that that harmless cataclysm in the theater of the opera of Wallace, Indiana, excited not a person in Europe but me, and so came near to not being worth cabling to Florence by way of France. But it does excite me. It excites me because I cannot make out, for sure, what it was that moved that spectator to resist the officer. I was gliding along smoothly and without obstruction or accident, until I came to that word "spalleggiato," then the bottom fell out. You notice what a rich gloom, what a somber and pervading mystery, that word sheds all over the whole Wallachian tragedy. That is the charm of the thing, that is the delight of it. This is where you begin, this is where you revel. You can guess and guess, and have all the fun you like; you need not be afraid there will be an end to it; none is possible, for no amount of guessing will ever furnish you a meaning for that word that you can be sure is the right one. All the other words give you hints, by their form, their sound, or their spelling—this one doesn't, this one throws out no hints, this one keeps its secret. If there is even the slightest slight shadow of a hint anywhere, it lies in the very meagerly suggestive fact that "spalleggiato" carries our word "egg" in its stomach. Well, make the most of it, and then where are you at? You conjecture that the spectator which was smoking in spite of the prohibition and become re-prohibited by the guardians, was "egged on" by his friends, and that it was owing to that evil influence that he initiated the revolveration in theater that has galloped under the sea and come crashing through the European press without exciting anybody but me. But are you sure, are you dead sure, that that was the way of it? No. Then the uncertainty remains, the mystery abides, and with it the charm. Guess again.

If I had a phrase-book of a really satisfactory sort I would

study it, and not give all my free time to undictionarial read-
ings, but there is no such work on the market. The existing
phrase-books are inadequate. They are well enough as far as
they go, but when you fall down and skin your leg they don't
tell you what to say.

THEY SHOOT CANOES, DON'T THEY?

A while back my friend Retch Sweeney and I were hiking through a wilderness area and happened to come across these three guys who were pretending to cling to the side of a mountain as if their lives depended on it. They were dressed in funny little costumes and all tied together on a long rope. Their leader was pounding what looked like a big spike into a crack in the rock. We guessed right off what they were up to. They were obviously being initiated into a college fraternity, and this was part of the hazing. Not wishing to embarrass them any more than was absolutely necessary, Retch and I just let on as if everything was normal and that scarcely a day went by that we didn't see people in funny costumes hammering nails into rock.

"We seem to have taken a wrong turn back there a ways," I said to them. "Could you give us some idea where we are?"

The three pledgies seemed both angered and astonished at seeing us. "Why, this is the North Face of Mount Terrible," the leader said. "We're making an assault on it. You shouldn't be up here!"

"You're telling me!" I said. "We're supposed to be on our way to Wild Rose Lake."

"Say, it's none of my business," Retch put in, "but this thing you're makin', don't you think you would get it built a lot faster if you found some level ground? It's pretty steep up here."

That didn't seem to set too well with them, or at least so I interpreted from their flared nostrils and narrowed eyes.

"Say, don't let a couple of flabby, middle-aged men disturb you," I said. "We'll just mosey on past you and climb up to the top of this hill and get out of your way. Maybe we can get a bearing on Wild Rose Lake from up there."

Well, I was glad they were all roped together and the rope was fastened to one of the spikes they had hammered into the rock. Otherwise, I think they would have taken off after us, and that slope was so steep you could just barely walk on it, let alone run. They would have caught us for sure.

"Those guys certainly weren't too friendly, were they?" Retch said later.

"No, they weren't," I said. "The very least they could have done was offer to give us a hand with the canoe."

Upon later reflection, I came to the conclusion that it was probably the canoe itself that had disturbed the pledgies. There are people who can't get within fifteen feet of a canoe without turning psychotic or, as my psychiatrist puts it, "going bananas."

I've been around canoes most of my life and have high regard for them. They're versatile and efficient and serve the angler and hunter well. But I have no truck with the sentimental nonsense often associated with them. Some years back I wrecked an old canoe of mine that I had spent hundreds of happy hours in. When I saw there was no way to salvage it, I tossed it on top of the car rack and hauled it out to the city dump. That was it. There was no sentimental nonsense involved. Just to show you some of the strange things that can happen, though, a few days later my wife went out to clean the garage and found the canoe back in its old place.

I had to laugh. "Well, I'll be darned," I said. "The old thing must have followed me home from the dump! Well, if it cares that much about me, I guess we'll let it stay."

After babbling sentimentality, the next most prevalent form of irrational behavior evoked by canoes is raw terror (occasionally there is boiled terror or even fried terror, but usually it's raw). Take my neighbor Al Finley, the city coun-

cilperson, for example. I figured that anyone so adept at floating bond issues as Finley certainly wouldn't have any trouble
floating a canoe—a duck to water, so to speak. I've taught
him most of the paddle strokes and he is quite proficient at
them, but he has never gotten over his fear of canoes.

"Careful!" he screams. "It's tipping! It's tipping! Watch
that rock! Careful!"

The way he acts is absolutely pathetic. I don't know what
he'd do if we ever put the canoe in the water.

Some canoe-induced behavior is so odd you can't even put
a name to it. Take the time I was canoeing up in Canada with
Dork Simp, a chap who had been a staunch atheist for as long
as I could remember. When we saw that we had made a mistake and had to shoot the Good God Almighty Rapids (named
by the first trapper to take a raft of furs down the river), Dork
yelled out that he had recently had some serious doubts about
the intellectual validity of atheism.

"Forget philosophy, for pete's sake!" I screamed at him.
"It's getting rough! Get off that seat and kneel down in the
canoe!"

"Amen to that," he yelled back. "You say the words first
and I'll try to follow along!"

We smacked into a rock and broke several ribs, two of
which, incidentally, seemed to be mine. As we slid sideways
off the rock, Dork shouted out that he had just found religion.

A few seconds later, as we were paddling up out of the vor-
tex of a whirlpool, he swore off smoking, drinking, and pro-
fanity, the last of which cut his vocabulary by approximately
half. When we were at last forcibly ejected from the lower end
of the rapids, Dork said that he had decided to enter the min-
istry.

"It's been a lifelong ambition of mine," he added.

"What!" I said. "Why, not more than fifteen minutes ago
you were an atheist."

"Was it only fifteen minutes?" he said. "I could have sworn
it was a lifetime!"

The weirdest reaction to canoes that I've ever observed
took place in Kelly's Bar & Grill. I had just walked in and

mounted a barstool next to Doc Moos, owner and operator of Doc's Boat Works, where I had Zelda, my old wood-and-canvas canoe, in for repairs. Doc was chatting with a new bartender Kelly had hired, a great dull slab of a man but pleasant enough, or so he seemed at first.

"How's my Zelda doing, Doc?" I asked.

"I got bad news for you," Doc said. "I couldn't save her."

"Oh no!" I moaned. "I can't get along without her."

The bartender gave me a sympathetic look. "Gee, I'm sorry fella," he said. "Here, have a drink on Kelly."

I thanked him brusquely, not wanting him to mistake my concern about Zelda for maudlin sentimentality.

"What went wrong?" I asked Doc.

"Well, first of all, as you know, she was cracked and peeling all over, but that was no real problem since we could have put a new fiberglass skin on her. But . . ."

"You can do that now, can you, Doc, put on a fiberglass skin?" the bartender asked.

"Sure," Doc told him. "It's quite a bit of work and expensive, but it wears forever."

"I bet it does," the bartender said. "But how does it look?"

"Just like new," Doc said. "Paint it a nice glossy red or green and it'll knock your eye out."

The bartender looked astounded. "I would've thought pink," he said.

"Pink!" Doc and I both shuddered. The man was totally without taste.

"Anyway," Doc went on, doing his best to ignore the bartender, "some of her ribs were busted up pretty bad. I was going to work up some new ones out of some oak boards I got in the shop . . ."

"What won't they think of next!" the bartender said. "Wood ribs!"

"But as I was saying," Doc continued, shaking his head, "that was when we found the dry rot."

"Oh no, not dry rot!" I moaned.

"Gee, dry rot," the bartender said. "I think my brother got that once from not washin' between his toes."

"Well, it was fatal for Zelda," Doc said.

"Here, have another drink on Kelly," the bartender said.

Up to this time the bartender had seemed like a decent enough fellow, if only slightly smarter than a grapefruit. Now he started to act a bit weird, particularly after I had said something about how much I enjoyed paddling Zelda, even when she was loaded down with all my camping gear. Then Doc asked me what I wanted to do with Zelda's remains. As I say, I'm not much on sentimentality so I told him just to keep them around the shop and use them for parts.

"It's about time I got myself a new one anyway," I said.

"So much for grief, hunh, fella?" the bartender snarled. "Beat the old thing, make her carry all your campin' junk, and then forget her, just like that!" He snapped his fingers so close to my face I jumped.

"What's with you?" I said. "All along I thought you were a canoeist."

That was when he tossed Doc and me out of the bar.

"Call me a canoeist, will you!" he shouted from the doorway. "Listen, fella, I may not be too smart, but I'm a lot more normal than you!"

I suppose these strange attitudes toward canoes are to be expected of persons who don't establish a meaningful relationship with them early in life. My own association with canoes began at age ten. That was when I built my first one. Even if I do say so myself, it was one of the most beautiful canoes I've ever seen.

I built it in a vacant upstairs bedroom out of some old lumber I found in the hog pen. The lumber was dirty and heavy, and I had great difficulty dragging it through the house and up to the bedroom. Most of the difficulty was caused by my mother and grandmother, who kept making nasty remarks about my character and trying to strike me with blunt objects.

It took me about three weeks to build the canoe. If you've never built a canoe, you probably don't realize that the hardest part is shaping the bow and stern just right. I came up with an ingenious solution to this problem that, if it had caught on, would have revolutionized canoe design. I put

square ends on it. There were a couple of other minor modifi-
cations that also simplified construction—the bottom and
sides were flat! I painted it with some red barn paint as a final
touch, and the end result was a sharp-looking canoe. Everyone else in my family thought so, too, except Gram. She said it
looked like a coffin for someone's pet boa constrictor. Gram, of
course, knew next to nothing about boat design.

The canoe's one drawback was that it weighed just slightly
less than a Buick, and since I was the only man in the family,
we had to ask the old woodsman Rancid Crabtree to come
over and help us carry it out of the house.

As Rancid was walking up the stairs, he sniffed the air and
asked, "You been keepin' hogs up here? Smells like . . ."

"Never mind what it smells like," Gram snapped. "Just
help us carry that contraption out of the house."

Mom, Gram, and I got at one end of the canoe and Rancid
at the other, and with a great deal of shouting and groaning
managed to lift it until it was resting on our shoulders. We
carried it out of the bedroom to the head of the stairs, at
which point Rancid gasped that he couldn't hold up his end a
second longer. While he was looking around frantically for
something to rest the canoe on, he accidentally stepped down
backwards onto the stairs. We at the rear end of the canoe
naturally assumed from this gesture that he had changed his
mind about resting, so we charged forward. It was just one of
those innocent misunderstandings. As it turned out, no one
was seriously injured, but some of the language would have
made the hair of a wart hog stand on end. The only ill effect I
suffered was psychological. As we all galloped around the
sharp turn at the landing, I caught a glimpse of the expression on Rancid's face, and it just wasn't the sort of thing a
ten-year-old boy should be allowed to see. For years afterwards, it would cause me to wake up whimpering in the
night.

When Rancid came into the kitchen for coffee after the or-
deal was over, he complained that he felt two feet shorter.
Gram pointed out to him that he was walking on his knees.
Rancid was always doing comical things like that.

Beautiful as it was, my first canoe was never launched but sat for years in the yard at the place where it was dropped. My mother later filled it with dirt and planted flowers in it. Strangers sometimes got the mistaken impression from it that we were holding a funeral for a tall, thin gangster.

The first store-bought canoe with which I had a meaningful relationship was hidden in some brush on the banks of a creek near where I lived. During the spring of the year, the creek was deep and fast with some nice rapids in it, but I had enough sense to realize that it would be dangerous for me to attempt to paddle the canoe down it. The main reason it would have been dangerous was that the big kid who owned the canoe had threatened to put me in a sack and toss the sack in the creek if he caught me messing around with it.

The big kid's name was Buster, and he divided his time among eating, sleeping, and beating up people, although not necessarily in that order. Sometimes he would catch me down by the creek and practice his beating-up techniques on me. Although these sessions were more monotonous than painful, they were sufficiently instructive to make me realize that I didn't want Buster performing real beating-up on me.

Nevertheless, I could not force myself to stay entirely away from the canoe, a lovely little fifteen-footer, mostly green but with a patch of white on the side where Buster had attempted to paint over the words PROPERTY OF SUNSET RESORT. Once, I even slipped the canoe into the water just to see how it floated. It floated fine. After giving considerable thought to the questions (1) how much fun would it be to paddle the canoe around a bit, and (2) how difficult would it be to swim while confined in a sack, I slipped the canoe back into its hiding place and wiped off my fingerprints.

About a mile from my home, the creek wound through a swamp that was full of dead trees, rotting stumps, quicksand, mud flats, snakes, frogs, slime—all the usual neat swamp stuff. Brook trout the size of alligators were said to inhabit the deeper waters of the swamp, and I would occasionally pole my log raft into the dark interior in search of them. It was on one of these excursions that I happened to come upon Buster's canoe, bobbing gently among the cattails that surrounded a small, brush-covered island. My heart leaped up.

"Well, I'll be darned!" I said to myself. "Ol' Buster's canoe has somehow slid itself into the crick and drifted into the swamp. Won't he be tickled pink when I bring it back to him—in a day or two or the week after next at the latest?"

My elation, however, was diluted by a sense of foreboding, even though there wasn't a sign of human life in any direction. I eased myself silently into the canoe and set the raft adrift, just in case someone might get the notion of using it as a means of pursuing me.

That the canoe had somehow drifted upstream and tied itself to a branch with a length of clothesline and a square knot were matters of no little curiosity to me, and I remember making a mental note to ask my arithmetic teacher what the odds of such an occurrence might be. As I was untying the square knot, I happened to glance out from among the cattails. What I saw momentarily freeze-dried my corpuscles. Strolling right toward me, arm-in-arm from out of the brush in the middle of the island, were Buster and a girl by the name of Alvira Holstein. Even as it was locked in the grip of terror, my fertile mind groped with the question of what the two of them could be doing on the island, Buster never having struck me as much of a picnicker. On the other hand, the occasion didn't seem appropriate for casual conversation. I did take some comfort in the fact that Buster did not appear to have a sack with him.

Upon seeing me crouched in his canoe, Buster let out a roar that is best described as approximating that of a grizzly bear having a bicuspid extracted without benefit of anesthetic. I had never paddled a canoe before, but at that instant, such was the inspiration of seeing Buster charging toward me, I instantly discovered that I had a talent for it bordering on genius. Within seconds I had the canoe moving at sufficient momentum to plane easily over half-submerged logs, mud flats, and flocks of waterfowl caught unawares. I looked back once, and Buster was still in hot pursuit, even though he was up to his armpits in swamp slime. He was screeching almost incoherently, something to the effect that he would make sweeping but imaginative alterations on my anatomy once he laid hands on it. Alvira Holstein was jumping up and down on the island, crying and screaming, and yelling out, "Don't kill him, Buster, don't kill him!" Even to this day it sets my nerves on edge to hear a woman yell something like that.

I paddled the canoe halfway to my house, which was remarkable only in that the water ended some distance short of that. My grandmother was in the kitchen when I burst through the door.

"Land sakes, what's after you?" she said.

"Never mind that now," I said. "Just tell me this. Is there really quicksand in the swamp?"

"There certainly is," she said. "And you just stay out of that swamp if you don't want to get swallowed up by it!"

I crossed my fingers. "Come on, *quicksand!*" I said.

Actually, it was Gram who finally saved me from the sack or, at best, going through life as a very odd-looking person. When she found out Buster was after me, she just scoffed.

"Buster ain't going to hurt you," she said, neglecting to mention why I should be an exception to the rule. "If he does, you just tell the sheriff on him. The sheriff's a tough man, and he don't stand for no nonsense."

"Yeah, he's tough all right," I said, pulling back the window curtain an inch to peer out. "But he don't bother about kids' fightin'. He says it's just natural."

"Oh, I don't know," Gram said. "Sheriff Holstein's a pretty sensible man, and I think if you just told him . . ."

"Holstein?" I said. "That's right, it *is* Sheriff Holstein, isn't it?" I walked away from the window, cut myself a slab of fresh-baked bread, and smeared on a layer of raspberry jam.

"Well, forget about Buster, Gram," I told her. "I got to go paddle my canoe."

THE WORLD OF TOMORROW

MAY 1939

I wasn't really prepared for the World's Fair last week, and it certainly wasn't prepared for me. Between the two of us there was considerable of a mixup.

The truth is that my ethmoid sinuses broke down on the eve of Fair Day, and this meant I had to visit the Fair carrying a box of Kleenex concealed in a copy of the *Herald Tribune*. When you can't breathe through your nose, Tomorrow seems strangely like the day before yesterday. The Fair, on its part, was having trouble too. It couldn't find its collar button. Our mutual discomfort established a rich bond of friendship between us, and I realize that the World's Fair and myself actually both need the same thing—a nice warm day.

The road to Tomorrow leads through the chimney pots of Queens. It is a long, familiar journey, through Mulsified Shampoo and Mobilgas, through Bliss Street, Kix, Astring-O-Sol, and the Majestic Auto Seat Covers. It winds through Textene, Blue Jay Corn Plasters; through Musterole and the delicate pink blossoms on the fruit trees in the ever-hopeful back yards of a populous borough, past Zemo, Alka-Seltzer, Baby Ruth, past Iodent and the Fidelity National Bank, by trusses, belts, and the clothes that fly bravely on the line under the trees with the new little green leaves in Queens' incomparable springtime. Suddenly you see the first intimation of the future, of man's dream—the white ball and spire—and there are the ramp and the banners flying from the pavilions and the brave hope of a glimpsed destination. Except for the Kleenex, I might have been approaching the lists at Camelot, for I felt that perhaps here would be the tournament all men wait for, the field of honor, the knights and the ladies under these bright banners, beyond these great walls. A closer inspection, however, on the other side of the turnstile, revealed that it was merely Heinz jousting with Beech-Nut—the same old contest on a somewhat larger field, with accommodations for more spectators, and rather better facilities all round.

The place is honeycombed with streets—broad, gusty streets, with tulips bending to the gale and in the air the sound of distant choirs. There are benches all along for the weary and the halt, but though science's failure to cope with the common cold had embittered my heart and slowed my step, the ball and spire still beckoned me on. It was not particularly surprising, somehow, when at last after so many months of anticipation and after so much of actual travail and suffering, when at last I arrived, paper handkerchiefs in hand, at the very threshold of Tomorrow, when I finally presented myself there at the base of the white phallus, face to face with the girl in the booth behind the little bars behind the glass window with the small round hole, expectant, ready, to see at last what none had ever seen, Tomorrow—it was not, somehow, particularly surprising to see the window close in my face and hear a bald contemporary voice say, "There will be a short wait of a few minutes, please."

That's the way it is with the future. Even after Grover Whalen has touched it with his peculiar magic, there is still a short wait.

The lady behind me was not surprised either, but she seemed apprehensive.

"Anything wrong in there?" she asked testily.

"No, madam," said the guard. "Just some minor difficulty in the Perisphere."

The lady was not satisfied. "Is there anything in there to scare you?" she asked, looking at the Perisphere rolling motionless in the gray vapors that have hung for centuries above the Flushing Meadows.

"No, madam," he replied. "The longest escalator in the world moves very slowly."

I clocked the wait. It was twenty minutes. Not bad, for a man who's waited all his life.

Much depends, when you ascend into the interior of the Perisphere, on the moment at which you happen to arrive at the top of the escalator and teeter off in a sidewise direction onto one of the two great moving rings that turn endlessly above the City of Man. If you arrive just as day has faded into night, and without any advance information about being shunted from an upward moving stairway onto a sideways moving balcony, the experience is something that stays with you. I was lucky. The City of Man, when it first broke on my expectant sight, was as dark as a hall bedroom, and for a second or two I didn't catch on that I myself was in motion—except celestially. If I hadn't recognized Mr. Kaltenborn's electric voice, I would have felt lonelier than perhaps the situation warranted.

"As day fades into night," he said, with the majestic huskiness which science has given speech, "each man seeks home, for here are children, comfort, neighbors, recreation—the good life of the well-planned city."

Trembling in violet light beneath me, there it was—the towers, now to the adjusted eye dimly visible—"a brave new world [such a big voice you have, Grandpa!] built by united hands and hearts. Here brain and brawn, faith and courage, are linked in high endeavor as men march on toward unity and peace. Listen! From office, farm, and factory they come with joyous song."

I don't know how long it takes in there. Ten minutes, maybe. But when I emerged from the great ball, to begin the descent of the Helicline, it had come on to rain.

To be informative about the Fair is a task for someone with a steadier nose than mine. I saw all as in a dream, and I cherish the dream and have put it away in lavender. The great size of the place has been a temporary disadvantage these first few days, when the draftiness, the chill, the disorder, the murky bath of canned reverence in which many of the commercial exhibits are steeped have conspired to give the place the clammy quality of a seaside resort in mid-November. But this same great size, come the first warm, expansive days, will suddenly become the most valuable asset of the Fair. The refurbished ash heap, rising from its own smolder, is by far the biggest show that has ever been assembled on God's earth, and it is going to be a great place to go on a fine summer night, a great place to go on a sunny spring morning. After all, nobody can embrace Culture in a topcoat.

The architecture is amusing enough, the buildings are big enough, to give the visitor that temporary and exalted feeling of being in the presence of something pretty special, something full of aspiration, something which at times is even exciting. And the exhibition is cock-eyed enough to fall, as it naturally does, in line with all carnivals, circuses, and wonderlands. The buildings (there are two hundred of them) have color and a certain dash, here and there a certain beauty. They are of the type that shows up best in strong light. Like any Miami Beach cottage, they look incredibly lovely in sunlight, adorned with a necklace of vine shadow against a clear white skin, incredibly banal and gloom-infested on cloudy days, when every pimple of plaster shows up in all its ugly pretension. The designers of this twentieth-century bazaar have been resourceful and have kept the comfort of the people in mind. Experience has taught them much. The modern technique of sightseeing is this: you sit in a chair (wired for sound) or stand on a platform (movable, glass-embowered) and while sitting, standing, you are brought mysteriously and reverently into easy view of what you want to see. There is no shoving in the exhibit hall of Tomorrow. There is no loitering and there is usually no smoking. Even in the girl show in the amusement area, the sailor is placed in a rather astringent attitude, behind glass, for the adoration of the female form. It is all rather serious-minded, this World of Tomorrow, and extremely impersonal. A ride on the Futurama of General Motors induces approximately the same emotional response as a trip through the Cathedral of St. John the Divine. The countryside unfolds before you in $5-million micro-loveliness, conceived in motion and executed by Norman Bel Geddes. The voice is a voice of utmost respect, of complete religious faith in the eternal benefaction of faster travel. The highways unroll in ribbons of perfection through the fertile and rejuvenated America of 1960—a vision of the day to come, the unobstructed left turn, the vanished grade crossing, the town which beckons but does not impede, the millennium of passionless motion. When night falls in the General Motors exhibit and you lean back in the cushioned chair (yourself in motion and the world so still) and hear (from the depths of the chair) the soft electric assurance of a better life—the life which rests on wheels alone—there is a strong, sweet poison which infects the blood. I didn't want to wake up. I liked 1960 in purple light, going a hundred miles an hour around impossible turns ever onward toward the certified cities of the flawless future. It wasn't till I passed an apple orchard and saw the trees, each blooming under its own canopy of glass, that I perceived that even the General Motors dream, as dreams so often do, left some questions unanswered about the future. The apple tree of Tomorrow, abloom under its inviolate hood, makes you stop and wonder. How will the little boy climb it? Where will the little bird build its nest?

I made a few notes at the Fair, a few hints of what you may expect of Tomorrow, its appointments, its characteristics.

In Tomorrow, people and objects are lit not from above but from below. Trees are lit from below. Even the cow on the rotolactor appears to be lit from below—the buried flood lamp illuminates the distended udder.

In Tomorrow one voice does for all. But it is a little unsure of itself; it keeps testing itself; it says, "Hello! One, two, three, four. Hello! One, two, three, four."

Rugs do not slip in Tomorrow, and the bassinets of newborn infants are wired against kidnappers.

There is no talking back in Tomorrow. You are expected to take it or leave it alone. There are sailors there (which makes you feel less lonely) and the sound of music.

The living room of Tomorrow contains the following objects: a broadloom carpet, artificial carnations, a television
radio victrola incessantly producing an image of someone or
something which is somewhere else, a glass bird, a chrome
steel lamp, a terracotta zebra, some veneered book cabinets
containing no visible books, another cabinet out of which a
small newspaper slowly pours in a never-ending ribbon, and a
small plush love seat in the shape of a new moon.

In Tomorrow, most sounds are not the sounds themselves
but a memory of sounds, or an electrification. In the case of a
cow, the moo will come to you not from the cow but from a
small aperture above your head.

Tomorrow is a little on the expensive side. I checked this
with my cabdriver in Manhattan to make sure. He was full of
praise about the Fair, but said he hadn't seen it and might, in
fact, never see it. "I hack out there, but I got it figured that for
me and the wife to go all through and do it right—no cheap-
skate stuff—it would break the hell out of a five-dollar bill. In
my racket, I can't afford it."

Tomorrow does not smell. The World's Fair of 1939 has
taken the body odor out of man, among other things. It is all
rather impersonal, this dream. The country fair manages better, where you can hang over the rail at the ox-pulling and
smell the ox. It's not only that the sailors can't get at the girls
through the glass, but even so wholesome an exhibit as
Swift's Premium Bacon produces twenty lovesick maidens in
a glass pit hermetically sealed from the ultimate consumer.

The voice of Mr. Kaltenborn in the City of Man says, "They
come with joyous song," but the truth is there is very little joyous song in the Fair grounds. There is a great deal of electri-
cally transmitted joy, but very little spontaneous joy.
Tomorrow's music, I noticed, came mostly from Yesterday's
singer. In fact, if Mr. Whalen wants a suggestion from me as
to how to improve his show (and I am reasonably confident
he doesn't), it would be to snip a few wires, hire a couple of
bands, and hand out ticklers. Gaiety is not the keynote in Tomorrow. I finally found it at the tag end of a chilly evening, far
along in the amusement area, in a tent with some black peo-

ple. There was laughing and shouting there, and a beautiful brown belly-dancer.

Another gay spot, to my surprise, was the American Telephone & Telegraph Exhibit. It took the old Telephone Company to put on the best show of all. To anyone who draws a lucky number, the company grants the privilege of making a long-distance call. This call can be to any point in the United States, and the bystanders have the exquisite privilege of listening in through earphones and of laughing unashamed. To understand the full wonder of this, you must reflect that there are millions of people who have never either made or received a long-distance call, and that when Eddie Pancha, a waiter in a restaurant in El Paso, Texas, hears the magic words "New York is calling . . . go ahead, please," he is transfixed in holy dread and excitement. I listened for two hours and ten minutes to this show, and I'd be there this minute if I were capable of standing up. I had the good luck to be listening at the earphone when a little boy named David Wagstaff won the toss and put in a call to tell his father in Springfield, Mass., what a good time he was having at the World's Fair. David walked resolutely to the glass booth before the assembled kitbitzers and in a tiny, timid voice gave the operator his call, his little new cloth hat set all nicely on his head. But his father wasn't there, and David was suddenly confronted with the necessity of telling his story to a man named Mr. Henry, who happened to answer the phone and who, on hearing little David Wagstaff's voice calling from New York, must surely have thought that David's mother had been run down in the BMT and that David was doing the manly thing.

"Yes, David," he said, tensely.

"Tell my father this," began David, slowly, carefully, determined to go through with the halcyon experience of winning a lucky call at the largest fair the world had yet produced.

"Yes, David."

"We got on the train, and . . . and . . . had a nice trip, and at New Haven, when they were taking off the car and putting another car on, it was *awfully* funny because the car gave a great—big—BUMP!"

Then followed David's three-minute appreciation of the World of Tomorrow and the Citadel of Light, phrased in the crumbling remnants of speech that little boys are left with when a lot of people are watching, and when their thoughts begin to run down, and when Perispheres begin to swim mistily in time. Mr. Henry—the invisible and infinitely surprised Mr. Henry—maintained a respectful and indulgent silence. I don't know what he was thinking, but I would swap the Helicline for a copy of his attempted transcription of David's message to his father.

My own memory of the Fair, like David's, has begun to dim. From so much culture, from so much concentrated beauty and progress, one can retain only a fragment. I remember the trees at night, shivering in their burlap undershirts, the eerie shadows clinging to the wrong side of their branches. I remember the fountains playing in the light, I remember the girl who sat so still, so clean, so tangible, producing with the tips of her fingers the synthetic speech—but the words were not the words she wanted to say, they were not the words that were in her mind. I remember the little old Stourbridge Lion, puffing in under its own steam to start the railroads bursting across America. But mostly the Fair has vanished, leaving only the voice of little David Wagstaff and the rambling ecstasy of his first big trip away from home; so many million dollars spent on the idea that our trains and our motorcars should go fast and smoothly, and the child remembering, not the smoothness, but the great—big—BUMP.

So (as the voice says) man dreams on. And the dream is still a contradiction and an enigma—the biologist peeping at bacteria through his microscope, the sailor peeping at the strip queen through binoculars, the eyes so watchful, and the hopes so high. Out in the honky-tonk section, in front of the Amazon show, where the ladies exposed one breast in deference to the fleet, kept one concealed in deference to Mr. Whalen, there was an automaton—a giant man in white tie and tails, with enormous rubber hands. At the start of each show, while the barker was drumming up trade, a couple of the girls would come outside and sit in the robot's lap. The effect was peculiarly lascivious—the extra-size man, exploring with his gigantic rubber hands the breasts of the little girls, the girls with their own small hands (by comparison so small, by comparison so terribly real) restrainingly on his, to check the unthinkable impact of his mechanical passion. Here was the Fair, all fairs, in pantomime; and here the strange mixed dream that made the Fair: the heroic man, bloodless and per-fect and enormous, created in his own image, and in his hand (rubber, aseptic) the literal desire, the warm and living breast.

MADDENED BY MYSTERY: OR, THE DEFECTIVE DETECTIVE

The great detective sat in his office. He wore a long green gown and half a dozen secret badges pinned to the outside of it.

Three or four pairs of false whiskers hung on a whisker-stand beside him.

Goggles, blue spectacles and motor glasses lay within easy reach.

He could completely disguise himself at a second's notice.

Half a bucket of cocaine and a dipper stood on a chair at his elbow.

His face was absolutely impenetrable.

A pile of cryptograms lay on the desk. The Great Detective hastily tore them open one after the other, solved them, and threw them down the cryptogram-shute at his side.

There was a rap at the door.

The Great Detective hurriedly wrapped himself in a pink domino, adjusted a pair of false black whiskers and cried, "Come in."

His secretary entered. "Ha," said the detective, "it is you!"

He laid aside his disguise.

"Sir," said the young man in intense excitement, "a mystery has been committed!"

"Ha!" said the Great Detective, his eye kindling, "is it such as to completely baffle the police of the entire continent?"

"They are so completely baffled with it," said the secretary, "that they are lying collapsed in heaps; many of them have committed suicide."

"So," said the detective, "and is the mystery one that is absolutely unparalleled in the whole recorded annals of the London police?"

"It is."

"And I suppose," said the detective, "that it involves names which you would scarcely dare to breathe, at least without first using some kind of atomizer or throat-gargle."

"Exactly."

"And it is connected, I presume, with the highest diplomatic consequences, so that if we fail to solve it England will be at war with the whole world in sixteen minutes?"

His secretary, still quivering with excitement, again answered yes.

"And finally," said the Great Detective, "I presume that it was committed in broad daylight, in some such place as the entrance of the Bank of England, or in the cloak-room of the House of Commons, and under the very eyes of the police?"

"Those," said the secretary, "are the very conditions of the mystery."

"Good," said the Great Detective, "now wrap yourself in this disguise, put on these brown whiskers and tell me what it is."

The secretary wrapped himself in a blue domino with lace insertions, then, bending over, he whispered in the ear of the Great Detective:

"The Prince of Wurttemberg has been kidnapped."

The Great Detective bounded from his chair as if he had been kicked from below.

A prince stolen! Evidently a Bourbon! The scion of one of the oldest families in Europe kidnapped. Here was a mystery indeed worthy of his analytical brain.

His mind began to move like lightning.

"Stop!" he said, "how do you know this?"

The secretary handed him a telegram. It was from the Prefect of Police of Paris. It read: "The Prince of Wurttemberg stolen. Probably forwarded to London. Must have him here for the opening day of Exhibition. £1,000 reward."

So! The Prince had been kidnapped out of Paris at the very time when his appearance at the International Exposition would have been a political event of the first magnitude.

With the Great Detective to think was to act, and to act was to think. Frequently he could do both together.

"Wire to Paris for a description of the Prince."

The secretary bowed and left.

At the same moment there was a slight scratching at the door.

A visitor entered. He crawled stealthily on his hands and knees. A hearthrug thrown over his head and shoulders disguised his identity.

He crawled to the middle of the room.

Then he rose.

Great Heaven!

It was the Prime Minister of England.

"You!" said the detective.

"Me," said the Prime Minister.

"You have come in regard to the kidnapping of the Prince of Wurttemberg?"

The Prime Minister started.

"How do you know?" he said.

The Great Detective smiled his inscrutable smile.

"Yes," said the Prime Minister. "I will use no concealment. I am interested, deeply interested. Find the Prince of Wurttemberg, get him safe back to Paris and I will add £500 to the reward already offered. But listen," he said impressively as he left the room, "see to it that no attempt is made to alter the marking of the prince, or to clip his tail."

So! To clip the Prince's tail! The brain of the Great Detective reeled. So! a gang of miscreants had conspired to—but no! the thing was not possible.

There was another rap at the door.

A second visitor was seen. He wormed his way in, lying almost prone upon his stomach, and wriggling across the floor.

He was enveloped in a long purple cloak. He stood up and peeped over the top of it.

Great Heaven!

It was the Archbishop of Canterbury!

"Your Grace!" exclaimed the detective in amazement— "pray do not stand, I beg you. Sit down, lie down, anything rather than stand."

The Archbishop took off his mitre and laid it wearily on the whisker-stand.

"You are here in regard to the Prince of Wurttemberg."

The Archbishop started and crossed himself. Was the man a magician?

"Yes," he said, "much depends on getting him back. But I have only come to say this: my sister is desirous of seeing you. She is coming here. She has been extremely indiscreet and her fortune hangs upon the Prince. Get him back to Paris or I fear she will be ruined."

The Archbishop regained his mitre, uncrossed himself, wrapped his cloak about him, and crawled stealthily out on his hands and knees, purring like a cat.

The face of the Great Detective showed the most profound sympathy. It ran up and down in furrows. "So," he muttered, "the sister of the Archbishop, the Countess of Dashleigh!" Accustomed as he was to the life of the aristocracy, even the Great Detective felt that there was here intrigue of more than customary complexity.

There was a loud rapping at the door.

There entered the Countess of Dashleigh. She was all in furs.

She was the most beautiful woman in England. She strode imperiously into the room. She seized a chair imperiously and seated herself on it, imperial side up.

She took off her tiara of diamonds and put it on the tiara-holder beside her and uncoiled her boa of pearls and put it on the pearl-stand.

"You have come," said the Great Detective, "about the Prince of Wurttemburg."

"Wretched little pup!" said the Countess of Dashleigh in disgust.

So! A further complication! Far from being in love with the Prince, the Countess denounced the young Bourbon as a pup!

"You are interested in him, I believe."

"Interested!" said the Countess. "I should rather say so. Why, I bred him!"

"You which?" gasped the Great Detective, his usually impassive features suffused with a carmine blush.

"I bred him," said the Countess, "and I've got £10,000 upon his chances, so no wonder I want him back in Paris. Only listen," she said, "if they've got hold of the Prince and cut his tail or spoiled the markings of his stomach it would be far better to have him quietly put out of the way here."

The Great Detective reeled and leaned up against the side of the room. So! The cold-blooded admission of the beautiful woman for the moment took away his breath! Herself the mother of the young Bourbon, misallied with one of the greatest families of Europe, staking her fortune on a Royalist plot, and yet with so instinctive a knowledge of European politics as to know that any removal of the hereditary birth-marks of the Prince would forfeit for him the sympathy of the French populace.

The Countess resumed her tiara.

She left.

The secretary re-entered.

"I have three telegrams from Paris," he said, "they are completely baffling."

He handed over the first telegram.

It read:

"The Prince of Wurttemberg has a long, wet snout, broad ears, very long body, and short hind legs."

The Great Detective looked puzzled.

He read the second telegram.

"The Prince of Wurttemberg is easily recognized by his deep bark."

And then the third.

"The Prince of Wurttemberg can be recognized by the patch of white hair across the centre of his back."

The two men looked at one another. The mystery was maddening, impenetrable.

The Great Detective spoke.

"Give me my domino," he said. "These clues must be followed up," then pausing, while his quick brain analysed and summed up the evidence before him—"a young man," he muttered, "evidently young since described as a 'pup,' with a long, wet snout (ha! addicted obviously to drinking), a streak of white hair across his back (a first sign of the results of his abandoned life)—yes, yes," he continued, "with this clue I shall find him easily."

The Great Detective rose.

He wrapped himself in a long black cloak with white whiskers and blue spectacles attached.

Completely disguised, he issued forth.

He began the search.

For four days he visited every corner of London.

He entered every saloon in the city. In each of them he drank a glass of rum. In some of them he assumed the disguise of a sailor. In others he entered as a soldier. Into others he penetrated as a clergyman. His disguise was perfect. Nobody paid any attention to him as long as he had the price of a drink.

The search proved fruitless.

Two young men were arrested under suspicion of being the Prince, only to be released.

The identification was incomplete in each case.

One had a long wet snout but no hair on his back.

The other had hair on his back but couldn't bark.

Neither of them was the young Bourbon.

The Great Detective continued his search.

He stopped at nothing.

Secretly, after nightfall, he visited the home of the Prime Minister. He examined it from top to bottom. He measured all the doors and windows. He took up the flooring. He inspected the plumbing. He examined the furniture. He found nothing.

With equal secrecy he penetrated into the palace of the Archbishop. He examined it from top to bottom. Disguised as a choir-boy he took part in the offices of the church. He found nothing.

Still undismayed, the Great Detective made his way into the home of the Countess of Dashleigh. Disguised as a house-maid, he entered the service of the Countess.

Then at last the clue came which gave him a solution of the mystery.

On the wall of the Countess' boudoir was a large framed engraving.

It was a portrait.

Under it was a printed legend:

THE PRINCE OF WURTTEMBURG

The portrait was that of a Dachshund.

The long body, the broad ears, the unclipped tail, the short hind legs—all was there.

In the fraction of a second the lightning mind of the Great Detective had penetrated the whole mystery.

THE PRINCE WAS A DOG!!!!

Hastily throwing a domino over his housemaid's dress, he rushed to the street. He summoned a passing hansom, and in a few moments was at his house.

"I have it," he gasped to his secretary, "the mystery is solved. I have pieced it together. By sheer analysis I have rea-soned it out. Listen—hind legs, hair on back, wet snout, pup—eh, what? does that suggest nothing to you?"

"Nothing," said the secretary; "it seems perfectly hope-less."

The Great Detective, now recovered from his excitement, smiled faintly.

"It means simply this, my dear fellow. The Prince of Wurt-temburg is a dog, a prize Dachshund. The Countess of Dash-leigh bred him, and he is worth some £25,000 in addition to the prize of £10,000 offered at the Paris dog show. Can you wonder that—"

At that moment the Great Detective was interrupted by the scream of a woman.

"Great Heaven!"

The Countess of Dashleigh dashed into the room.

Her face was wild.

Her tiara was in disorder.

Her pearls were dripping all over the place.

She wrung her hands and moaned.

"They have cut his tail," she gasped, "and taken all the hair off his back. What can I do? I am undone!!"

"Madame," said the Great Detective, calm as bronze, "do yourself up. I can save you yet."

"You!"

"Me!"

"How?"

"Listen. This is how. The Prince was to have been shown at Paris."

The Countess nodded.

"Your fortune was staked on him?"

The Countess nodded again.

"The dog was stolen, carried to London, his tail cut and his marks disfigured."

Amazed at the quiet penetration of the Great Detective, the Countess kept on nodding and nodding.

"And you are ruined?"

"I am," she gasped, and sank down on the floor in a heap of pearls.

"Madame," said the Great Detective, "all is not lost."

He straightened himself up to his full height. A look of inflinchable unflexibility flickered over his features.

The honour of England, the fortune of the most beautiful woman in England was at stake.

"I will do it," he murmured.

"Rise, dear lady," he continued. "Fear nothing. I WILL IMPERSONATE THE DOG!!!"

That night the Great Detective might have been seen on the deck of the Calais packet boat with his secretary. He was on his hands and knees in a long black cloak, and his secretary had him on a short chain.

He barked at the waves exultingly and licked the secretary's hand.

"What a beautiful dog," said the passengers.

The disguise was absolutely complete.

The Great Detective had been coated over with mucilage to which dog hairs had been applied. The markings on his back were perfect. His tail, adjusted with an automatic coupler, moved up and down responsive to every thought. His deep eyes were full of intelligence.

Next day he was exhibited in the Dachshund class at the International show.

He won all hearts.

"Quel beau chien!" cried the French people.

"Ach! was ein Dog!" cried the Spanish.

The Great Detective took the first prize!

The fortune of the Countess was saved.

Unfortunately as the Great Detective had neglected to pay the dog tax, he was caught and destroyed by the dog-catchers. But that is, of course, quite outside of the present narrative, and is only mentioned as an odd fact in conclusion.

WEDDING ANNOUNCEMENTS

The society page, especially that part that deals with wedding and engagement announcements, is more than just a way to save printing and postage costs in telling of a son's or daughter's betrothal; it is a clarion declaration of one's bloodlines and accomplishments.

Now to some of you bloodlines may not seem important, either because you do not have any, or because they run thin in spots; but to the rich of cell they are even more important than the considerable fortunes passed on to them by their wise and farsighted ancestors.

Indeed, while bloodlines may come first, accomplishments such as the inheritance of a New York Stock Exchange company or acceptance into a secret society are also steely marks of worth not to be ignored. Large looms the small-town plumber who is also a member of Skull and Bones.

Personally I find reading the society announcements every bit as fascinating as the Egyptian Book of the Dead, the special crypto-words and names telling me not only a family's history, but its current rank and standing; whether it has depth in greenbacks or just blue erythrocytes.

There is no easy Rosetta stone for deciphering these, but practice will increase your facility. Start with the following blurbs culled from my local paper and see how you do.

Frick—Popover

Mr. and Mrs. Van Wyck Frick have announced the engagement of their daughter Doo Doo to Mr. C. Livingston Popover, who manages his own trust.

Doo Doo, who is known to her friends as Puff Puff, or to her very close friends as Dee Dee, or to the senior class at Dartmouth as Eee Zee, attended Miss Pinball's School in South Braintree where she was voted most likely to become pregnant during inclement weather.

Her grandfather, Col. Summerfield Frick, invented the cummerbund and was chairman of the Frick Formalwear Corp., which dispensed free cummerbunds to our troops during the Vietnam War. Her father, Van Wyck Frick, runs a polo league for advantaged children in Palm Beach.

Mr. Popover is the son of "Pop" Popover, the World War II ace who was twice decorated by President Truman and later sent to Leavenworth penitentiary for shooting down four civilian aircraft en route to Miami Beach. His mother is the former Abigail Oaktop, whose family has large holdings in real estate, banking, and the United States government. The couple plan a June wedding.

Allison Peaworth
Engaged to Nobody

Allison Peaworth, daughter of Admiral and "Moneybags" Turner Peaworth, has become affianced to Jeffery Sider, a nobody.

Miss Peaworth, who attended Hollyville Academy, Le Nevrose in Geneva, and Bennington College where she was graduated magna cum laude in creative movement, is working at the Morgan Guaranty Trust bank in New York as a blank check. Her maternal grandfather, Hoghorn Pill, discovered money.

The couple plan to be married in June and honeymoon aboard the family yacht U.S.S. *Lexington*.

C. W. Corleone
Weds Fifi Dubois

In the Wood Presbyterian Church yesterday afternoon, Fifi Aubusson Dubois, daughter of Mr. and Mrs. Brian Dubois of New York and Block Island, was married to Carmine (The Wrench) Corleone, son of Don and Mrs. Rocco Corleone of West New York, certain parts of Detroit, and Las Vegas, Nevada. The ceremony was performed by Rev. Castiglia Maione, an employee of the bridegroom's family. Miss Camilia Dubois, sister of the bride, was maid of honor. For the groom, Angelo (The Sub) Argutti served as best man in place of Bongo (The Nerve) Tuttifiore, who was detained when his head got unexpectedly lodged in the tail pipe of a Boeing 747 bound for Okinawa.

The bride was presented at a dinner given by her parents in 1971 and was a member of the Junior League, the Junior Assemblies, and "Bunions For Bertha," a militant podiatric group out of South Orange. She attended the Tingly Country Day School and was graduated from Le Snoot College in Marseilles, France. Her father is retired board chairman of Fenton, Hargewick, McDiggle, and Dubois, makers of "Groverly." The bride's maternal grandfather, Auchindrake Foxglove, was master of the hounds at Le Club.

Mr. Corleone is an alumnus of the "Cavoon" school in Castellamare, Sicily, where he was a member of "Wire and Shiv" and editor of *On The Take*. His father, who recently acquired Chicago as part payment of an outstanding debt, is a presser at the C & D laundry in lower Manhattan.

After a brief honeymoon the couple will go into hiding.

HANGING ALDERMEN

Chicago is always on the point of hanging some one and quartering him and boiling him in hot pitch, and assuring him that he has lost the respect of all honorable men. Rumors of a characteristic agitation had come faintly up Archey Road, and Mr. Hennessy had heard of it.

"I hear they're goin' to hang th' aldhermen," he said. "If they thry it on Willum J. O'Brien, they'd betther bombard him first. I'd hate to be th' man that 'd be called to roll with him to his doom. He cud lick th' whole Civic Featheration."

"I believe ye," said Mr. Dooley. "He's a powerful man. But I hear there is, as ye say, what th' pa-apers 'd call a movement on fut f'r to dec'rate Chris'mas threes with aldhermen, an' 'tis wan that ought to be encouraged. Nawthin' cud be happyer, as Hogan says, thin th' thought iv cillybratin' th' season be sthringin' up some iv th' fathers iv th' city where th' childher cud see thim. But I'm afraid, Hinnissy, that you an' me won't see it. 'Twill all be over soon, an' Willum J. O'Brien 'll go by with his head just as near his shoulders as iver. 'Tis har-rd to hang an aldherman, annyhow. Ye'd have to suspind most iv thim be th' waist.

"Man an' boy, I've been in this town forty year an' more; an' divvle th' aldherman have I see hanged yet, though I've sthrained th' eyes out iv me head watchin' f'r wan iv thim to be histed anny pleasant mornin'. They've been goin' to hang thim wan week an' presintin' thim with a dimon' star th' next iver since th' year iv th' big wind, an' there's jus' as manny iv thim an' jus' as big robbers as iver there was.

"An' why shud they hang thim, Hinnissy? Why shud they? I'm an honest man mesilf, as men go. Ye might have ye'er watch, if ye had wan, on that bar f'r a year, an' I'd niver touch it. It wudden't be worth me while. I'm an honest man. I pay me taxes, whin Tim Ryan isn't assessor with Grogan's boy on th' books. I do me jooty; an' I believe in th' polis foorce, though not in polismen. That's diff'rent. But honest as I am, between you an' me, if I was an aldherman, I wudden't say, be hivins, I think I'd stand firm; but—well, if some wan come to me an' said, 'Dooley, here's fifty thousan' dollars f'r ye'er vote to betray th' sacred inthrests iv Chicago,' I'd go to Father Kelly an' ask th' prayers iv th' congregation.

" 'Tis not, Hinnissy, that this man Yerkuss goes up to an aldherman an' says out sthraight, 'Here, Bill, take this bundle, an' be an infamyous scoundhrel.' That's th' way th' man in Mitchigan Avnoo sees it, but 'tis not sthraight. D'ye mind Dochney that was wanst aldherman here? Ye don't. Well, I do. He ran a little conthractin' business down be Halsted Sthreet. 'Twas him built th' big shed f'r th' ice comp'ny. He was a fine man an' a sthrong wan. He begun his political career be lickin' a plasthrer be th' name iv Egan, a man that had th' County Clare thrip an' was thought to be th' akel iv anny man in town. Fr'm that he growed till he bate near ivry man he knew, an' become very pop'lar, so that he was sint to th' council. Now Dochney was an honest an' sober man whin he wint in; but wan day a man come up to him, an' says he, 'Ye know that ordhnance Schwartz inthrajooced?' 'I do,' says Dochney, 'an' I'm again it. 'Tis a swindle,' he says. 'Well,' says th' la-ad, 'they'se five thousan' in it f'r ye,' he says. They had to pry Dochney off iv him. Th' nex' day a man he knowed well come to Dochney, an' says he, 'That's a fine ordhnance iv Schwartz.' 'It is, like hell,' says Dochney. ''Tis a plain swindle,' he says. ''Tis a good thing f'r th' comp'nies,' says this man; 'but look what they've done f'r th' city,' he says, 'an' think,' he says, 'iv th' widdies an' orphans,' he says, 'that has their har-rd-earned coin invisted,' he says. An' a tear rolled

down his cheek. 'I'm an orphan mesilf,' says Dochney; 'an' as
f'r th' widdies, anny healthy widdy with sthreet-car stock
ought to be ashamed iv hersilf if she's a widdy long,' he says.
An' th' man wint away.

"Now Dochney thought he'd put th' five thousan' out iv his
mind, but he hadn't. He'd on'y laid it by, an' ivry time he
closed his eyes he thought iv it. 'Twas a shame to give th'
comp'nies what they wanted, but th' five thousan' was a lot iv
money. 'Twud lift th' morgedge. 'Twud clane up th' notes on
th' new conthract. 'Twud buy a new dhress f'r Mrs. Dochney.
He begun to feel sorrowful f'r th' widdies an' orphans. 'Poor
things!' says he to himsilf, says he. 'Poor things, how they
must suffer!' he says; 'an' I need th' money. Th' sthreet-car
comp'nies is robbers,' he says; 'but 'tis thrue they've built up
th' city,' he says, 'an' th' money'd come in handy,' he says.
'No wan'd be hurted, annyhow,' he says; 'an', sure, it ain't a
bribe f'r to take money f'r doin' something ye want to do,
annyhow,' he says. 'Five thousan' widdies an' orphans,' he
says; an' he wint to sleep.

"That was th' way he felt whin he wint down to see ol'
Simpson to renew his notes, an' Simpson settled it. 'Dochney,' he says, 'I wisht ye'd pay up,' he says. 'I need th'
money,' he says. 'I'm afraid th' council won't pass th'
Schwartz ordhnance,' he says; 'an' it manes much to me,' he
says. 'Be th' way,' he says, 'how're ye goin' to vote on that
ordhance?' he says. 'I dinnaw,' says Dochney. 'Well,' says
Simpson (Dochney tol' me this himsilf), 'whin ye find out,
come an' see me about th' notes,' he says. An' Dochney wint
to th' meetin'; an', whin his name was called, he hollered
'Aye,' so loud a chunk iv plaster fell out iv th' ceilin' an' stove
in th' head iv a rayform aldherman."

"Did they hang him?" asked Mr. Hennessy.

"Faith, they did not," said Mr. Dooley. "He begun missin'
his jooty at wanst. Aldhermen always do that after th' first few
weeks. 'Ye got ye'er money,' says Father Kelly; 'an' much
good may it do ye,' he says. 'Well,' says Dochney, 'I'd be a
long time prayin' mesilf into five thousan',' he says. An' he
become leader in th' council. Th' las' ordhnance he inthro-

jooced was wan establishin' a license f'r churches, an' compellin' thim to keep their fr-ront dure closed an' th' blinds drawn on Sundah. He was expelled fr'm th' St. Vincent de Pauls, an' ilicted a director iv a bank th' same day.

"Now, Hinnissy, that there man niver knowed he was bribed—th' first time. Th' second time he knew. He ast f'r it. An' I wudden't hang Dochney. I wudden't if I was sthrong enough. But some day I'm goin' to let me temper r-run away with me, an' get a comity together, an' go out an' hang ivry dam widdy an' orphan between th' rollin' mills an' th' foundlin's' home. If it wasn't f'r thim raypechious crathers, they'd be no boodle annywhere."

"Well, don't forget Simpson," said Mr. Hennessy.

"I won't," said Mr. Dooley. "I won't."

A SHORT HISTORY OF DEEDLE

The culturally obtuse who still cling to the notion that scat—that is, the singing of a musical phrase made up of an idiotic syllable or syllables—was invented by Louis Armstrong or Ella Fitzgerald would do well to approach Munce Peasley's new book, "The Meaningless in Music: Six Centuries, from Fa-la to Ooblie-dot" (Niggling Press, New Haven. Six pages; $18), with extreme caution. Dr. Peasley, curator of rare beineckes at the Beinecke collection at Yale University, has assembled cast-iron proof that the first nonsense syllables were sung not by a man in Chicago with a wide tie and zoot pants but by an unknown fourteenth-century English thresher, whose magnificent contribution altered the course of Western culture, though he himself was trampled to death by kine the following week. Peasley, using blunt scissors and a jar of mucilage, has reconstructed this and other significant events in his field, and we can but stand slack-jawed at the quality of his research, to say nothing of his general appearance. A short précis follows, after which the reader may continue to stare vacantly out the window.

FOLK BEGINNINGS: The earliest known record of primitive scat, or *scutte,* occurs in Weir's "Synggebok" (1345)—a collection of English country airs sung at harvest time to celebrate the continuing failure of all known farming methods.

Weir, a London scrivener and curdsmonger, obtained a contemporary version of the Scots ballad "Wha Haue Ye Gae?":

Oh, wha haue ye gae,
Ma' billy-dilly glorn?
Wha haue ye gae, ma' birney?
Ich bene ta' ye toon,
Wi' ma' nelkins all a-blorn.
Synge lack-a-day, witherey-boo,
lack-a-day, tarn—

Here the fragment ends, probably because of Weir's falling into the mill and being ground into a fine white powder. (The event was celebrated in another popular ballad of the day, "Weir Haue Bene Grynde Intae Whyte Poudre, Ye Stupe" [1346].) However, the evidence is incontrovertible. "Lack-a-day, witherey-boo," dating from this period, was instantly recognized as the most infuriating musical phrase in the language, remaining unchallenged until the introduction, over six hundred years later, of "tootie-fruitie, o-rootie" by Charles Berry.

Transition to Other Modes: The classical school begins with the appearance, in Italy, of Fra Antonio de'Nonentati, a modest seventeenth-century cleric who was the *maestro di concerti* for the Pietà Ospedale during the period when it was entirely under water (1689-90). In an era already celebrated for the hysterical productivity of its artists, he stands out as the preeminent freak. In addition to performing his regular duties at the hospital (he was responsible for the daily taunting of the *incurabili*), he provided for his patron, the Duc M'anti, thousands of masses, cantatas, capriccios, preludes, and fugues, plus hundreds of occasional pieces designed, in the fashion of the time, to aid the aging nobleman in the execution of his daily regimen: a sicilienne to help him sleep, a brisk rondo to wake him up, a tuneful courante to make him eat his peas, a merry allemande to encourage him to pitch face forward into the canal. This creative cataract, dwarfing even the combined œuvre of Haydn, Scarlatti *père,* and Paul (the Tiny Dynamo) Williams, allowed the Duke to dominate the social and cultural life of Italy for over a decade, until the Vatican impounded his Rolodex.

It is no secret that Nonentati's endless inspiration severely taxed his collaborators, notably the castrato Calamari (Fruggio Spedini, nicknamed the Squid because he was fat and rubbery and darted about the stage in an obnoxious manner). The relationship, though unproductive, was not entirely cordial, judging from this entry in the monk's journal:

July 29. A long hot summer. In two weeks it will be July 43. How slowly the time goes! Up at 3 A.M. for matins and some light composition. Completed a commission from the Grand Magistrate to devise a new tuning for his mandolin; viz:

He was quite enchanted with it and sent along a scroll entitling me to have my nose twisted any time I am at the palace. Finished today's opera, but the bewigged ponce is again late with the text. What to do? Without words I cannot rehearse the singers. Without singers, you got no opera. Without no opera, you got nothing.[1]

The story is taken up here by Langoustino, another *soprano naturale*, about whom Handel said, ". . . his singing can make the birds come down from the sky and walk around for a while. If that is what you want." From Langoustino's famous letter to his horse:

. . in the absence of any text, Maestro asked me for tonight's performance to sing "anything at all—even something imbecilic, like your name." By the second act, however, the inordinately damp weather had shrunk my

[1] Translation by Fabrizio Linen Supply and Translation Service.

costume (a leather jerkin) to one-quarter of its original size, totally constricting my chesst and rendering impossible any but the tiniest of breaths. "La—" I sang, over and over, in a series of strangulated mouse-like inhalations. From beyond the footlights came a telltale rustling and shifting as the audience gleefully anticipated a major fiasco. Tartini smirked behind his fan; humiliation seemed inescapable. My embarrassment turned to rage. "La . . . la . . . la . . ." I persisted, forcing each breath, until my field of vision was replaced by a pleasant series of bright pinwheels against a black background. Upon being revived, I learned that the performance, far from a disaster, had thoroughly charmed the Duke (who is a swine), and he awarded me twelve florins and a thaler, though I would have preferred money.

THE BAROQUE MASTERS: Baroque scat had its origins in the work of Johann Joachim Quantz, the German flautist who was clever enough to be called a contemporary of Buxtehude even though they did not both live at the same time. Quantz taught his students to speak the word "did'll" into their flutes to achieve proper articulation. The novelty caught on quickly, as the only other diversion available in eighteenth-century Berlin was the weekly placing of large stones upon an ugly person, or "critic." Quantz died a wealthy man, and, as befitted a person of his stature, was buried upside down to see if he had any loose change in his bib.

THE CLASSICAL SCHOOL: It is probable that the young Mozart was familiar with Quantz's work, most likely through the efforts of the Baron van Swieten, an amateur who also ran the catcall concession at the Munich Spielhaus. Van Swieten was a friend and patron of the young Salzburg genius, and occasionally let him see the works of the Baroque masters. As he was mortally afraid of adulterating the pure musical wellspring of the prodigy, he permitted him to view his copy of Bach's Goldberg Variations only through a telescope while the

Baron rode by in a carriage, opening and shutting the book very quickly.

In his memoirs, the Baron himself recalls, "Today I chanced to overhear the lad singing to himself in the act of composing a song. It was a bittersweet, haunting melody":

We now know this fragment belonged not to a song at all but to the opening few measures of the "Leipzig" Symphony, or "St. Anne's Jitters," as it is known in England. With typical unself-consciousness, Mozart here takes the antiquated "dee"—a product of the lyrical but unsophisticated Italian school—and combines it with the more intellectual "did'll" of the German Quantz and arrives at the brilliant synthesis "deedle," thus effecting in one masterstroke a blending of the affettuoso with the rubato, and the creation of a style that can be either played at home for friends or worn after dark for an evening of casual elegance. Mozart himself was quite pleased with the phrase, writing to his father, "I'm certain you'll agree it has wonderful potential if used correctly, and should garner hefty ducat in local situations." He went on to say, "It has become a favorite of Prince Leopold, who sponsored an outdoor musicale on my behalf, even joining the orchestra to blow a little flute (called a *piccolo*). When the concert was halted, due to a rain shower, he was kind enough to draw me aside, saying, 'Someday you and your deedles will be more famous than Mozart.' Since I *am* Mozart, I found his remark perverse, until I recalled that he had been repeatedly struck by lightning during the afternoon."

THE NINETEENTH-CENTURY SCHOOL: The early Romantics (Berlioz, Mendelssohn, Chopin, and the Shapiros—the last not composers, but inseparable) brought scat out from the musty corridors of classicism into the bright sunshine of what Liszt called "the emotive rebobazoid" (the Abbé was over seventy at the time and may have meant something else entirely). In any event, strict adherence to classical syllables was abandoned for a freer, more poetic style. Mendelssohn hummed the opening theme of his Violin Concerto to Ferdinand David thus:

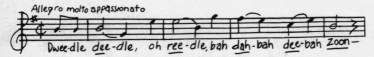

An illuminating anecdote about Brahms illustrates how the artistic personality transcends formalistic limitations, but we do not have this anecdote. Yet it is known that Brahms, at the dress rehearsal of his "Ein Deutsches Requiem," admonished the chorus, saying, "Text, schmext, just keep it peppy. And don't fidget during the solos."

THE MODERNISTS AND BEYOND: If there is one composer who developed a truly contemporary technique, it is either Maurice Ravel or someone who looked just like him and lived in his apartment. Ravel, a great admirer of American jazz, heard an early Louis Armstrong performance of "Honeysuckle Rose" containing the following phrase:

Like all great innovators, Ravel took great risks, often saying, as he twirled his upper lip (he had no mustache), "Now I take these great risks, isn't it?" and, stimulated by Satchmo's brilliant improvisation on the Waller tune, attempted to dictate the cadenza of an unpublished saxophone concerto (two hundred bars, all thirty-second notes) on the syllable "dwane;" viz:

By the third bar, his jaw had dislocated, and Honegger later reported that he had to sponge foam from the Master's cravat.

Ravel was of course the victim of a rapidly worsening situation—one that Schoenberg characterized as the lack of a simple, universal "zot-sprechen," capable of being understood by anyone, regardless of style or nationality. Toward that end, a worldwide artistic conference was convened in April, 1938, in a nice room at the Europa Hotel, in Vienna, with folding chairs for up to three hundred people and light refreshments promised afterward. The steering committee, co-chaired by Francis Poulenc and Fats Waller, urged the adoption of the simplified, or metric, vout system, a workable compromise in which all previous syllables, from "fa-la" to "vaus-o-zootie," were immediately replaced by a simple "zot," while the irregular hyphenates ("zobba-zide," "po-zide," and "re-bop") were to be slowly phased out. In the keynote address, delivered to almost three hundred folding chairs, rooney-master Slim Gaillard captured the spirit of the evening when he said,

Yip rock, heh-ree-sey,
Kay biss-ay knee, kib-bee bah,
Ah-la-ha mish-a-Mac voutie!
La-ha, la-ha Macrooney-mo.

Seven years later, in occupied Austria, Anton von Webern paused to light a cigarette in the doorway of his home and was struck down by a bullet. An old era had ended, and so far nothing has replaced it.

MISSION TO MANDALA

In last month's issue of *First Brigade,* we saw Joe and Jim launch the flying skiff *Capability* from the U.S.S. *Enterprise,* Floating HQ of the famous First, and set course for Mandala, mysterious island stronghold of the treacherous Celanese. Hours passed. To anxious buddies waiting for word—Rocco, Izzy, Chief Thunder, Mojo, Mike, Captain O'Connor, Nurse Nancy—they seemed like days. *"Mama mia!* It's-a no use-a," said Rocco, manning the scanner that was fine-tuned to pick up faint flickers from Joe and Jim's solar-powered laser signal rings. "Keep trying, Rock!" muttered Captain O'Connor grimly. "I know the boys are trying to get through to us—I just know it!" Suddenly Izzy heard taps on his headset. *"Oy veh,"* he sighed. "If it's bed news you vant, Keptain, boy, hef I got da bed news!" Faithful to their orders, the two youths had maintained radio silence, but by tapping on solid subterranean surfaces they had managed to send a Morse-code message by way of the Brigade's highly sensitive seismograph, informing HQ that they were trapped in an abandoned mine shaft and hopelessly surrounded by screaming Celanese terrorists crazed by anti-American rhetoric and dominated by their Cuban Communist mercenary masters! On the decks of the *Enterprise,* initial dismay and disbelief were quickly replaced by quiet determination as the ship swung hard to starboard. Communications Control crackled with crisp orders. "Them little gimps think America says 'uncle,' I reckon it's up to us to give 'em a lesson in *English,*" Mike said confidently. "C'mon, Marie and Louise," Mojo whispered to his fists. "Time for you to do the *talkin'.*"

Can the First do the job? Can a New York City cabdriver, an ex-welterweight champ, a San Francisco short-order cook, a Nebraska farm boy, a direct descendant of Crazy Horse, a former tailback for the Fighting Irish, and the first woman to perform successfully an arterial bypass on a mountaintop in a blizzard—can a crack team of diehard individuals intervene and, with minimal loss of human life, rescue Joe and Jim—a veteran C.I.A. operative and an A.D.A. vice-president who loves opera? Or does Mandala mean curtains? Is it time to turn tail, run up the white flag, call off the dogs, and generally cheese it? Is it time to cash in Old Glory?

More from Mandala in a minute. First, this month's mail-bag:

> *Here's a big salute to all you guys at Able Baker Comics, especially the artists. Jerry's work on the preventive air strike in the November ish was superb—great action, beautiful color! Just one complaint. How could Joe and Jim walk into an abandoned mine shaft? It has "TRAP" written all over it. These guys are supposedly trained in anti-terrorist tactics (A.T.T.), but sometimes they don't have the smarts to dial Information. Did they eat Dumb Flakes for breakfast? C'mon! Let's get both oars in the water!*
>
> L.F., NEW HAVEN

A low blow, L. F., and it hurts, man, no lie. You're calling two guys dumb who rigged up a makeshift bombsight from a beer bottle and a mess kit when the *Capability* came through Chinese ack-ack looking like Swiss cheese and planted 500-pounders in Mao's chow mein, giving Chiang Kai-shek time to reach Taiwan ("Yanks Over Yangtze")? You say two soldiers are stupid who snuck behind V.C. lines, disguising themselves by squinting, and blazed a fake Ho Chi Minh Trail that led two thousand N.V.D. regulars straight into the arms of the Third Division ("Tête-à-Tet")? It's armchair commanders like you, L. F., who make fighting for democracy the thankless job that it is. Glad you like November's art, though. We plan more preventive air strikes in the very near future, so be on the lookout.

I have every Able Baker comic going back to 1942. First Brigade is tops in my book, followed by Screaming Leathernecks, Charlie Squadron, Still Subs Run Deep, Slim Smith—Secret Agent, Battling Seabees, Defense Plant Workers in War and Peace, and Wally Randolph—Air Raid Warden, in that order. One question—

Fire away.

In Vol. IV, No. 8, after witnessing the Japanese surrender, Joe plans to return to Middleburg and become an inventor. In Vol. XII, No. 4, at Panmunjom, Jim asks Sgt. Monica York to marry him. In more recent issues, the boys frequently mention wanting to settle down Stateside. Now, trapped in the mine shaft, Jim says he'd give anything for a Coke and cheeseburger. Are these hints of upcoming retirement, possibly of disbanding the entire Brigade?

B.D., SAN LUIS OBISPO

Not on your ever-lovin' life, B.D. That question was answered once and for all when carrier-based Zeros approached Oahu one quiet Sunday morning years ago. When word was flashed to the U.S. of A., Joe was in his garage-workshop, attaching airbrakes with C-clamps to his landau, and Jim was listening to Act III of *Aïda*. They left home and never looked back. Sure, they miss it—Mom, Bud, Sis, the shady streets, Sunday dinner, swimming in the Mississippi, the sweet smell of sassafras, sarsaparilla, and blackstrap molasses—but don't mistake homesickness for lack of resolve. Joe and Jim intend to stay up front for as long as it takes. Why? Check your back yard. See enemy troops digging foxholes in the sandbox? No? Good. Let's keep it that way.

I wish that First Brigade *could be read in every college classroom in America. Maybe it would show today's generation that a volunteer army is an army only if people volunteer. It's up to them. Why is it we always run when we should do what must be done? We'd always rather joke and kid and talk about the things we did, or fret and worry, moan and stew, than tackle the job that's ours to do. If Americans would only fight for everything we know is right, we soon would have a better life free of suffering and strife.*

D.M., OMAHA

Consider the nail hit on the head, D.M. Wake up and smell the coffee, students.

The First Brigade is great, especially Mojo and Chief Thunder. Good to see members of so-called "minority" groups who are willing to fight for the land they love. My only complaint has to do with smoking. I know Captain O'Connor is under a great deal of pressure, but it makes me sick to see cigarettes dangling from his lips. Cigarettes sap a person's vital resources. It's just plain wrong to show them as a sign of manliness.

B.T., ORLANDO

Good point, B.T., and we'll pass it on. A word to the wise should be sufficient. Meanwhile, let's not forget "Allies über Alles" when the Captain lobbed a Zippo into the Nazi fuel dump, or the exploding cigar in "A Gift for Göring."

The Mandala crisis puts me in mind of two similar adventures. In 1942, trapped in a deep bunker on Corregidor, Joe and Jim fasted forty days until, thin *enough to wriggle up the secret airshaft, they escaped the Imperial Japanese Army and reached the open Pacific in time to guide MacArthur's landing boats through mine-infested waters. In 1966, trapped in a Viet Cong cave beneath Hill 109, Joe and Jim called in an air strike right on top of them, and the Air Force, in a textbook display of precision bombing, hit the geological fault right on the money, surgically splitting open the hill and enabling the boys to climb out and be rescued by commandos. I'm confident the First will find a way this time too. Just one little quibble: when the Celanese attack the mouth of the mine shaft, you have their SM-82s going "B*LAM-BLAAAMMM."* *According to the latest* Jane's Guns, *that would be "R*A-A-A-T-R*A-A-A-A-A-T*." Keep up the good work.*

M.G., PHOENIX

Our faces are red, M.G. We confused the SM-82 with the C-24. Your vigilance gives Joe and Jim an even better chance of surviving the attack until the First arrives—as you know, the SM-82 lacks the anti-rock capability of the C-24. Precious minutes have been won. Accept our thanks.

A few years ago, in the Mayaguez incident, Joe and Jim employed stink bombs to render enemy forces helpless with disgust. Now here they are trapped in a mine shaft where stink bombs would be highly effective and on page 24 Joe even points out to Jim that Celanese can't wear gas masks because their heads are too small—but where are the bombs??? What gives? Don't go barefoot to a snake-stomping, as my Dad used to say. Did the guys just plain forget them or what?

G.E., NASHVILLE

Hold on there, G.E. Don't run off half-cocked. Stink bombs come under chemical warfare, and thanks to bleeding hearts in Washington, these valuable tools have been taken out of the hands of the First Brigade. So don't complain to us. Write your Congressman.

Now back to our story.

Deep beneath Mandala, dodging Celanese shells that ricocheted off the mine-shaft walls (BLAAANGG! KACHINGGG!) and hand grenades bouncing down the steeply slanted floor (THUNK-THUNK-THUNK-THUNK-THUNK-THUNK-BLAAAAMMMMMM!!), armed only with M-16s (KRRAKK! KRRAKK!), a flamethrower (KER-WHOOOOSHHHH!), and a bullhorn (WE HAVE JUST ONE RE-SPONSE, ONSE-ONSE-ONSE . . . TO YOUR DEMAND FOR SURREN-DER-ER-ER-ER: NUTS!-TS!-TS!-TS!), Joe and Jim crouched behind a large rock, which Celanese firepower was slowly making smaller and smaller. "Where in blazes is the First?" Jim shouted over the din. "Sometimes—sometimes I get the feeling—oh, never mind," he murmured.

"What??!! Get *what* feeling??!!" Joe answered. Twenty-seven years spent crouched next to Jim in one hellhole after another made him sensitive to the feelings of his younger partner, a liberal and a graduate of a small liberal-arts college, who, unlike Joe—who, like most men of scientific bent, expressed himself plainly and forthrightly—often hesitated and had to be coaxed.

"Sometimes I get the feeling the First is only symbolic," said Jim. "Ever-present—sure! but symbolism all the same."

Joe's eyes rolled up in his smoke-blackened face. He sighed wearily, lighting his last cigarette as he did so. Although he knew that he would always count on the young activist when the chips were down, he had long since come to distrust Jim's doubts, his ever-present skepticism, not to mention his tendency, common among liberals, to want to get into long discussions just when it's time to hunker down and aim for the eyeballs.

"Listen," he rasped. "H_2O is a symbol too. Does that mean you don't believe in water?" He paused, hoping the message would sink in, when suddenly Jim grabbed him.

"That's it!" Jim yelled. "Listen!"

From a narrow crevice beneath their feet came the unmistakable sound of running water. "It's an underground river," said Jim. "Smells like fresh water. That means it runs *to* the sea."

Joe smiled. "See if you can squeeze through that crevice," he said. "I'll hold 'em off."

Meanwhile, aboard the *Enterprise*, Captain O'Connor awaited the arrival of powerful magnets from Midway Island, magnets that, according to physicists, could be mounted in the bellies of low-flying B-52s, yanking the little heads of the Celanese up by the chin-straps of their iron helmets and preventing them from aiming accurately at Joe and Jim as the boys fled from the mine shaft. It had been Nurse Nancy's idea—a whiplash attack—and she watched the Captain anxiously now as he paced the windswept deck. "How much longer can he go on like this?" she asked herself, silently. "The aneurysm is as big as a fist. How can I tell him?" Unaware of her, unaware that Joe and Jim had been carried from Mandala by the underground river and even now were swimming hand over fist in the wrong direction against powerful waves dotted with the fins of killer sharks, he strode back and forth, his eyes fixed eastward, exhaling through his nostrils.

PIGS IS PIGS

Mike Flannery, the Westcote agent of the Interurban Express Company, leaned over the counter of the express office and shook his fist. Mr. Morehouse, angry and red, stood on the other side of the counter, trembling with rage. The argument had been long and heated, and at last Mr. Morehouse had talked himself speechless. The cause of the trouble stood on the counter between the two men. It was a soap box across the top of which were nailed a number of strips, forming a rough but serviceable cage. In it two spotted guinea-pigs were greedily eating lettuce leaves.

"Do as you loike, then!" shouted Flannery, "pay for thim an' take thim, or don't pay for thim and leave them be. Rules is rules, Mister Morehouse, an' Mike Flannery's not goin' to be called down fer breakin' of thim."

"But you everlastingly stupid idiot!" shouted Mr. Morehouse, madly shaking a flimsy printed book beneath the agent's nose, "can't you read it here—in your own plain printed rates? 'Pets, domestic, Franklin to Westcote, if properly boxed, twenty-five cents each.' " He threw the book on the counter in disgust. "What more do you want? Aren't they pets? Aren't they domestic? Aren't they properly boxed? What?"

He turned and walked back and forth rapidly; frowning ferociously.

Suddenly he turned to Flannery, and forcing his voice to an artifical calmness spoke slowly but with intense sarcasm.

"Pets," he said "P-e-t-s! Twenty-five cents each. There are two of them. One! Two! Two times twenty-five are fifty! Can you understand that? I offer you fifty cents."

Flannery reached for the book. He ran his hand through the pages and stopped at page sixty-four.

"An' I don't take fifty cints," he whispered in mockery. "Here's the rule for ut. 'Whin the agint be in anny doubt regardin' which of two rates applies to a shipment, he shall charge the larger. The consign-ey may file a claim for the overcharge.' In this case, Misther Morehouse, I be in doubt. Pets thim animals may be, an' domestic they be, but pigs I'm blame sure they do be, an' me rules says plain as the nose on yer face, 'Pigs Franklin to Westcote, thirty cints each.' An' Misther Morehouse, by me arithmetical knowledge two times thurty comes to sixty cints."

Mr. Morehouse shook his head savagely. "Nonsense!" he shouted, "confounded nonsense, I tell you! Why, you poor ignorant foreigner, that rule means common pigs, domestic pigs, not guinea-pigs!"

Flannery was stubborn.

"Pigs is pigs," he declared firmly. "Guinea-pigs, or dago pigs or Irish pigs is all the same to the Interurban Express Company an' to Mike Flannery. Th' nationality of the pig creates no differentiality in the rate, Misther Morehouse! 'Twould be the same was they Dutch pigs or Rooshun pigs. Mike Flannery," he added, "is here to tind to the expriss business and not to hould conversation wid dago pigs in sivinteen languages fer to discover be they Chinese or Tipperary by birth an' nativity."

Mr. Morehouse hesitated. He bit his lip and then flung out his arms wildly.

"Very well!" he shouted, "you shall hear of this! Your president shall hear of this! It is an outrage! I have offered you fifty cents. You refuse it! Keep the pigs until you are ready to take the fifty cents, but, by George, sir, if one hair of those pigs' heads is harmed I will have the law on you!"

He turned and stalked out, slamming the door. Flannery carefully lifted the soap box from the counter and placed it in a corner. He was not worried. He felt the peace that comes to a faithful servant who has done his duty and done it well.

Mr. Morehouse went home raging. His boy, who had been awaiting the guinea-pigs, knew better than to ask him for them. He was a normal boy and therefore always had a guilty conscience when his father was angry. So the boy slipped quietly around the house. There is nothing so soothing to a guilty conscience as to be out of the path of the avenger.

Mr. Morehouse stormed into the house. "Where's the ink?" he shouted at his wife as soon as his foot was across the doorsill.

Mrs. Morehouse jumped, guiltily. She never used ink. She had not seen the ink, nor moved the ink, nor thought of the ink, but her husband's tone convicted her of the guilt of having borne and reared a boy, and she knew that whenever her husband wanted anything in a loud voice the boy had been at it.

"I'll find Sammy," she said meekly.

When the ink was found Mr. Morehouse wrote rapidly, and he read the completed letter and smiled a triumphant smile.

"That will settle that crazy Irishman!" he exclaimed. "When they get that letter he will hunt another job, all right!"

A week later Mr. Morehouse received a long official envelope with the card of the Interurban Express Company in the upper left corner. He tore it open eagerly and drew out a sheet of paper. At the top it bore the number A6754. The letter was short. "Subject—Rate on guinea-pigs," it said, "Dr. Sir—We are in receipt of your letter regarding rate on guinea-pigs between Franklin and Westcote, addressed to the president of this company. All claims for overcharge should be addressed to the Claims Department."

Mr. Morehouse wrote to the Claims Department. He wrote six pages of choice sarcasm, vituperation and argument, and sent them to the Claims Department.

A few weeks later he received a reply from the Claims Department. Attached to it was his last letter.

"Dr. Sir," said the reply. "Your letter of the 16th inst., addressed to this Department, subject rate on guinea-pigs from Franklin to Westcote, rec'd. We have taken up the matter with our agent at Westcote, and his reply is attached herewith. He informs us that you refused to receive the consignment or to pay the charges. You have therefore no claim against this company, and your letter regarding the proper rate on the consignment should be addressed to our Tariff Department."

Mr. Morehouse wrote to the Tariff Department. He stated his case clearly, and gave his arguments in full, quoting a page or two from the encyclopedia to prove that guinea-pigs were not common pigs.

With the care that characterizes corporations when they are systematically conducted, Mr. Morehouse's letter was numbered, O.K'd, and started through the regular channels. Duplicate copies of the bill of lading, manifest, Flannery's receipt for the package and several other pertinent papers were pinned to the letter, and they were passed to the head of the Tariff Department.

The head of the Tariff Department put his feet on his desk and yawned. He looked through the papers carelessly.

"Miss Kane," he said to his stenographer, "take this letter. 'Agent, Westcote, N. J. Please advise why consignment referred to in attached papers was refused domestic pet rates.' "

Miss Kane made a series of curves and angles on her note book and waited with pencil poised. The head of the department looked at the papers again.

"Huh! guinea-pigs!" he said. "Probably starved to death by this time! Add this to that letter: 'Give condition of consignment at present.' "

He tossed the papers on to the stenographer's desk, took his feet from his own desk and went out to lunch.

When Mike Flannery received the letter he scratched his head.

"Give prisint condition," he repeated thoughtfully. "Now what do thim clerks be wantin' to know, I wonder! 'Prisint condition,' is ut? Thim pigs, praise St. Patrick, do be in good health, so far as I know, but I niver was no veternairy surgeon to dago pigs. Mebby thim clerks wants me to call in the pig docther and have their pulses took. Wan thing I do know, howiver, which is they've glorious appytites for pigs of their soize. Ate? They'd ate the brass padlocks off of a barn door! If the paddy pig, by the same token, ate as hearty as these dago pigs do, there'd be a famine in Ireland."

To assure himself that his report would be up to date, Flannery went to the rear of the office and looked into the cage. The pigs had been transferred to a larger box—a dry goods box.

"Wan,—two,—t'ree,—four,—foive,—six,—sivin,—eight!" he counted. "Sivin spotted an' wan all black. All well an' hearty an' all eatin' loike ragin' hippypottymusses." He went back to his desk and wrote.

"Mr. Morgan, Head of Tariff Department," he wrote. "Why do I say dago pigs is pigs because they is pigs and will be til you say they ain't which is what the rule book says stop your jollying me you know it as well as I do. As to health they are all well and hoping you are the same. P.S. There are eight now the family increased all good eaters. P.S. I paid out so far two dollars for cabbage which they like shall I put in bill for same what?"

Morgan, head of the Tariff Department, when he received this letter, laughed. He read it again and became serious.

"By George!" he said, "Flannery is right, 'pigs is pigs.' I'll have to get authority on this thing. Meanwhile, Miss Kane, take this letter: Agent, Westcote, N. J. Regarding shipment guinea-pigs, File No. A6754. Rule 83, General Instruction to Agents, clearly states that agents shall collect from consignee all costs of provender, etc., etc., required for live stock while in transit or storage. You will proceed to collect same from consignee."

Flannery received this letter next morning, and when he read it he grinned.

"Proceed to collect," he said softly. "How thim clerks do loike to be talkin'! *Me* proceed to collect two dollars and twenty-foive cints off Misther Morehouse! I wonder do thim clerks *know* Misther Morehouse? I'll git it! Oh, yes! 'Misther Morehouse, two an' a quarter, plaze.' 'Cert'nly, me dear frind F'annery. Delighted!' *Not!"*

Flannery drove the express wagon to Mr. Morehouse's door. Mr. Morehouse answered the bell.

"Ah, ha!" he cried as soon as he saw it was Flannery. "So you've come to your senses at last, have you? I thought you would! Bring the box in."

"I hev no box," said Flannery coldly. "I hev a bill agin Misther John C. Morehouse for two dollars and twenty-foive cints for kebbages aten by his dago pigs. Wud you wish to pay ut?"

"Pay—Cabbages—!" gasped Mr. Morehouse. "Do you mean to say that two little guinea-pigs—"

"Eight!" said Flannery. "Papa an' mamma an' the six childer. Eight!"

For answer Mr. Morehouse slammed the door in Flannery's face. Flannery looked at the door reproachfully.

"I take ut the con-*sign*-y don't want to pay for thim kebbages," he said. "If I know signs of refusal, the con-*sign*-y refuses to pay for wan dang kebbage leaf an' be hanged to me!"

Mr. Morgan, the head of the Tariff Department, consulted the president of the Interurban Express Company regarding guinea-pigs, as to whether they were pigs or not pigs. The president was inclined to treat the matter lightly.

"What is the rate on pigs and on pets?" he asked.

"Pigs thirty cents, pets twenty-five," said Morgan.

"Then of course guinea-pigs are pigs," said the president.

"Yes," agreed Morgan, "I look at it that way, too. A thing that can come under two rates is naturally due to be classed as the higher. But are guinea-pigs, pigs? Aren't they rabbits?"

"Come to think of it," said the president, "I believe they are more like rabbits. Sort of half-way station between pig and rabbit. I think the question is this—are guinea-pigs of the domestic pig family? I'll ask Professor Gordon. He is authority on such things. Leave the papers with me."

The president put the papers on his desk and wrote a letter

to Professor Gordon. Unfortunately the Professor was in South America collecting zoological specimens, and the letter was forwarded to him by his wife. As the Professor was in the highest Andes, where no white man had ever penetrated, the letter was many months in reaching him. The president forgot the guinea-pigs, Morgan forgot them, Mr. Morehouse forgot them, but Flannery did not. One-half of his time he gave to the duties of his agency; the other half was devoted to the guinea-pigs. Long before Professor Gordon received the president's letter Morgan received one from Flannery.

"About them dago pigs," it said, "what shall I do they are great in family life, no race suicide for them, there are thirty-two now shall I sell them do you take this express office for a menagerie, answer quick."

Morgan reached for a telegraph blank and wrote:

"Agent, Westcote. Don't sell pigs."

He then wrote Flannery a letter calling his attention to the fact that the pigs were not the property of the company but were merely being held during a settlement of a dispute regarding rates. He advised Flannery to take the best possible care of them.

Flannery, letter in hand, looked at the pigs and sighed. The dry-goods box cage had become too small. He boarded up twenty feet of the rear of the express office to make a large and airy home for them, and went about his business. He worked with feverish intensity when out on his rounds, for the pigs required attention and took most of his time. Some months later, in desperation, he seized a sheet of paper and wrote "160" across it and mailed it to Morgan. Morgan returned it asking for explanation. Flannery replied:

"There be now one hundred sixty of them dago pigs, for heavens sake let me sell off some, do you want me to go crazy, what."

"Sell no pigs," Morgan wired.

Not long after this the president of the express company received a letter from Professor Gordon. It was a long and scholarly letter, but the point was that the guinea-pig was the

Cavia aparoea, while the common pig was the genius *Sus* of the family *Suidae.* He remarked that they were prolific and multiplied rapidly.

"They are not pigs," said the president, decidedly, to Morgan. "The twenty-five cent rate applies."

Morgan made the proper notation on the papers that had accumulated in File A6754, and turned them over to the Audit Department. The Audit Department took some time to look the matter up, and after the usual delay wrote Flannery that as he had on hand one hundred and sixty guinea-pigs, the property of consignee, he should deliver them and collect charges at the rate of twenty-five cents each.

Flannery spent a day herding his charges through a narrow opening in their cage so that he might count them.

"Audit Dept." he wrote, when he had finished the count, "you are way off there may be was one hundred and sixty dago pigs once, but wake up don't be a back number. I've got even eight hundred, now shall I collect for eight hundred or what, how about sixty-four dollars I paid out for cabbages."

It required a great many letters back and forth before the Audit Department was able to understand why the error had been made of billing one hundred and sixty instead of eight hundred, and still more time for it to get the meaning of the "cabbages."

Flannery was crowded into a few feet at the extreme front of the office. The pigs had all the rest of the room and two boys were employed constantly attending to them. The day after Flannery had counted the guinea-pigs there were eight more added to his drove, and by the time the Audit Department gave him authority to collect for eight hundred Flannery had given up all attempts to attend to the receipt or the delivery of goods. He was hastily building galleries around the express office, tier above tier. He had four thousand and sixty-four guinea-pigs to care for! More were arriving daily.

Immediately following its authorization the Audit Department sent another letter, but Flannery was too busy to open it. They wrote another and then they telegraphed:

"Error in guinea-pig bill. Collect for two guinea-pigs, fifty cents. Deliver all to consignee."

Flannery read the telegram and cheered up. He wrote out a bill as rapidly as his pencil could travel over paper and ran all the way to the Morehouse home. At the gate he stopped suddenly. The house stared at him with vacant eyes. The windows were bare of curtains and he could see into the empty rooms. A sign on the porch said, "To Let." Mr. Morehouse had moved! Flannery ran all the way back to the express office. Sixty-nine guinea-pigs had been born during his absence. He ran out again and made feverish inquiries in the village. Mr. Morehouse had not only moved, but he had left Westcote. Flannery returned to the express office and found that two hundred and six guinea-pigs had entered the world since he left it. He wrote a telegram to the Audit Department.

"Can't collect fifty cents for two dago pigs consignee has left town address unknown what shall I do? Flannery."

The telegram was handed to one of the clerks in the Audit Department, and as he read it he laughed.

"Flannery must be crazy. He ought to know that the thing to do is to return the consignment here," said the clerk. He telegraphed Flannery to send the pigs to the main office of the company at Franklin.

When Flannery received the telegram he set to work. The six boys he had engaged to help him also set to work. They worked with the haste of desperate men, making cages out of soap boxes, cracker boxes, and all kinds of boxes, and as fast as the cages were completed they filled them with guinea-pigs and expressed them to Franklin. Day after day the cages of guinea-pigs flowed in a steady stream from Westcote to Franklin, and still Flannery and his six helpers ripped and nailed and packed—relentlessly and feverishly. At the end of the week they had shipped two hundred and eighty cases of guinea-pigs, and there were in the express office seven hundred and four more pigs than when they began packing them.

"Stop sending pigs. Warehouse full," came a telegram to Flannery. He stopped packing only long enough to wire back.

"Can't stop," and kept on sending them. On the next train up from Franklin came one of the company's inspectors. He had instructions to stop the stream of guinea-pigs at all hazards. As his train drew up at Westcote station he saw a cattle-car standing on the express company's siding. When he reached the express office he saw the express wagon backed up to the door. Six boys were carrying bushel baskets full of guinea-pigs from the office and dumping them into the wagon. Inside the room Flannery, with his coat and vest off, was shoveling guinea-pigs into bushel baskets with a coal scoop. He was winding up the guinea-pig episode.

He looked up at the inspector with a snort of anger.

"Wan wagonload more an' I'll be quit of thim, an' niver will ye catch Flannery wid no more foreign pigs on his hands. No, sur! They near was the death o' me. Nixt toime I'll know that pigs of whativer nationality is domistic pets—an' go at the lowest rate."

He began shoveling again rapidly, speaking quickly between breaths.

"Rules may be rules, but you can't fool Mike Flannery twice wid the same thrick—whin ut comes to live stock, dang the rules. So long as Flannery runs this expriss office—pigs is pets—an' cows is pets—an' horses is pets—an' lions an' tigers an' Rocky Mountain goats is pets—an' the rate on thim is twinty-foive cints."

He paused long enough to let one of the boys put an empty basket in the place of the one he had just filled. There were only a few guinea-pigs left. As he noted their limited number his natural habit of looking on the bright side returned.

"Well, annyhow," he said cheerfully, " 'tis not so bad as ut might be. What if thim dago pigs had been elephants!"

NERO

Nero was the son of Agrippina the Younger and Cnaeus Domitius Ahenobarbus, combining the worst features of each. His father was fond of running down little children with his chariot and gouging out people's eyes, and there were rumors I'd rather not mention.[1] Agrippina was a sister of Caligula. You don't get over a thing like that.[2]

Nero was born at Antium on December 15, A.D. 37. He was named Lucius Domitius Ahenobarbus, so he is known as Nero Claudius Caesar Drusus Germanicus. Any relationship to Germanicus opened all doors at this period. Nowadays it wouldn't get you a thing.[3]

In some respects Nero was ahead of his time. He boiled his drinking water to remove the impurities and cooled it with unsanitary ice to put them back again. He renamed the month of April after himself, calling it Neroneus, but the idea never caught on because April is not Neroneus and there is no use pretending that it is. During his reign of fourteen years, the outlying provinces are said to have prospered. They were farther away.

[1] The Ahenobarbi, or Bronzebeards, all had red beards because the black beard of Lucius Domitius Ahenobarbus, founder of the family, had been changed to red by Castor and Pollux, I forget why.

[2] Suetonius states that when Tiberius, Agrippina's uncle, was in exile and looking for favorable omens, "as he was changing his clothes, his tunic appeared to be all on fire." It probably *was* on fire.

[3] By the way, just who was Germanicus?

Since Nero's character leaves much to be desired, we are apt to forget his good side. We should try to remember that he did not murder his mother until he was twenty-one years old. Besides, he only did it to please his sweetheart, Poppaea Sabina, whom he later married and kicked to death while she was with child.[4] It was her own fault, in a way, as she nagged him for coming home late from the races.

Octavia, Nero's first wife, a daughter of the Emperor Claudius, was not quite satisfactory. She was the kind that bears a grudge. She disliked Nero for poisoning her young brother Britannicus. He would have died anyhow, sooner or later, but Octavia tried to make something out of it. Nero banished her, then had her smothered in a steam bath and married Poppaea, for love will find a way.

His next wife was Statilia Messalina, who was not the Messalina you're thinking of. That was Valeria Messalina, Nero's cousin and the third wife of the Emperor Claudius. She was the worst woman in Rome and she just loved being it. She was so wicked that she hated well-behaved people on principle. She said they made her tired.[5] Statilia was not nearly so intelligent as Valeria. She took to brooding after a while. She had been married four times, but nothing like this.

Mentally, Nero was fair to middling. He could speak Latin fluently. His tutor, Lucius Annaeus Seneca, was a Stoic, or humbug. Seneca taught the vanity of worldly wealth and was immensely rich. When it was suggested that he stop lending money at ruinous rates if he felt that way about it, he said it would be against all the tenets of the Stoic philosophy and beneath him as a member in good standing to give that much attention to so indifferent a subject when his mind should be on higher things. This established his reputation as a thinker.[6]

---

[4] Poppaea Sabina was the daughter of Poppaea Sabina, who was the daughter of C. Poppaeus Sabinus.

[5] Claudius finally had her killed, but not until she'd had an awfully good time. If you don't know the details of her career, you're just as well off.

[6] When Seneca was exiled for a time under the *Lex de adulteriis,* he said nothing at all. There was nothing to say.

Nero finally had enough of Seneca's thoughts and told him to go and drop dead, which he did. He gave the same order to a senator named P. Clodius Paetas Thrasea just for looking like a thinker. Senator P. Clodius Thrasea hadn't a thought in his whole system, but he gave that impression somehow, at least when he wasn't talking.

Agrippina was a wonderful mother to Nero, except that she was inclined to be bossy. A matron of the old school, she was head of the reform party in Rome and in charge of its murders as well as her own private ones.[7] She did not murder her first husband, the father of Nero. She only drove him to drink. Her second, Crispus Passienus, died suddenly after making a will in her favor, and she is often accused of feeding mushrooms poisoned with arsenic to her third, the Emperor Claudius, so that Nero could succeed him, the quicker the better. Let's not be too sure of this. It is possible that the Emperor's basal metabolism was all out of whack and that the symptoms were confused with those of arsenic. Or Claudius may have tampered with his own food in one of his vague states.

Claudius was an old fellow who had been found hiding behind a curtain after the death of Caligula and made Emperor by mistake.[8] Caligula once threw him into the river to get rid of him and somebody fished him out.[9] Since that time he had been subject to nervous twitchings.[10] Most people regarded Claudius as feeble-minded because he wrote a mildly uninteresting collection of historical sketches and tried to be funny in company. He was interested only in the past. When his friends asked him, as they constantly did, why he didn't write about current events, he would start twitching again. None of his four marriages turned out very well. He was always reading a book.[11]

[7] Agrippina had two canine teeth on the right side of her mouth. This was always good for a laugh in some circles.
[8] His only friend was a little white poodle.
[9] He was the brother of Germanicus.
[10] Claudius had been neglected as a child. His mother, Antonia, refused to remarry after the death of Drusus, devoting herself entirely to a pet lamprey which may have reminded her of the deceased.
[11] Claudius' son Drusus by Plautia Urgulanillo was choked to death while tossing up pears and catching them in his mouth.

Yet Claudius accomplished some sound constructive work. He built the Via Claudia, a splendid road leading to the Danube Valley, over which the barbarians later traveled to conquer Italy. He also invented three new letters, one representing the consonant *u* as distinguished from the vowel *u*, one for a sound between *i* and *u*, and one for *bs* or *ps*. They had to be dropped, as nobody could pronounce them.[12]

Agrippina had long been a problem to Nero, always interfering as she did and quarreling about who should be murdered and who shouldn't. Since he owed her everything for murdering Claudius, he had hoped to kill her as gently as possible. He did not want her to suffer, and he went to some lengths to prevent it. He gave her quick poison three times without result, then he fixed the ceiling of her bedroom so it would fall and crush her as she slept. Of course that didn't work. It never does. Either the ceiling doesn't fall or the victim sleeps on the sofa that night.

Next, he attempted to drown her by means of a boat with a collapsible bottom, but the vessel sank too slowly and she swam away like a mink. Nero then lost his head completely, as who wouldn't, and told his freedman, Anicetus, to try anything. Anicetus, a rude but sensible fellow, went and got a club and beat her to death. Maybe the Cave Men knew best.

We cannot be sure how many others Nero murdered, since some of the stories are probably mere gossip. You know how it is. Once you kill a few people, you get a bad name. You're blamed for every corpse that turns up for miles around and anything else that goes wrong.

Take the great fire that destroyed most of Rome in A.D. 64. They say he started it. Be that as it may, he did not fiddle during the conflagration, for the violin had not yet been invented. He played the lyre and sang of the Fall of Troy. What's so awful about that? Of course he shouldn't have tortured so many Christians to prove that they did it. A few would have been plenty.[13]

[12] Ferrero holds that certain parts of his mind were highly developed. He doesn't say which parts.
[13] It is generally thought that no Christians were thrown to the lions

Anyhow, he rebuilt the city on a more modern plan. The chief improvement was his Golden House, as he called it, an imperial residence a mile long, equipped with a revolving banquet hall, walls of gold and jewels, machines for squirting perfume in all directions, a duplex apartment for his pet ape, and a statue of himself 120 feet high. When he moved in, he said that at least he was beginning to live like a human being. I have been unable to think of an adequate comeback to that remark. You try it.

Nero's singing has occasioned unfavorable comment, quite aside from the fire episode. He sang and sang, in private and in public, accompanied by his lyre, five thousand applauders chosen for their endurance, and a regiment of soldiers with drawn swords. He would step to the front of the stage with his personal bodyguard and ask his audience if they had ever heard a better singer. They always said no, they hadn't.[14] If you have been wondering why Nero sang, the answer is clear enough. People sing because they think they can sing.[15]

He made his professional debut at Naples five years after the death of his mother. She was spared that, at least. The theatre was shaken by an earthquake during the show and collapsed after the final section. Nero got away. Lightning frequently struck near the scene of his concerts. It missed him.

He also went to Greece and sang for a year and a half, after which he returned to Italy and sang. Forty-one citizens conspired to slaughter him, but something went wrong.[16] Then he announced a recital at which he would play the pipe organ, the flute, and the bagpipes and sing a tragedy set to music by himself. The legions rose in Gaul and the Senate declared him a public enemy. As the troops advanced on Rome, Nero pro-

---

until the reign of Marcus Aurelius Antoninus, whose *Meditations* you ought to read. Great stuff.

[14] Nero's voice was thin and weak. Had it possessed more volume, it would have been worse.

[15] At the age of twelve Nero had shown a lively interest in the arts, particularly music, painting, sculpture, and poetry. Why was nothing done about this?

[16] I don't mind singers so much, if only they wouldn't practice.

posed to go and meet them and win their hearts by singing a few songs. Somebody had to explain. Assisted by Epaphroditus, his private secretary, he cut his throat on June 9, A.D. 68, the anniversary of his first wife's murder. Well, we're none of us perfect.

THE ARTISTIC CAREER OF CORKY

You will notice, as you flit through these reminiscences of mine, that from time to time the scene of action is laid in and around the city of New York; and it is just possible that this may occasion the puzzled look and the start of surprise. "What," it is possible that you may ask yourselves, "is Bertram doing so far from his beloved native land?"

Well, it's a fairly longish story; but, reefing it down a bit and turning it for the nonce into a two-reeler, what happened was that my Aunt Agatha on one occasion sent me over to America to try to stop young Gussie, my cousin, marrying a girl on the vaudeville stage, and I got the whole thing so mixed up that I decided it would be a sound scheme to stop on in New York for a bit instead of going back and having long, cozy chats with her about the affair.

So I sent Jeeves out to find a decent flat, and settled down for a spell of exile.

I'm bound to say New York's a most sprightly place to be exiled in. Everybody was awfully good to me, and there seemed to be plenty of things going on; so, take it for all in all, I didn't undergo any frightful hardships. Blokes introduced me to other blokes, and so on and so forth, and it wasn't long before I knew squads of the right sort, some who rolled in the stuff in houses up by the Park, and others who lived with the gas turned down mostly around Washington Square—artists and writers and so forth. Brainy coves.

Corky, the bird I am about to treat of, was one of the artists. A portrait painter, he called himself, but as a matter of fact his score up to date had been nil. You see, the catch about portrait painting—I've looked into the thing a bit—is that you can't start painting portraits till people come along and ask you to, and they won't come and ask you to until you've painted a lot first. This makes it kind of difficult, not to say tough, for the ambitious youngster.

Corky managed to get along by drawing an occasional picture for the comic papers—he had rather a gift for funny stuff when he got a good idea—and doing bedsteads and chairs and things for the advertisements. His principal source of income, however, was derived from biting the ear of a rich uncle—one Alexander Worple, who was in the jute business. I'm a bit foggy as to what jute is, but it's apparently something the populace is pretty keen on, for Mr. Worple had made quite an indecently large stack out of it.

Now, a great many fellows think that having a rich uncle is a pretty soft snap, but, according to Corky, such is not the case. Corky's uncle was a robust sort of cove, who looked like living for ever. He was fifty-one, and it seemed as if he might go to par. It was not this, however, that distressed poor Corky, for he was not bigoted and had no objection to the man going on living. What Corky kicked at was the way the above Worple used to harry him.

Corky's uncle, you see, didn't want him to be an artist. He didn't think he had any talent in that direction. He was always urging him to chuck Art and go into the jute business and start at the bottom and work his way up. And what Corky said was that, while he didn't know what they did at the bottom of the jute business, instinct told him that it was something too beastly for words. Corky, moreover, believed in his future as an artist. Some day, he said, he was going to make a hit. Meanwhile, by using the utmost tact and persuasiveness, he was inducing his uncle to cough up very grudgingly a small quarterly allowance.

He wouldn't have got this if his uncle hadn't had a hobby. Mr. Worple was peculiar in this respect. As a rule, from what

I've observed, the American captain of industry doesn't do anything out of business hours. When he has put the cat out and locked up the office for the night, he just relapses into a state of coma from which he emerges only to start being a captain of industry again. But Mr. Worple in his spare time was what is known as an ornithologist. He had written a book called *American Birds,* and was writing another, to be called *More American Birds.* When he had finished that, the presumption was that he would begin a third, and keep on till the supply of American birds gave out. Corky used to go to him about once every three months and let him talk about American birds. Apparently you could do what you liked with old Worple if you gave him his head first on his pet subject, so these little chats used to make Corky's allowance all right for the time being. But it was pretty rotten for the poor chap. There was the frightful suspense, you see, and, apart from that, birds, except when broiled and in the society of a cold bottle, bored him stiff.

To complete the character study of Mr. Worple, he was a man of extremely uncertain temper, and his general tendency was to think that Corky was a poor chump and that whatever step he took in any direction on his own account was just another proof of his innate idiocy. I should imagine Jeeves feels very much the same about me.

So when Corky trickled into my apartment one afternoon, shooing a girl in front of him, and said, "Bertie, I want you to meet my fiancée, Miss Singer," the aspect of the matter which hit me first was precisely the one which he had come to consult me about. The very first words I spoke were, "Corky, how about your uncle?"

The poor chap gave one of those mirthless laughs. He was looking anxious and worried, like a man who has done the murder all right but can't think what the deuce to do with the body.

"We're so scared, Mr. Wooster," said the girl. "We were hoping that you might suggest a way of breaking it to him."

Muriel Singer was one of those very quiet, appealing girls who have a way of looking at you with their big eyes as if they thought you were the greatest thing on earth and wondered that you hadn't got on to it yet yourself. She sat there in a sort of shrinking way, looking at me as if she were saying to herself, "Oh, I do hope this great strong man isn't going to hurt me." She gave a fellow a protective kind of feeling, made him want to stroke her hand and say, "There, there, little one!" or words to that effect. She made me feel that there was nothing I wouldn't do for her. She was rather like one of those inno-cent-tasting American drinks which creep imperceptibly into your system so that, before you know what you're doing, you're starting out to reform the world by force if necessary and pausing on your way to tell the large man in the corner that, if he looks at you like that, you will knock his head off. What I mean is, she made me feel alert and dashing, like a knight-errant or something of that kind. I felt that I was with her in this thing to the limit.

"I don't see why your uncle shouldn't be most awfully bucked," I said to Corky. "He will think Miss Singer the ideal wife for you."

Corky declined to cheer up.

"You don't know him. Even if he did like Muriel, he wouldn't admit it. That's the sort of pigheaded ass he is. It would be a matter of principle with him to kick. All he would consider would be that I had gone and taken an important step without asking his advice, and he would raise Cain auto-matically. He's always done it."

I strained the old bean to meet this emergency.

"You want to work it so that he makes Miss Singer's ac-quaintance without knowing that you know her. Then you come along . . ."

"But how can I work it that way?"

I saw his point. That was the catch.

"There's only one thing to do," I said.

"What's that?"

"Leave it to Jeeves."

And I rang the bell.

"Sir?" said Jeeves, kind of manifesting himself. One of the

rummy things about Jeeves is that, unless you watch like a hawk, you very seldom see him come into a room. He's like one of those weird birds in India who dissolve themselves into thin air and nip through space in a sort of disembodied way and assemble the parts again just where they want them. I've got a cousin who's what they call a Theosophist, and he says he's often nearly worked the thing himself, but couldn't quite bring it off, probably owing to having fed in his boyhood on the flesh of animals slain in anger and pie.

The moment I saw the man standing there, registering respectful attention, a weight seemed to roll off my mind. I felt like a lost child who spots his father in the offing.

"Jeeves," I said, "we want your advice."

"Very good, sir."

I boiled down Corky's painful case into a few well-chosen words.

"So you see what it amounts to, Jeeves. We want you to suggest some way by which Mr. Worple can make Miss Singer's acquaintance without getting on to the fact that Mr. Corcoran already knows her. Understand?"

"Perfectly, sir."

"Well, try to think of something."

"I have thought of something already, sir."

"You have!"

"The scheme I would suggest cannot fail of success, but it has what may seem to you a drawback, sir, in that it requires a certain financial outlay."

"He means," I translated to Corky, "that he has got a pippin of an idea, but it's going to cost a bit."

Naturally the poor chap's face dropped, for this seemed to dish the whole thing. But I was still under the influence of the girl's melting gaze, and I saw that this was where I started in as the knight-errant.

"You can count on me for all that sort of thing, Corky," I said. "Only too glad. Carry on, Jeeves."

"I would suggest, sir, that Mr. Corcoran take advantage of Mr. Worple's attachment to ornithology."

"How on earth did you know that he was fond of birds?"

"It is the way these New York apartments are constructed, sir. Quite unlike our London houses. The partitions between the rooms are of the flimsiest nature. With no wish to overhear, I have sometimes heard Mr. Corcoran expressing himself with a generous strength on the subject I have mentioned."

"Oh! Well?"

"Why should not the young lady write a small volume, to be entitled—let us say—*The Children's Book of American Birds* and dedicate it to Mr. Worple? A limited edition could be published at your expense, sir, and a great deal of the book would, of course, be given over to eulogistic remarks concerning Mr. Worple's own larger treatise on the same subject. I should recommend the dispatching of a presentation copy to Mr. Worple, immediately on publication, accompanied by a letter in which the young lady asks to be allowed to make the acquaintance of one to whom she owes so much. This would, I fancy, produce the desired result, but as I say, the expense involved would be considerable."

I felt like the proprietor of a performing dog on the vaudeville stage when the tyke has just pulled off his trick without a hitch. I had betted on Jeeves all along, and I had known that he wouldn't let me down. It beats me sometimes why a man with his genius is satisfied to hang around pressing my clothes and what not. If I had half Jeeves's brain I should have a stab at being Prime Minister or something.

"Jeeves," I said, "that is absolutely ripping! One of your very best efforts."

"Thank you, sir."

The girl made an objection.

"But I'm sure I couldn't write a book about anything. I can't even write good letters."

"Muriel's talents," said Corky, with a little cough, "lie more in the direction of the drama, Bertie. I didn't mention it before, but one of our reasons for being a trifle nervous as to how Uncle Alexander will receive the news is that Muriel is in the chorus of that show *Choose Your Exit* at the Manhattan. It's absurdly unreasonable, but we both feel that that fact might increase Uncle Alexander's natural tendency to kick like a steer."

I saw what he meant. I don't know why it is—one of these psychology sharps could explain it, I suppose—but uncles and aunts, as a class, are always dead against the drama, legitimate or otherwise. They don't seem able to stick it at any price.

But Jeeves had a solution, of course.

"I fancy it would be a simple matter, sir, to find some impecunious author who would be glad to do the actual composition of the volume for a small fee. It is only necessary that the young lady's name should appear on the title page."

"That's true," said Corky. "Sam Patterson would do it for a hundred dollars. He writes a novelette, three short stories, and ten thousand words of a serial for one of the all-fiction magazines under different names every month. A little thing like this would be nothing to him. I'll get after him right away."

"Fine!"

"Will that be all, sir?" said Jeeves. "Very good, sir. Thank you, sir."

I always used to think that publishers had to be devilish intelligent fellows, loaded down with the gray matter; but I've got their number now. All a publisher has to do is to write checks at intervals, while a lot of deserving and industrious chappies rally round and do the real work. I know, because I've been one myself. I simply sat tight in the old flat with a fountain pen, and in due season a topping, shiny book came along.

I happened to be down at Corky's place when the first copies of *The Children's Book of American Birds* bobbed up. Muriel Singer was there, and we were talking of things in general when there was a bang at the door and the parcel was delivered.

It was certainly some book. It had a red cover with a fowl of some species on it, and underneath the girl's name in gold letters. I opened a copy at random.

"Often of a spring morning," it said at the top of page twenty-one, "as you wander through the fields, you will hear the sweet-toned, carelessly flowing warble of the purple finch linnet. When you are older you must read all about him in Mr. Alexander Worple's wonderful book, *American Birds*."

You see. A boost for the uncle right away. And only a few pages later there he was in the limelight again in connection with the yellow-billed cuckoo. It was great stuff. The more I read, the more I admired the chap who had written it and Jeeve's genius in putting us on to the wheeze. I didn't see how the uncle could fail to drop. You can't call a chap the world's greatest authority on the yellow-billed cuckoo without rousing a certain disposition towards chumminess in him.

"It's a cert!" I said.

"An absolute cinch!" said Corky.

And a day or two later he meandered up the Avenue to my flat to tell me that all was well. The uncle had written Muriel a letter so dripping with the milk of human kindness that if he hadn't known Mr. Worple's handwriting Corky would have refused to believe him the author of it. Any time it suited Miss Singer to call, said the uncle, he would be delighted to make her acquaintance.

Shortly after this I had to go out of town. Divers sound sportsmen had invited me to pay visits to their country places, and it wasn't for several months that I settled down in the city again. I had been wondering a lot, of course, about Corky, whether it all turned out right, and so forth, and my first evening in New York, happening to pop into a quiet sort of little restaurant which I go to when I don't feel inclined for the bright lights, I found Muriel Singer there, sitting by herself at a table near the door. Corky, I took it, was out telephoning. I went up and passed the time of day.

"Well, well, well, what?" I said.

"Why, Mr. Wooster! How do you do?"

"Corky around?"

"I beg your pardon?"

"You're waiting for Corky, aren't you?"

"Oh, I didn't understand. No, I'm not waiting for him."

It seemed to me that there was a sort of something in her voice, a kind of thingummy, you know.

"I say, you haven't had a row with Corky, have you?"

"A row?"

"A spat, don't you know—little misunderstanding—faults on both sides—er—and all that sort of thing."

"Why, whatever makes you think that?"

"Oh, well, as it were, what? What I mean is—I thought you usually dined with him before you went to the theatre."

"I've left the stage now."

Suddenly the whole thing dawned on me. I had forgotten what a long time I had been away.

"Why, of course, I see now! You're married!"

"Yes."

"How perfectly topping! I wish you all kinds of happiness."

"Thank you so much. Oh, Alexander," she said, looking past me, "this is a friend of mine—Mr. Wooster."

I spun around. A bloke with a lot of stiff gray hair and a red sort of healthy face was standing there. Rather a formidable Johnnie, he looked, though peaceful at the moment.

"I want you to meet my husband, Mr. Wooster. Mr. Wooster is a friend of Bruce's, Alexander."

The old boy grasped my hand warmly, and that was all that kept me from hitting the floor in a heap. The place was rocking. Absolutely.

"So you know my nephew, Mr. Wooster?" I heard him say. "I wish you would try to knock a little sense into him and make him quit this playing at painting. But I have an idea that he is steadying down. I noticed it first that night he came to dinner with us, my dear, to be introduced to you. He seemed altogether quieter and more serious. Something seemed to have sobered him. Perhaps you will give us the pleasure of your company at dinner tonight, Mr. Wooster? Or have you dined?"

I said I had. What I needed then was air, not dinner. I felt that I wanted to get into the open and think this thing out.

When I reached my flat I heard Jeeves moving about in his lair. I called him.

"Jeeves," I said, "now is the time for all good men to come to the aid of the party. A stiff b. and s. first of all, and then I've a bit of news for you."

He came back with a tray and a long glass.

"Better have one yourself, Jeeves. You'll need it."

"Later on, perhaps, thank you, sir."

"All right. Please yourself. But you're going to get a shock. You remember my friend, Mr. Corcoran?"

"Yes, sir."

"And the girl who was to slide gracefully into his uncle's esteem by writing a book on birds?"

"Perfectly, sir."

"Well, she's slid. She's married the uncle."

He took it without blinking. You can't rattle Jeeves.

"That was always a development to be feared, sir."

"You don't mean to tell me that you were expecting it?"

"It crossed my mind as a possibility."

"Did it, by Jove! Well, I think you might have warned us!"

"I hardly liked to take the liberty, sir."

Of course, as I saw after I had had a bite to eat and was in a calmer frame of mind, what had happened wasn't my fault, if you came down to it. I couldn't be expected to foresee that the scheme, in itself a crackerjack, would skid into the ditch as it had done, but all the same I'm bound to admit that I didn't relish the idea of meeting Corky again until time, the great healer, had been able to get in a bit of soothing work. I cut Washington Square out absolutely for the next few months. I gave it the complete miss-in-balk. And then, just when I was beginning to think I might safely pop down in that direction and gather up the dropped threads, so to speak, time, instead of working the healing wheeze, went and pulled the most awful bone and put the lid on it. Opening the paper one morning, I read that Mrs. Alexander Worple had presented her husband with a son and heir.

I was so dashed sorry for poor old Corky that I hadn't the heart to touch my breakfast. I was bowled over. Absolutely. It was the limit.

I hardly knew what to do. I wanted, of course, to rush down to Washington Square and grip the poor blighter silently by the hand; and then, thinking it over, I hadn't the nerve. Absent treatment seemed the touch. I gave it him in waves.

But after a month or so I began to hesitate again. It struck me that it was playing it a bit low-down on the poor chap, avoiding him like this just when he probably wanted his pals to surge round him most. I pictured him sitting in his lonely studio with no company but his bitter thoughts, and the pathos of it got me to such an extent that I bounded straight into a taxi and told the driver to go all out for the studio.

I rushed in, and there was Corky, hunched up at the easel, painting away, while on the model throne sat a severe-looking female of middle age, holding a baby.

A fellow has to be ready for that sort of thing.

"Oh, ah!" I said, and started to back out.

Corky looked over his shoulder.

"Hallo, Bertie. Don't go. We're just finishing for the day. That will be all this afternoon," he said to the nurse, who got up with the baby and decanted it into a perambulator which was standing in the fairway.

"At the same hour tomorrow, Mr. Corcoran?"

"Yes, please."

"Good afternoon."

"Good afternoon."

Corky stood there, looking at the door, and then he turned to me and began to get it off his chest. Fortunately, he seemed to take it for granted that I knew all about what had happened, so it wasn't as awkward as it might have been.

"It's my uncle's idea," he said. "Muriel doesn't know about it yet. The portrait's to be a surprise for her on her birthday. The nurse takes the kid out ostensibly to get a breather, and they beat it down here. If you want an instance of the irony of fate, Bertie, get acquainted with this. Here's the first commission I have ever had to paint a portrait, and the sitter is that human poached egg that has butted in and bounced me out of my inheritance. Can you beat it! I call it rubbing the thing in to expect me to spend my afternoons gazing into the ugly face of a little brat who to all intents and purposes has hit me behind the ear with a blackjack and swiped all I possess. I can't refuse to paint the portrait, because if I did my uncle would stop my allowance; yet every time I look up and catch that kid's vacant eye, I suffer agonies. I tell you, Bertie, sometimes when he gives me a patronizing glance and then turns away and is sick, as if it revolted him to look at me, I come within an ace of occupying the entire front page of the evening papers as the latest murder sensation. There are moments when I can almost see the headlines: PROMISING YOUNG ARTIST BEANS BABY WITH AXE."

I patted his shoulder silently. My sympathy for the poor old scout was too deep for words.

I kept away from the studio for some time after that, because it didn't seem right to me to intrude on the poor chappie's sorrow. Besides, I'm bound to say that nurse intimidated me. She reminded me so infernally of Aunt Agatha. She was the same gimlet-eyed type.

But one afternoon Corky called me on the phone.

"Bertie!"

"Hallo?"

"Are you doing anything this afternoon?"

"Nothing special."

"You couldn't come down here, could you?"

"What's the trouble? Anything up?"

"I've finished the portrait."

"Good boy! Stout work!"

"Yes." His voice sounded rather doubtful. "The fact is, Bertie, it doesn't look quite right to me. There's something about it . . . My uncle's coming in half an hour to inspect it, and—I don't know why it is, but I kind of feel I'd like your moral support!"

I began to see that I was letting myself in for something. The sympathetic coöperation of Jeeves seemed to me to be indicated.

"You think he'll cut up rough?"

"He may."

I threw my mind back to the red-faced chappie I had met at the restaurant, and tried to picture him cutting up rough. It was only too easy. I spoke to Corky firmly on the telephone.

"I'll come," I said.

"Good!"

"But only if I may bring Jeeves."

"Why Jeeves? What's Jeeves got to do with it? Who wants Jeeves? Jeeves is the fool who suggested the scheme that has led . . ."

"Listen, Corky, old top! If you think I am going to face that uncle of yours without Jeeves's support, you're mistaken. I'd sooner go into a den of wild beasts and bite a lion on the back of the neck."

"Oh, all right," said Corky. Not cordially, but he said it; so I rang for Jeeves, and explained the situation.

"Very good, sir," said Jeeves.

We found Corky near the door, looking at the picture with one hand up in a defensive sort of way, as if he thought it might swing on him.

"Stand right where you are, Bertie," he said, without moving. "Now, tell me honestly, how does it strike you?"

The light from the big window fell right on the picture. I took a good look at it. Then I shifted a bit nearer and took another look. Then I went back to where I had been at first, because it hadn't seemed quite so bad from there.

"Well?" said Corky anxiously.

I hesitated a bit.

"Of course, old man, I only saw the kid once, and then only for a moment, but—but it *was* an ugly sort of kid, wasn't it, if I remember rightly?"

"As ugly as that?"

I looked again, and honesty compelled me to be frank.

"I don't see how it could have been, old chap."

Poor old Corky ran his fingers through his hair in a temperamental sort of way. He groaned.

"You're quite right, Bertie. Something's gone wrong with the darned thing. My private impression is that, without knowing it, I've worked that stunt that Sargent used to pull—painting the soul of the sitter. I've got through the mere outward appearance, and have put the child's soul on canvas."

"But could a child of that age have a soul like that? I don't see how he could have managed it in the time. What do you think, Jeeves?"

"I doubt it, sir."

"It—it sort of leers at you, doesn't it?"

"You've noticed that, too?" said Corky.

"I don't see how one could help noticing."

"All I tried to do was to give the little brute a cheerful expression. But, as it has worked out, he looks positively dissipated."

"Just what I was going to suggest, old man. He looks as if he were in the middle of a colossal spree, and enjoying every minute of it. Don't you think so, Jeeves?"

"He has a decidedly inebriated air, sir."

Corky was starting to say something, when the door opened and the uncle came in.

For about three seconds all was joy, jollity, and good will. The old boy shook hands with me, slapped Corky on the back, said he didn't think he had ever seen such a fine day, and whacked his leg with his stick. Jeeves had projected himself into the background, and he didn't notice him.

"Well, Bruce, my boy; so the portrait is really finished, is it—really finished? Well, bring it out. Let's have a look at it. This will be a wonderful surprise for your aunt. Where is it? Let's . . ."

And then he got it—suddenly, when he wasn't set for the punch; and he rocked back on his heels.

"Oosh!" he exclaimed. And for perhaps a minute there was one of the scaliest silences I've ever run up against.

"Is this a practical joke?" he said at last, in a way that set about sixteen drafts cutting through the room at once.

I thought it was up to me to rally round old Corky.

"You want to stand a bit farther away from it," I said.

"You're perfectly right!" he snorted. "I do! I want to stand so far away from it that I can't see the thing with a telescope!" He turned on Corky like an untamed tiger of the jungle who has just located a chunk of meat. "And this—this—is what you have been wasting your time and my money for all these years! A painter! I wouldn't let you paint a house of mine. I gave you this commission, thinking that you were a competent worker, and this—this—this—extract from a comic supplement is the result!" He swung towards the door, lashing his tail and growling to himself. "This ends it. If you wish to continue this foolery of pretending to be an artist because you want an excuse for idleness, please yourself. But let me tell you this. Unless you report at my office on Monday morning, prepared to abandon all this idiocy and start in at the bottom of the business to work your way up, as you should have done half a dozen years ago, not another cent—not another cent—not another . . . Boosh!"

Then the door closed and he was no longer with us. And I crawled out of the bombproof shelter.

"Corky, old top!" I whispered faintly.

Corky was standing staring at the picture. His face was set. There was a hunted look in his eye.

"Well, that finishes it!" he muttered brokenly.

"What are you going to do?"

"Do? What can I do? I can't stick on here if he cuts off supplies. You heard what he said. I shall have to go to the office on Monday."

I couldn't think of a thing to say. I knew exactly how he felt about the office. I don't know when I've been so infernally uncomfortable. It was like hanging round trying to make conversation to a pal who's just been sentenced to twenty years in quod.

And then a soothing voice broke the silence.

"If I might make a suggestion, sir!"

It was Jeeves. He had slid from the shadows and was gazing gravely at the picture. Upon my word, I can't give you a better idea of the shattering effect of Corky's Uncle Alexander when in action than by saying that he had absolutely made me forget for the moment that Jeeves was there.

"I wonder if I have ever happened to mention to you, sir, a Mr. Digby Thistleton, with whom I was once in service? Perhaps you have met him? He was a financier. He is now Lord Bridgworth. It was a favorite saying of his that there is always a way. The first time I heard him use the expression was after the failure of a patent depilatory which he promoted."

"Jeeves," I said, "what on earth are you talking about?"

"I mentioned Mr. Thistleton, sir, because his was in some respects a parallel case to the present one. His depilatory failed, but he did not despair. He put it on the market again under the name of Hair-o, guaranteed to produce a full crop of hair in a few months. It was advertised, if you remember, sir, by a humorous picture of a billiard ball, before and after taking, and made such a substantial fortune that Mr. Thistleton was soon afterwards elevated to the peerage for services to his Party. It seems to me that, if Mr. Corcoran looks into the matter, he will find, like Mr. Thistleton, that there is always a way. Mr. Worple himself suggested the solution of the difficulty. In the heat of the moment he compared the portrait to an extract from a colored comic supplement. I consider the suggestion a very valuable one, sir. Mr. Corcoran's portrait may not have pleased Mr. Worple as a likeness of his only child, but I have no doubt that editors would gladly consider it as a foundation for a series of humorous drawings. If Mr. Corcoran will allow me to make the suggestion, his talent has always been for the humorous. There is something about this picture—something bold and vigorous, which arrests the attention. I feel sure it would be highly popular."

Corky was glaring at the picture, and making a sort of dry, sucking noise with his mouth. He seemed completely overwrought.

And then suddenly he began to laugh in a wild way.

"Corky, old man!" I said, massaging him tenderly. I feared the poor blighter was hysterical.

He began to stagger about all over the floor.

"He's right! The man's absolutely right! Jeeves, you're a

lifesaver. You've hit on the greatest idea of the age. Report at the office on Monday! Start at the bottom of the business! I'll buy the business if I feel like it. I know the man who runs the comic section of the *Sunday Star*. He'll eat this thing. He was telling me only the other day how hard it was to get a good new series. He'll give me anything I ask for a real winner like this. I've got a gold mine. Where's my hat? I've got an income for life! Where's that confounded hat? Lend me a five, Bertie. I want to take a taxi down to Park Row!"

Jeeves smiled paternally. Or, rather, he had a kind of paternal muscular spasm about the mouth, which is the nearest he ever gets to smiling.

"If I might make the suggestion, Mr. Corcoran—for a title of the series which you have in mind—'The Adventures of Baby Blobbs.' "

Corky and I looked at the picture, then at each other in an awed way. Jeeves was right. There could be no other title.

"Jeeves," I said. It was a few weeks later, and I had just finished looking at the comic section of the *Sunday Star*. "I'm an optimist. I always have been. The older I get, the more I agree with Shakespeare and those poet Johnnies about it always being darkest before the dawn and there's a silver lining and what you lose on the swings you make up on the roundabouts. Look at Mr. Corcoran, for instance. There was a fellow, one would have said, clear up to the eyebrows in the soup. To all appearances he had got it right in the neck. Yet look at him now. Have you seen these pictures?"

"I took the liberty of glancing at them before bringing them to you, sir. Extremely diverting."

"They have made a big hit, you know."

"I anticipated it, sir."

I leaned back against the pillows.

"You know, Jeeves, you're a genius. You ought to be drawing a commission on these things."

"I have nothing to complain of in that respect, sir, Mr. Corcoran has been most generous. I am putting out the brown suit, sir."

"No, I think I'll wear the blue with the faint red stripe."
"Not the blue with the faint red stripe, sir."
"But I rather fancy myself in it."
"Not the blue with the faint red stripe, sir."
"Oh, all right, have it your own way."
"Very good, sir. Thank you, sir."

BREEDING WILL TELL:
A FAMILY TREATMENT

There once appeared in a magazine a photograph of myself taken under obviously youthful circumstances. I assumed that it would be readily apparent to all that this was my high school yearbook picture. I neglected, however, to take into consideration that I number among my acquaintances some people of decidedly lofty background. I was first jarred into awareness of this by a well-born young fashion model, who, in reference to said photograph, offered, "I really loved your deb picture, Fran." Had that been the end of it I would undoubtedly have forgotten the incident, but later on that very same evening an almost identical remark was made by a minor member of the Boston aristocracy. As far as I was concerned this constituted a trend. I therefore felt faced with a decision: either snort derisively at the very idea or create an amusing fiction appropriate to such thinking. Being at least peripherally in the amusing fiction business, I chose the latter and thus have prepared the following genealogy.

Margaret Lebovitz, my paternal grandmother, was born in Ghetto Point, Hungary (a restricted community), at the very dawn of the Gay Nineties. An appealing child, she was often left in the care of trusted family retainers (my Aunt Sadie and Uncle Benny), as her father's far-flung business affairs—which were mainly concerned with being conscripted into the army—frequently kept him away from home. Although her mother spent most of her time amusing herself in the cabbage fields, she nevertheless made it a point to visit the nursery every evening and stand guard while little Margaret said her prayers. Margaret's childhood was a happy one—she and her chums exchanged confidences and babushkas as they whiled away the carefree hours picking beets and playing hide and seek with the Cossacks. Tariff, the family estate, where the Lebovitzes wintered (*and* summered) was indeed a wondrous place and it was therefore not surprising when Margaret balked at being sent away to school. Her father, home on a brief desertion, took her into his straw-lined study—which was affectionately called "Daddy's hideout"—and explained patiently that unbreakable tradition demanded that girls of Margaret's class acquire the necessary social graces such as fleeing demurely and staying properly alive. Margaret listened respectfully and agreed to begin her freshman year at Miss Belief's.

Margaret was a great success at Miss Belief's, where her taste in footwear quickly won her the nickname Bootsie. Bootsie was an excellent student and demonstrated such a flair for barely audible breathing that she was unanimously elected chairman of the Spring Day Escape Committee. That is not to say that Bootsie was a grind—quite the contrary. An irrepressible madcap, Bootsie got herself into such bad scrapes that the fellow members of her club, the Huddled Masses, were frequently compelled to come to her rescue. Fond of outdoor sports, Bootsie longed for summer vacation and happily joined in the girlish cries of "Serf's up!" that greeted the season.

Upon reaching her eighteenth birthday, Bootsie made her debut into society and her beauty, charm, and way with a hoe soon gained her a reputation as the Brenda Frazier of Ghetto Point. All of the young men in her set were smitten with Bootsie and found it absolutely necessary to secure the promise of a waltz days in advance of a party, as her dance pogrom was invariably full. Bootsie's favorite beau was Tibor, a tall, dashing young deserter and two-time winner of the Hungarian Cup Race, which was held yearly in a lavishly irrigated wheat field. Tibor was fond of Bootsie, but he was not unmindful of the fact that she would one day come into her father's great plowshare, and this was his primary interest in her. The discovery that Tibor was a fortune hunter had a devastating effect upon Bootsie and she took to her bed. Bootsie's family, understandably concerned about her condition, held a meeting to discuss the problem. It was concluded that a change of scenery would do her a world of good. A plan of action was decided upon and thus Bootsie Lebovitz was sent steerage to Ellis Island in order that she might forget.

THE DARLINGS AT THE TOP OF THE STAIRS

Childhood used to end with the discovery that there is no Santa Claus. Nowadays, it too often ends when the child gets his first adult, the way Hemingway got his first rhino, with the difference that the rhino was charging Hemingway, whereas the adult is usually running from the child. This has brought about a change in the folklore and mythology of the American home, and of the homes of other offspring-beleaguered countries. The dark at the top of the stairs once shrouded imaginary bears that lay in wait for tiny tots, but now parents, grandparents, and other grown relatives are afraid there may be a little darling lurking in the shadows, with blackjack, golf club, or .32-caliber automatic.

The worried psychologists, sociologists, anthropologists, and other ologists, who jump at the sound of every backfire or slammed door, have called our present jeopardy a "child-centered culture." Every seven seconds a baby is born in the United States, which means that we produce, every two hours, approximately five companies of infantry. I would say this amounts to a child-overwhelmed culture, but I am one of those who do not intend to surrender meekly and unconditionally. There must be a bright side to this menacing state of civilization, and if somebody will snap on his flashlight, we'll take a look around for it.

More has been written about the child than about any other age of man, and it is perhaps fortunate that the literature is now so extensive a child would have become twenty-one before its parents could get through half the books on how to bring it up. The trouble with the "child expert" is that he is so often a dedicated, or desiccated, expository writer and lecturer, and the tiny creative talents he attempts to cope with are beyond him. Margaret Mead, the American anthropologist, is an exception, for she realizes the dangers inherent in twisting infantile creativity into the patterns of adult propriety, politeness, and conformity. Let us glance at a few brief examples of creative literature in the very young, for which they should have been encouraged, not admonished.

The small girl critic who wrote, "This book tells me more about penguins than I wanted to know," has a technique of clarity and directness that might well be studied by the so-called mature critics of England and the United States, whose tendency, in dealing with books about penguins or anything else, is to write long autobiographical rambles.

Then there was a little American girl who was asked by her teacher to write a short story about her family. She managed it in a single true and provocative sentence: "Last night my daddy didn't come home at all." I told this to a five-year-old moppet I know and asked her if she could do as well, and she said, "Yes," and she did. Her short story, in its entirety, went like this: "My daddy doesn't take anything with him when he goes away except a nightie and whiskey."

I am known to parents as a disruptive force, if not indeed a naughty influence, upon my small colleagues in the field of imaginative writing. When Sally, aged four, told me, "I want to be a ghost," her mother said quickly, "No, you don't," and I said, "Yes, she does. Let her be a ghost. Maybe she will become another W. E. Henley, who wrote, 'And the world's a ghost that gleams, flickers, vanishes away.' "

"Who is W. E. Henley?" the child's mother asked uneasily.

"Wilhelmina Ernestine Henley," I explained. "A poet who became a ghost."

Her mother said she didn't want Sally to become a poet or a ghost, but a good wife and mother.

Finally, there was Lisa, aged five, whose mother asked her

to thank my wife for the peas we had sent them the day before from our garden. "I thought the peas were awful, I wish you and Mrs. Thurber was dead, and I hate trees," said Lisa, thus conjoining in one creative splurge the nursery rhyme about pease porridge cold, the basic plot sense of James M. Cain, and Birnam wood moving upon Dunsinane. Lisa and I were the only unhorrified persons in the room when she brought this out. We knew that her desire to get rid of her mother and my wife at one fell swoop was a pure device of creative literature. As I explained to the two doomed ladies later, it is important to let your little daughters and sons kill you off figuratively, because this is a natural infantile urge that cannot safely be channeled into amenity or what Henry James called "the twaddle of graciousness." The child that is scolded or punished for its natural human desire to destroy is likely to turn later to the blackjack, the golf club, or the .32-caliber automatic.

The tiny twaddler of ungraciousness has my blessing, as you can see. You can also see that I am mainly concerned with the incipient, or burgeoning, creativity of the female child. This is because I am more interested in Thurber's theory of Elaine Vital, the female life force, than in Bergson's theory of Elan Vital, the masculine life force, which it seems to me is all he isolated. Elaine Vital, if properly directed—that is, let alone—may become the hope of the future. God knows we have enough women writers (at least one too many, if you ask me), but I believe they are the product of a confined and constrained infantile creativity. Being females, they have turned to the pen and the typewriter, instead of the blackjack, golf club, and .32-caliber automatic.

Boys are perhaps beyond the range of anybody's sure understanding, at least when they are between the ages of eighteen months and ninety years. They have got us into the human quandary, dilemma, plight, predicament, pickle, mess, pretty pass, and kettle of fish in which we now find ourselves. Little boys are much too much for me at my age, for it is they who have taken over the American home, physically. They are in charge of running everything, usually into the ground.

Most American parents will not answer the telephone when it rings, but will let a little boy do it. Telephone operators, I have been informed, now frequently say to a mumbling toddler, "Is there anyone older than you in the house?" Many of the tradespeople and artisans I deal with, or try to, in my part of Connecticut, go in for this form of evasionism. A small male child will pick up the receiver and burble into the transmitter. In this way urgency, or even crisis, is met with baby talk, or prattle tattle. The fact that my plumbing has let go or a ceiling is falling down is reduced, in this new system of noncommunication, to a tiny, halting, almost inaudible recital of what happened to a teddy bear, or why cereal is not good with sliced bananas and should be thrown at Daddy. The tradesman or artisan and his wife are spared the knowledge of a larger disaster at the expense of the nerves and mental balance of the caller. I shall set down here an exasperating personal experience in this area of obfuscation.

"Oo tiss?" a tiny voice demanded when I called the plumber one day.

"This is Tanta Twaus," I said, "and Tanta Twaus won't give you any Twissmas pwesents this Twissmas if you do not put Mommy or Daddy on the other end of this doddam apparatus."

"Appawana?" asked the tiny voice. At this point his mother, like a woman in transport and on her third martini, grabbed up the receiver.

"He said, 'Appomattox,' didn't he?" she cried. "Isn't that wonderful?"

"Madam," I said, chilling the word, "the answer to the question I just put to your son is Waterloo, not Appomattox. The next voice you hear will be that of me, dying in the flood of broken pipes and the rubble of fallen ceilings." And I slammed up the receiver.

Ours is indeed a child-centered culture in the sense that the little boys have got me squarely centered in their gun sights. I shall continue to urge on the little girls who hate trees, are indifferent to penguins, envy Banquo, wish Mother were with the angels, and can read Daddy like a book. What you are going to do, I don't know, but I advise you to keep glancing over your shoulder, and look out for the darlings at the top of the stairs.

HOSTAGES TO MOMUS

I

I never got outside of the legitimate line of graft but once. By the legitimate I mean something a little more risky than burglarizing a police-station in New York, and not quite as unsafe as operating a glove contract for the United States government. I always did like a graft that you could explain satisfactorily when they asked you about it—something that began to look like a torpedo-boat as soon as it made a noise like a trawler. But, one time, as I say, I reversed the decision of the revised statutes, and undertook a thing that I'd have to apologize for even under the New Jersey trust laws.

Me and Caligula Polk, of Muskogee in the Creek Nation, was down in the Mexican State of Tamaulipas running a peripatetic lottery and monte game. Now, selling lottery tickets is a government graft in Mexico, just like selling forty-eight cents' worth of postage-stamps for forty-nine cents is over here. So Uncle Porfirio he instructs the *rurales* to attend to our case.

Rurales? They're a sort of country police; but don't draw any mental crayon portraits of the worthy constable with a tin star and a gray goatee. The *rurales*—well, if we'd mount our Supreme Court on broncos, arm 'em with Winchesters, and start 'em out after John Doe *et al.*, we'd have about the same thing.

When the *rurales* started for us we started for the States. They chased us as far as Matamoras. We hid in a brickyard;

and that night we swum the Rio Grande, Caligula with a brick in each hand, absent-minded, which he drops upon the soil of Texas, forgetting he had 'em.

From there we emigrated to San Antone, and then over to New Orleans, where we took a rest. And in that town of cotton bales and other adjuncts to female beauty we made the acquaintance of drinks invented by the Creoles during the period of Louey Cans, in which they are still served at the side doors. The most I can remember of that town is that me and Caligula and a Frenchman named McCarty—wait a minute; Adolph McCarty—was trying to make the French Quarter pay up the back trading-stamps due on the Louisiana Purchase, when somebody hollers that the johndarms are coming. I have an insufficient recollection of buying two yellow tickets through a window; and I seemed to see a man swing a lantern and say "All aboard!" I remembered no more, except that the train butcher was covering me and Caligula up with Augusta J. Evans' works and figs.

When we become conscientious, we find that we have collided up against the State of Georgia at a spot hitherto unaccounted for in print except by an asterisk, which means that trains stop every other Thursday on signal by tearing up a rail. We was waked up in a yellow pine hotel by the noise of flowers and the smell of birds. Yes, sir, for the wind was banging sunflowers as big as buggy wheels against the weather-boarding, and the chicken coop was right under the window. Me and Caligula dressed and went downstairs. The landlord was shelling peas on the front porch. He was six feet of chills and fever, and Hongkong in complexion, though in other respects he seemed amenable in the exercise of his sentiments and features.

Caligula, who is a spokesman by birth, and a small man, though red-haired and impatient of painfulness of any kind, speaks up.

"Pardner," says he, "good-morning, and be darned to you. Would you mind telling us why we are at? We know the reason we are where, but can't exactly figure out on account of at what place."

"Well, gentlemen," says the landlord, "I reckoned you-all would be inquiring this morning. You-all dropped off of the nine thirty train here last night; and you was right tight. Yes, you was right smart in liquor. I can inform you that you are now in the town of Mountain Valley, in the State of Georgia."

"On top of that," says Caligula, "don't say that we can't have anything to eat."

"Sit down, gentlemen," says the landlord, "and in twenty minutes I'll call you to the best breakfast you can get anywhere in town."

That breakfast turned out to be composed of fried bacon and a yellowish edifice that proved up something between pound cake and flexible sandstone. The landlord calls it corn pone; and then he sets out a dish of the exaggerated breakfast food known as hominy; and so me and Caligula makes the acquaintance of the celebrated food that enabled every Johnny Reb to lick one and two-thirds Yankees for nearly four years on a stretch.

"The wonder to me is," says Caligula, "that Uncle Robert Lee's boys didn't chase the Grant and Sherman outfit clear up into Hudson's Bay. It would have made me that mad to eat this truck they call mahogany!"

"Hog and hominy," I explains, "is the staple food of this section."

"Then," says Caligula, "they ought to keep it where it belongs. I thought this was a hotel and not a stable. Now, if we was in Muskogee at the St. Lucifer House, I'd show you some breakfast grub. Antelope steaks and fried liver to begin on, and venison cutlets with *chili con carne* and pineapple fritters, and then some sardines and mixed pickles; and top it off with a can of the yellow clings and a bottle of beer. You won't find a layout like that on the bill of affairs of any of your Eastern restauraws."

"Too lavish," says I. "I've traveled, and I'm unprejudiced. There'll never be a perfect breakfast eaten until some man grows arms long enough to stretch down to New Orleans for his coffee and over to Norfolk for his rolls, and reaches up to

Vermont and digs a slice of butter out of a spring-house, and then turns over a beehive close to a white clover patch out in Indiana for the rest. Then he'd come pretty close to making a meal on the amber that the gods eat on Mount Olympia."

"Too ephemeral," says Caligula, "I'd want ham and eggs, or rabbit stew, anyhow, for a chaser. What do you consider the most edifying and casual in the way of a dinner?"

"I've been infatuated from time to time," I answers, "with fancy ramifications of grub such as terrapines, lobsters, reed birds, jambolaya, and canvas-covered ducks; but after all there's nothing less displeasing to me than a beekfsteak smothered in mushrooms on a balcony in sound of the Broadway streetcars, with a hand-organ playing down below, and the boys hollering extras about the latest suicide. For the wine, give me a reasonable Ponty Cany. And that's all, except a *demi-tasse*."

"Well," says Caligula, "I reckon in New York you get to be a conniseer; and when you go around with the *demi-tasse* you are naturally bound to buy stylish grub."

"It's a great town for epicures," says I. "You'd soon fall into their ways if you was there."

"I've heard it was," says Caligula. "But I reckon I wouldn't. I can polish my fingernails all they need myself."

II

After breakfast we went out on the front porch, lighted up two of the landlord's *flor de upas* perfectos, and took a look at Georgia.

The instalment of scenery visible to the eye looked mighty poor. As far as we could see was red hills all washed down with gullies and scattered over with patches of piny woods. Blackberry bushes was all that kept the rail fences from falling down. About fifteen miles over to the north was a little range of well-timbered mountains.

That town of Mountain Valley wasn't going. About a dozen people permeated along the sidewalks; but what you saw mostly was rain-barrels and roosters, and boys poking around with sticks in piles of ashes made by burning the scenery of Uncle Tom shows.

And just then there passes down on the other side of the street a high man in a long black coat and a beaver hat. All the people in sight bowed, and some crossed the street to shake hands with him; folks came out of stores and houses to holler at him; women leaned out of windows and smiled; and all the kids stopped playing to look at him. Our landlord stepped out on the porch and bent himself double like a carpenter's rule, and sung out "Good-morning, colonel" when he was a dozen yards gone by.

"And is that Alexander, pa?" says Caligula to the landlord; "and why is he called great?"

"That, gentlemen," says the landlord, "is no less than Colonel Jackson T. Rockingham, the president of the Sunrise & Edenville Tap Railroad, mayor of Mountain Valley, and chairman of the Perry County board of immigration and public improvements."

"Been away a good many years, hasn't he?" I asked.

"No, sir; Colonel Rockingham is going down to the post-office for his mail. His fellow-citizens take pleasure in greeting him thus every morning. The colonel is our most prominent citizen. Besides the height of the stock of the Sunrise & Edenville Tap Railroad, he owns a thousand acres of that land across the creek. Mountain Valley delights, sir, to honor a citizen of such worth and public spirit."

For an hour that afternoon Caligula sat on the back of his neck on the porch and studied a newspaper, which was unusual in a man who despised print. When he was through he took me to the end of the porch among the sunlight and drying dishtowels. I knew that Caligula had invented a new graft. For he chewed the ends of his mustache and ran the left catch of his suspenders up and down, which was his way.

"What is it now?" I asks. "Just so it ain't floating mining stocks or raising Pennsylvania pinks, we'll talk it over."

Pennsylvania pinks? Oh, that refers to a coin-raising scheme of the Keystoners. They burn the soles of old women's feet to make them tell where their money's hid.

Caligula's words in business was always few and bitter.

"You see them mountains," said he, pointing. "And you seen that colonel man that owns railroads and cuts more ice when he goes to the post-office than Roosevelt does when he cleans 'em out. What we're going to do is to kidnap the latter into the former, and inflict a ransom of ten thousand dollars."

"Illegality," says I, shaking my head.

"I knew you'd say that," says Caligula. "At first sight it does seem to jar peace and dignity. But it don't. I got the idea out of that newspaper. Would you commit aspersions on a equitable graft that the United States itself has condoned and indorsed and ratified?"

"Kidnapping," said I, "is an immoral function in the derogatory list of the statutes. If the United States upholds it, it must be a recent enactment of ethics, along with race suicide and rural delivery."

"Listen," says Caligula, "and I'll explain the case set down in the papers. Here was a Greek citizen named Burdick Harris," says he, "captured for a graft by Africans; and the United States sends two gunboats to the State of Tangiers and makes the King of Morocco give up seventy thousand dollars to Raisuli."

"Go slow," says I. "That sounds too international to take in all at once. It's like 'thimble, thimble, who's got the naturalization papers?' Are you sure you haven't been reading an account of a theatrical trust trying to fire a critic out of a musical comedy?"

" 'Twas press despatches from Constantinople," says Caligula. "You'll see, six months from now. They'll be confirmed by the monthly magazines; and then it won't be long till you'll notice 'em with photos alongside of Governor La Follette and the new Czarooski in the while-you-get-your-hair-cut weeklies. It's all right, Pick. This African man Raisuli hides Burdick Harris up in the mountains, and advertises his price to the governments of different nations. Now, you wouldn't think for a minute," goes on Caligula, "that John Hay would chip in and help this graft along if it wasn't a square game, would you?"

"Why, no," says I. "I've always stood right with Mr. Bryan in politics; and I couldn't consciously say a word against the Republican administration just now. But if Harris was a Greek, on what system of international protocols does Hay interfere?"

"It ain't exactly set forth in the papers," says Caligula. "I suppose it's a matter of sentiment. You know he wrote this poem 'Little Breeches'; and them Greeks wear little or none. But anyhow, John Hay sends the Brooklyn and the Olympia over, and they cover Africa with thirty-inch guns. And then Hay cables after the health of the *persona grata*. 'And how are they this morning?' he wires. 'Is Burdick Harris alive yet, or Mr. Raisuli dead?' And the King of Morocco sends up the seventy thousand dollars, and they turn Burdick Harris loose. And there's not half the hard feelings among the nations about this little kidnapping matter as there was about the peace congress. And Burdick Harris says to the reporters, in the Greek language, that he's often heard about the United States, and he admires Roosevelt, next to Raisuli, who is one of the whitest and most gentlemanly kidnappers that he ever worked alongside of. So you see, Pick," winds up Caligula, "we've got the law of nations on our side. We'll cut this colonel man out of the herd, and corral him in them little mountains, and stick up his heirs and assigns for ten thousand dollars."

"Well, you seldom little red-headed territorial terror," I answers, "you can't bluff your uncle Tecumseh Pickens! I'll be your company in this graft. But I misdoubt if you've absorbed the inwardness of this Burdick Harris case, Calig; and if on any morning we get a telegram from John Hay asking about the health of the scheme, I propose to acquire the most propinquitous and celeritous mule in this section and gallop diplomatically over into the neighboring and peaceful nation of Alabama."

III

Me and Caligula spent the next three days investigating the bunch of mountains into which we proposed to kidnap Colonel Jackson T. Rockingham. We finally selected an upright slice of topography covered with bushes and trees that you could only reach by a secret path that we cut out up the side of it. And the only way to reach the mountain was to follow up the bed of a branch that wound among the elevations.

Then I took in hand an important subdivision of the proceedings. I went up to Atlanta on the train and laid in a two-hundred-and-fifty-dollar supply of the most gratifying and efficient lines of grub that money could buy. I always was an admirer of viands in their more palliative and revised stages. Hog and hominy are not only inartistic to my stomach, but they give indigestion to my moral sentiments. And I thought of Colonel Jackson T. Rockingham, president of the Sunrise & Edenville Tap Railroad, and how he would miss the luxury of his home fare as is so famous among wealthy Southerners. So I sunk half of mine and Caligula's capital in as elegant a layout of fresh and canned provisions as Burdick Harris or any other professional kidnappee ever saw in a camp.

I put another hundred in a couple of cases of Bordeaux, two quarts of cognac, two hundred Havana regalias with gold bands, and a camp stove and stools and folding cots. I wanted Colonel Rockingham to be comfortable; and I hoped after he gave up the ten thousand dollars he would give me and Caligula as good a name for gentlemen and entertainers as the Greek man did the friend of his that made the United States his bill collector against Africa.

When the goods came down from Atlanta, we hired a wagon, moved them up on the little mountain, and established camp. And then we laid for the colonel.

We caught him one morning about two miles out from Mountain Valley, on his way to look after some of his burnt umber farm land. He was an elegant old gentleman, as thin and tall as a trout rod, with frazzled shirt-cuffs and specs on a black string. We explained to him, brief and easy, what we wanted; and Caligula showed him, careless, the handle of his forty-five under his coat.

"What?" says Colonel Rockingham. "Bandits in Perry County, Georgia! I shall see that the board of immigration and public improvements hears of this!"

"Be so unfoolhardly as to climb into that buggy," says Caligula, "by order of the board of perforation and public depravity. This is a business meeting, and we're anxious to adjourn *sine qua non.*"

We drove Colonel Rockingham over to the mountain and up the side of it as far as the buggy would go. Then we tied the horse, and took our prisoner on foot up to the camp.

"Now, colonel," I says to him, "we're after the ransom, me and my partner; and no harm will come to you if the King of Mor—if your friends send up the dust. In the mean time, we are gentlemen the same as you. And if you give us your word not to try to escape, the freedom of the camp is yours."

"I give you my word," says the colonel.

"All right," says I; "and now it's eleven o'clock, and me and Mr. Polk will proceed to inoculate the occasion with a few well-timed trivialities in the line of grub."

"Thank you," says the colonel; "I believe I could relish a slice of bacon on a plate of hominy."

"But you won't," says I emphatic. "Not in this camp. We soar in higher regions than them occupied by your celebrated but repulsive dish."

While the colonel read his paper, me and Caligula took off our coats and went in for a little luncheon *de luxe* just to show him. Caligula was a fine cook of the Western brand. He could toast a buffalo or fricassee a couple of steers as easy as a woman could make a cup of tea. He was gifted in the way of knocking together edibles when haste and muscle and quantity was to be considered. He held the record west of the Arkansaw River for frying pancakes with his left hand, broiling venison cutlets with his right, and skinning a rabbit with his teeth at the same time. But I could do things *en casserole* and *à la creole,* and handle the oil and tabasco as gently and nicely as a French *chef.*

So at twelve o'clock we had a hot lunch ready that looked like a banquet on a Mississippi River steamboat. We spread it on the tops of two or three big boxes, opened two quarts of the red wine, set the olives and a canned oyster cocktail and a ready-made Martini by the colonel's plate, and called him to grub.

Colonel Rockingham drew up his campstool, wiped off his specs, and looked at the things on the table. Then I thought he was swearing; and I felt mean because I hadn't taken more pains with the victuals. But he wasn't; he was asking a blessing; and me and Caligula hung our heads, and I saw a tear drop from the colonel's eye into his cocktail.

I never saw a man eat with so much earnestness and application—not hastily, like a grammarian, or one of the canal, but slow and appreciative, like a anaconda or a real *vive bonjour*.

In an hour and a half the colonel leaned back. I brought him a pony of brandy and his black coffee, and set the box of Havana regalias on the table.

"Gentlemen," says he, blowing out the smoke and trying to breathe it back again, "when we view the eternal hills and the smiling and beneficent landscape, and reflect upon the goodness of the Creator who—"

"Excuse me, colonel," says I, "but there's some business to attend to now;" and I brought out paper and pen and ink and laid 'em before him. "Who do you want to send to for the money?" I asks.

"I reckon," says he, after thinking a bit, "to the vice-president of our railroad, at the general offices of the company in Edenville."

"How far is it to Edenville from here?" I asked.

"About ten miles," says he.

Then I dictated these lines, and Colonel Rockingham wrote them out:

I am kidnapped and held a prisoner by two desperate outlaws in a place which is useless to attempt to find. They demand ten thousand dollars at once for my release. The amount must be raised immediately, and these directions followed. Come alone with the money to Stony Creek, which runs out of Blacktop Mountains. Follow the bed of the creek till you come to a big flat rock on the left bank, on which is marked a cross in red chalk. Stand on the rock and wave a white flag. A guide will come to you and conduct you to where I am held. Lose no time.

After the colonel had finished this, he asked permission to tack on a postscript about how white he was being treated, so the railroad wouldn't feel uneasy in its bosom about him. We agreed to that. He wrote down that he had just had lunch with the two desperate ruffians; and then he set down the whole bill of fare, from cocktails to coffee. He wound up with the remark that dinner would be ready about six, and would probably be a more licentious and intemperate affair than lunch.

Me and Caligula read it, and decided to let it go; for we, being cooks, were amenable to praise, though it sounded out of place on a sight draft for ten thousand dollars.

I took the letter over to the Mountain Valley road and watched for a messenger. By and by a colored equestrian came along on horseback, riding toward Edenville. I gave him a dollar to take the letter to the railroad offices; and then I went back to camp.

IV

About four o'clock in the afternoon, Caligula, who was acting as lookout, calls to me:

"I have to repawt a white shirt signaling on the starboard bow, sir."

I went down the mountain and brought back a fat, red man in an alpaca coat and no collar.

"Gentlemen," says Colonel Rockingham, "allow me to introduce my brother, Captain Duval C. Rockingham, vice-president of the Sunrise & Edenville Tap Railroad."

"Otherwise the King of Morocco," says I. "I reckon you

don't mind my counting the ransom, just as a business formality."

"Well, no, not exactly," says the fat man, "not when it comes. I turned that matter over to our second vice-president. I was anxious after Brother Jackson's safetiness. I reckon he'll be along right soon. What does the lobster salad you mentioned taste like, Brother Jackson?"

"Mr. Vice-President," says I, "you'll oblige us by remaining here till the second V. P. arrives. This is a private rehearsal, and we don't want any roadside speculators selling tickets."

In half an hour Caligula sings out again:

"Sail ho! Looks like an apron on a broomstick."

I perambulated down the cliff again, and escorted up a man six foot three, with a sandy beard and no other dimensions that you could notice. Thinks I to myself, if he's got ten thousand dollars on his person it's in one bill and folded lengthwise.

"Mr. Patterson G. Coble, our second vice-president," announces the colonel.

"Glad to know you, gentlemen," says this Coble. "I came up to disseminate the tidings that Major Tallahassee Tucker, our general passenger agent, is now negotiating a peach-crate full of our railroad bonds with the Perry County Bank for a loan. My dear Colonel Rockingham, was that chicken gumbo or cracked goobers on the bill of fare in your note? Me and the conductor of fifty-six was having a dispute about it."

"Another white wings on the rocks!" hollers Caligula. "If I see any more I'll fire on 'em and swear they was torpedo-boats!"

The guide goes down again, and convoys into the lair a person in blue overalls carrying an amount of inebriety and a lantern. I am so sure that this is Major Tucker that I don't even ask him until we are up above; and then I discover that it is Uncle Timothy, the yard switchman at Edenville, who is sent ahead to flag our understandings with the gossip that Judge Pendergast, the railroad's attorney, is in the process of mortgaging Colonel Rockingham's farming lands to make up the ransom.

While he is talking, two men crawl from under the bushes into camp, and Caligula, with no white flag to disinter him from his plain duty, draws his gun. But again Colonel Rockingham intervenes and introduces Mr. Jones and Mr. Batts, engineer and fireman of train number forty-two.

"Excuse us," says Batts, "but me and Jim have hunted squirrels all over this mounting, and we don't need no white flag. Was that straight, colonel, about the plum pudding and pineapples and real store cigars?"

"Towel on a fishing-pole in the offing!" howls Caligula. "Suppose it's the firing line of the freight conductors and brakemen."

"My last trip down," says I, wiping off my face. "If the S. & E. T. wants to run an excursion up here just because we kidnapped their president, let 'em. We'll put out our sign, 'The Kidnappers' Café and Trainmen's Home.' "

This time I caught Major Tallahassee Tucker by his own confession, and I felt easier. I asked him into the creek, so I could drown him if he happened to be a track-walker or caboose porter. All the way up the mountain he driveled to me about asparagus on toast, a thing that his intelligence in life had skipped.

Up above I got his mind segregated from food and asked if he had raised the ransom.

"My dear sir," says he, "I succeeded in negotiating a loan on thirty thousand dollars' worth of the bonds of our railroad, and—"

"Never mind just now, major," says I. "It's all right, then. Wait till after dinner, and we'll settle the business. All of you gentlemen," I continues to the crowd, "are invited to stay to dinner. We have mutually trusted one another, and the white flag is supposed to wave over the proceedings."

"The correct idea," says Caligula, who was standing by me. "Two baggage-masters and a ticket-agent dropped out of a tree while you was below the last time. Did the major man bring the money?"

"He says," I answered, "that he succeeded in negotiating the loan."

If any cooks ever earned ten thousand dollars in twelve hours, me and Caligula did that day. At six o'clock we spread the top of the mountain with as fine a dinner as the personnel of any railroad ever engulfed. We opened all the wine, and we concocted entrées and *pièces de resistance,* and stirred up little savory *chef de cuisines* and organized a mass of grub such as has been seldom instigated out of canned and bottled goods. The railroad gathered around it, and the wassail and diversions was intense.

After the feast me and Caligula, in the line of business, takes Major Tucker to one side and talks ransom. The major pulls out an agglomeration of currency about the size of the price of a town lot in the suburbs of Rabbitville, Arizona, and makes this outcry.

"Gentlemen," says he, "the stock of the Sunrise & Edenville railroad has depreciated some. The best I could do with thirty thousand dollars' worth of the bonds was to secure a loan of eighty-seven dollars and fifty cents. On the farming lands of Colonel Rockingham, Judge Pendergast was able to obtain, on a ninth mortgage, the sum of fifty dollars. You will find the amount, one hundred and thirty-seven fifty, correct."

"A railroad president," said I, looking this Tucker in the eye, "and the owner of a thousand acres of land; and yet—"

"Gentlemen," says Tucker, "the railroad is ten miles long. There don't any train run on it except when the crew goes out in the pines and gathers enough lightwood knots to get up steam. A long time ago, when times was good, the net earnings used to run as high as eighteen dollars a week. Colonel Rockingham's land has been sold for taxes thirteen times. There hasn't been a peach crop in this part of Georgia for two years. The wet spring killed the watermelons. Nobody around here has money enough to buy fertilizer; and land is so poor the corn crop failed, and there wasn't enough grass to support the rabbits. All the people have had to eat in this section for over a year is hog and hominy, and—"

"Pick," interrupts Caligula, mussing up his red hair, "what are you going to do with that chicken-feed?"

I hands the money back to Major Tucker; and then I goes over to Colonel Rockingham and slaps him on the back.

"Colonel," says I, "I hope you've enjoyed our little joke. We don't want to carry it too far. Kidnappers! Well, wouldn't it tickle your uncle? My name's Rhinegelder, and I'm a nephew of Chauncey Depew. My friend's a second cousin of the editor of *Puck*. So you can see. We are down South enjoying ourselves in our humorous way. Now, there's two quarts of cognac to open yet, and then the joke's over."

What the use to go into the details? One or two will be enough. I remember Major Tallahassee Tucker playing on a jew's-harp, and Caligula waltzing with his head on the watch pocket of a tall baggage-master. I hesitate to refer to the cakewalk done by me and Mr. Patterson G. Coble with Colonel Jackson T. Rockingham between us.

And even on the next morning, when you wouldn't think it possible, there was a consolation for me and Caligula. We knew that Raisuli himself never made half the hit with Burdick Harris that we did with the Sunrise & Edenville Tap Railroad.

THE METTERLING LISTS

Venal & Sons has at last published the long-awaited first volume of Metterling's laundry lists (*The Collected Laundry Lists of Hans Metterling,* Vol. I, 437 pp., plus XXXII-page introduction; indexed; $18.75), with an erudite commentary by the noted Metterling scholar Gunther Eisenbud. The decision to publish this work separately, before the completion of the immense four-volume *œuvre,* is both welcome and intelligent, for this obdurate and sparkling book will instantly lay to rest the unpleasant rumors that Venal & Sons, having reaped rich rewards from the Metterling novels, play, and notebooks, diaries, and letters, was merely in search of continued profits from the same lode. How wrong the whisperers have been! Indeed, the very first Metterling laundry list

List No. 1
6 prs. shorts
4 undershirts
6 prs. blue socks
4 blue shirts
2 white shirts
6 handkerchiefs
    No Starch

serves as a perfect, near-total introduction to this troubled genius, known to his contemporaries as the "Prague Weirdo."

The list was dashed off while Metterling was writing *Confess-ions of a Monstrous Cheese,* that work of stunning philosophi-cal import in which he proved not only that Kant was wrong about the universe but that he never picked up a check. Met-terling's dislike of starch is typical of the period, and when this particular bundle came back too stiff Metterling became moody and depressed. His landlady, Frau Weiser, reported to friends that "Herr Metterling keeps to his room for days, weeping over the fact that they have starched his shorts." Of course, Breuer has already pointed out the relation between stiff underwear and Metterling's constant feeling that he was being whispered about by men with jowls (*Metterling: Para-noid-Depressive Psychosis and the Early Lists,* Zeiss Press). This theme of a failure to follow instructions appears in Met-terling's only play, *Asthma,* when Needleman brings the cursed tennis ball to Valhalla by mistake.

The obvious enigma of the second list

LIST NO. 2
7 prs. shorts
5 undershirts
7 prs. black socks
6 blue shirts
6 handkerchiefs
   No Starch

is the seven pairs of black socks, since it has been long known that Metterling was deeply fond of blue. Indeed, for years the mention of any other color would send him into a rage, and he once pushed Rilke down into some honey because the poet said he preferred brown-eyed women. According to Anna Freud ("Metterling's Socks as an Expression of the Phallic Mother," *Journal of Psychoanalysis,* Nov., 1935), his sudden shift to the more sombre legwear is related to his unhappiness over the "Bayreuth Incident." It was there, during the first act of *Tristan,* that he sneezed, blowing the toupee off one of the opera's wealthiest patrons. The audience became con-

vulsed, but Wagner defended him with his now classic remark "Everybody sneezes." At this, Cosima Wagner burst
into tears and accused Metterling of sabotaging her husband's work.

That Metterling had designs on Cosima Wagner is undoubtedly true, and we know he took her hand once in Leipzig and again, four years later, in the Ruhr Valley. In Danzig,
he referred to her tibia obliquely during a rainstorm, and she
thought it best not to see him again. Returning to his home in
a state of exhaustion, Metterling wrote *Thoughts of a
Chicken,* and dedicated the original manuscript to the
Wagners. When they used it to prop up the short leg of a
kitchen table, Metterling became sullen and switched to dark
socks. His housekeeper pleaded with him to retain his beloved
blue or at least to try brown, but Metterling cursed her, saying, "Slut! And why not Argyles, eh?"

In the third list

List No. 3
6 handkerchiefs
5 undershirts
8 prs. socks
3 bedsheets
2 pillowcases

linens are mentioned for the first time: Metterling had a great
fondness for linens, particularly pillowcases, which he and his
sister, as children, used to put over their heads while playing
ghosts, until one day he fell into a rock quarry. Metterling
liked to sleep on fresh linen, and so do his fictional creations.
Horst Wasserman, the impotent locksmith in *Filet of Herring,*
kills for a change of sheets, and Jenny, in *The Shepherd's Finger,* is willing to go to bed with Klineman (whom she hates for
rubbing butter on her mother) "if it means lying between soft
sheets." It is a tragedy that the laundry never did the linens to
Metterling's satisfaction, but to contend, as Pfaltz has done,
that his consternation over it prevented him from finishing

Whither Thou Goest, Cretin is absurd. Metterling enjoyed the
luxury of sending his sheets out, but he was not dependent
on it.

What prevented Metterling from finishing his long-planned
book of poetry was an abortive romance, which figures in the
"Famous Fourth" list:

LIST NO. 4
7 prs. shorts
6 handkerchiefs
6 undershirts
7 prs. black socks
  No Starch
Special One-Day Service

In 1884, Metterling met Lou Andreas-Salomé, and suddenly,
we learn, he required that his laundry be done fresh daily.
Actually, the two were introduced by Nietzsche, who told Lou
that Metterling was either a genius or an idiot and to see if
she could guess which. At that time, the special one-day service was becoming quite popular on the Continent, particularly with intellectuals, and the innovation was welcomed by
Metterling. For one thing, it was prompt, and Metterling
loved promptness. He was always showing up for appointments early—sometimes several days early, so that he would
have to be put up in a guest room. Lou also loved fresh ship-
ments of laundry every day. She was like a little child in her
joy, often taking Metterling for walks in the woods and there
unwrapping the latest bundle. She loved his undershirts and
handkerchiefs, but most of all she worshipped his shorts. She
wrote Nietzsche that Metterling's shorts were the most sublime thing she had ever encountered, including *Thus Spake
Zarathustra*. Nietzsche acted like a gentleman about it, but
he was always jealous of Metterling's underwear and told
close friends he found it "Hegelian in the extreme." Lou Sa-
lomè and Metterling parted company after the Great Treacle
Famine of 1886, and while Metterling forgave Lou, she always said of him that "his mind had hospital corners."

The fifth list

LIST NO. 5
6 undershirts
6 shorts
6 handkerchiefs

has always puzzled scholars, principally because of the total
absence of socks. (Indeed, Thomas Mann, writing years later,
became so engrossed with the problem he wrote an entire
play about it, *The Hosiery of Moses,* which he accidentally
dropped down a grating.) Why did this literary giant suddenly
strike socks from his weekly list? Not, as some scholars say, as
a sign of his oncoming madness, although Metterling had by
now adopted certain odd behavior traits. For one thing, he believed that he was either being followed or was following
somebody. He told close friends of a government plot to steal
his chin, and once, on holiday in Jena, he could not say anything but the word "eggplant" for four straight days. Still,
these seizures were sporadic and do not account for the missing socks. Nor does his emulation of Kafka, who for a brief period of his life stopped wearing socks, out of guilt. But
Eisenbud assures us that Metterling continued to wear socks.
He merely stopped sending them to the laundry! And why?
Because at this time in his life he acquired a new housekeeper, Frau Milner, who consented to do his socks by
hand—a gesture that so moved Metterling that he left the
woman his entire fortune, which consisted of a black hat and
some tobacco. She also appears as Hilda in his comic allegory,
Mother Brandt's Ichor.

Obviously, Metterling's personality had begun to fragment
by 1894, if we can deduce anything from the sixth list:

LIST NO. 6
25 handkerchiefs
1 undershirt
5 shorts
1 sock

and it is not surprising to learn that it was at this time he entered analysis with Freud. He had met Freud years before in Vienna, when they both attended a production of *Oedipus,* from which Freud had to be carried out in a cold sweat. Their sessions were stormy, if we are to believe Freud's notes, and Metterling was hostile. He once threatened to starch Freud's beard and often said he reminded him of his laundryman. Gradually, Metterling's unusual relationship with his father came out. (Students of Metterling are already familiar with his father, a petty official who would frequently ridicule Metterling by comparing him to a wurst.) Freud writes of a key dream Metterling described to him:

> I am at a dinner party with some friends when suddenly a man walks in with a bowl of soup on a leash. He accuses my underwear of treason, and when a lady defends me her forehead falls off. I find this amusing in the dream, and laugh. Soon everyone is laughing except my laundryman, who seems stern and sits there putting porridge in his ears. My father enters, grabs the lady's forehead, and runs away with it. He races to a public square, yelling, "At last! At last! A forehead of my own! Now I won't have to rely on that stupid son of mine." This depresses me in the dream, and I am seized with an urge to kiss the Burgomaster's laundry. (Here the patient weeps and forgets the remainder of the dream.)

With insights gained from this dream, Freud was able to help Metterling, and the two became quite friendly outside of analysis, although Freud would never let Metterling get behind him.

In Volume II, it has been announced, Eisenbud will take up Lists 7–25, including the years of Metterling's "private laundress" and the pathetic misunderstanding with the Chinese on the corner.

THE WALTZ

Why, *thank you so much. I'd adore to.*

I don't want to dance with him. I don't want to dance with anybody. And even if I did, it wouldn't be him. He'd be well down among the last ten. I've seen the way he dances; it looks like something you do on Saint Walpurgis Night. Just think, not a quarter of an hour ago, here I was sitting, feeling so sorry for the poor girl he was dancing with. And now *I'm* going to be the poor girl. Well, well. Isn't it a small world?

And a peach of a world, too. A true little corker. Its events are so fascinatingly unpredictable, are not they? Here I was, minding my own business, not doing a stitch of harm to any living soul. And then he comes into my life, all smiles and city manners, to sue me for the favor of one memorable mazurka. Why, he scarcely knows my name, let alone what it stands for. It stands for Despair, Bewilderment, Futility, Degradation, and Premeditated Murder, but little does he wot. I don't wot his name, either; I haven't any idea what it is. Jukes, would be my guess from the look in his eyes. How do you do, Mr. Jukes? And how is that dear little brother of yours, with the two heads?

Ah, now why did he have to come around me, with his low requests? Why can't he let me lead my own life? I ask so little—just to be left alone in my quiet corner of the table, to do my evening brooding over all my sorrows. And he must come, with his bows and his scrapes and his may-I-have-this-ones.

And I had to go and tell him that I'd adore to dance with him.
I cannot understand why I wasn't struck right down dead.
Yes, and being struck dead would look like a day in the country, compared to struggling out a dance with this boy. But
what could I do? Everyone else at the table had got up to
dance, except him and me. There was I, trapped. Trapped like
a trap in a trap.

What can you say, when a man asks you to dance with
him? I most certainly will *not* dance with you, I'll see you in
hell first. Why, thank you, I'd like to awfully, but I'm having
labor pains. Oh, yes, *do* let's dance together—it's so nice to
meet a man who isn't a scaredy-cat about catching my beri-
beri. No. There was nothing for me to do, but say I'd adore to.
Well, we might as well get it over with. All right, Cannonball,
let's run out on the field. You won the toss; you can lead.

*Why, I think it's more of a waltz, really. Isn't it? We might
just listen to the music a second. Shall we? Oh, yes, it's a
waltz. Mind? Why, I'm simply thrilled. I'd love to waltz with
you.*

I'd love to waltz with you. I'd love to waltz with you. I'd love
to have my tonsils out, I'd love to be in a midnight fire at sea.
Well, it's too late now. We're getting under way. *Oh.* Oh, dear.
Oh, dear, dear, dear. Oh, this is even worse than I thought it
would be. I suppose that's the one dependable law of life—
everything is always worse than you thought it was going to
be. Oh, if I had any real grasp of what this dance would be
like, I'd have held out for sitting it out. Well, it will probably
amount to the same thing in the end. We'll be sitting it out on
the floor in a minute, if he keeps this up.

I'm so glad I brought it to his attention that this is a waltz
they're playing. Heaven knows what might have happened, if
he had thought it was something fast; we'd have blown the
sides right out of the building. Why does he always want to be
somewhere that he isn't? Why can't we stay in one place just
long enough to get acclimated? It's this constant rush, rush,
rush, that's the curse of American life. That's the reason that
we're all of us so—*Ow!* For God's sake, don't *kick*, you idiot;

this is only second down. Oh, my shin. My poor, poor shin, that I've had ever since I was a little girl!

Oh, no, no, no. Goodness, no. It didn't hurt the least little bit. And anyway it was my fault. Really it was. Truly. Well, you're just being sweet, to say that. It really was all my fault.

I wonder what I'd better do—kill him this instant, with my naked hands, or wait and let him drop in his traces. Maybe it's best not to make a scene. I guess I'll just lie low, and watch the pace get him. He can't keep this up indefinitely—he's only flesh and blood. Die he must, and die he shall, for what he did to me. I don't want to be of the over-sensitive type, but you can't tell me that kick was unpremeditated. Freud says there are no accidents. I've led no cloistered life, I've known dancing partners who have spoiled my slippers and torn my dress; but when it comes to kicking, I am Outraged Womanhood. When you kick me in the shin, *smile*.

Maybe he didn't do it maliciously. Maybe it's just his way of showing his high spirits. I suppose I ought to be glad that one of us is having such a good time. I suppose I ought to think myself lucky if he brings me back alive. Maybe it's captious to demand of a practically strange man that he leave your shins as he found them. After all, the poor boy's doing the best he can. Probably he grew up in the hill country, and never had no larnin'. I bet they had to throw him on his back to get shoes on him.

Yes, it's lovely, isn't it? It's simply lovely. It's the loveliest waltz. Isn't it? Oh, I think it's lovely, too.

Why, I'm getting positively drawn to the Triple Threat here. He's my hero. He has the heart of a lion, and the sinews of a buffalo. Look at him—never a thought of the consequences, never afraid of his face, hurling himself into every scrimmage, eyes shining, cheeks ablaze. And shall it be said that I hung back? No, a thousand times no. What's it to me if I have to spend the next couple of years in a plaster cast? Come on, Butch, right through them! Who wants to live forever?

Oh, Oh, dear. Oh, he's all right, thank goodness. For a

while I thought they'd have to carry him off the field. Ah, I couldn't bear to have anything happen to him. I love him. I love him better than anybody in the world. Look at the spirit he gets into a dreary, commonplace waltz; how effete the other dancers seem, beside him. He is youth and vigor and courage, he is strength and gaiety and—*Ow!* Get off my instep, you hulking peasant! What do you think I am, anyway—a gangplank? *Ow!*

No, of course it didn't hurt. Why, it didn't a bit. Honestly. And it was all my fault. You see, that little step of yours— well, it's perfectly lovely, but it's just a tiny bit tricky to follow at first. Oh, did you work it up yourself? You really did? Well, aren't you amazing! Oh, now I think I've got it. Oh, I think it's lovely. I was watching you do it when you were dancing before. It's awfully effective when you look at it.

It's awfully effective when you look at it. I bet I'm awfully effective when you look at me. My hair is hanging along my cheeks, my skirt is swaddling about me. I can feel the cold damp of my brow. I must look like something out of "The Fall of the House of Usher." This sort of thing takes a fearful toll of a woman my age. And he worked up his little step himself, he with his degenerate cunning. And it was just a tiny bit tricky at first, but now I think I've got it. Two stumbles, slip, and a twenty-yard dash: yes. I've got it. I've got several other things, too, including a split shin and a bitter heart. I hate this creature I'm chained to. I hated him the moment I saw his leering, bestial face. And here I've been locked in his noxious embrace for the thirty-five years this waltz has lasted. Is that orchestra never going to stop playing? Or must this obscene travesty of a dance go on until hell burns out?

Oh, they're going to play another encore. Oh, goody. Oh, that's lovely. Tired? I should say I'm not tired. I'd like to go on like this forever.

I should say I'm not tired. I'm dead, that's all I am. Dead, and in what a cause! And the music is never going to stop playing, and we're going on like this, Double-Time Charlie and I, throughout eternity. I suppose I won't care any more, after the first hundred thousand years. I suppose nothing will matter then, not heat nor pain nor broken heart nor cruel, aching weariness. Well. It can't come too soon for me.

I wonder why I didn't tell him I was tired. I wonder why I didn't suggest going back to the table. I could have said let's just listen to the music. Yes, and if he would, that would be the first bit of attention he has given it all evening. George Jean Nathan said that the lovely rhythms of the waltz should be listened to in stillness and not be accompanied by strange gyrations of the human body. I think that's what he said. I think it was George Jean Nathan. Anyhow, whatever he said and whoever he was and whatever he's doing now, he's better off than I am. That's safe. Anybody who isn't waltzing with this Mrs. O'Leary's cow I've got here is having a good time.

Still if we were back at the table, I'd probably have to talk to him. Look at him—what could you say to a thing like that! Did you go to the circus this year, what's your favorite kind of ice cream, how do you spell cat? I guess I'm as well off here. As well off as if I were in a cement mixer in full action.

I'm past all feeling now. The only way I can tell when he steps on me is that I can hear the splintering of bones. And all the events of my life are passing before my eyes. There was the time I was in a hurricane in the West Indies, there was the day I got my head cut open in the taxi smash, there was the night the drunken lady threw a bronze ash-tray at her own true love and got me instead, there was that summer that the sailboat kept capsizing. Ah, what an easy, peaceful time was mine, until I fell in with Swifty, here. I didn't know what trouble was, before I got drawn into this *danse macabre*. I think my mind is beginning to wander. It almost seems to me as if the orchestra were stopping. It couldn't be, of course; it could never, never be. And yet in my ears there is a silence like the sound of angel voices. . . .

Oh, they've stopped, the mean things. They're not going to play any more. Oh, darn. Oh, do you think they would? Do you really think so, if you gave them twenty dollars? Oh, that would be lovely. And look, do tell them to play this same thing. I'd simply adore to go on waltzing.

THE KENTUCKY DERBY IS DECADENT AND DEPRAVED

I got off the plane around midnight and no one spoke as I crossed the dark runway to the terminal. The air was thick and hot, like wandering into a steam bath. Inside, people hugged each other and shook hands . . . big grins and a whoop here and there: "By God! You old *bastard! Good* to see you, boy! *Damn* good . . . and I *mean* it!"

In the air-conditioned lounge I met a man from Houston who said his name was something or other—"but just call me Jimbo"—and he was here to get it on. "I'm ready for *anything,* by God! Anything at all. Yeah, what are you drinkin?" I ordered a Margarita with ice, but he wouldn't hear of it: "Naw, naw . . . what the hell kind of drink is that for Kentucky Derby time? What's *wrong* with you, boy?" He grinned and winked at the bartender. "Goddam, we gotta educate this boy. Get him some good *whiskey* . . ."

I shrugged. "Okay, a double Old Fitz on ice." Jimbo nodded his approval.

"Look." He tapped me on the arm to make sure I was listening. "I know this Derby crowd, I come here every year, and let me tell you one thing I've learned—this is no town to be giving people the impression you're some kind of faggot. Not in public, anyway. Shit, they'll roll you in a minute, knock you in the head and take every goddam cent you have."

I thanked him and fitted a Marlboro into my cigarette

holder. "Say," he said, "you look like you might be in the horse business . . . am I right?"

"No," I said. "I'm a photographer."

"Oh yeah?" He eyed my ragged leather bag with new interest. "Is that what you got there—cameras? Who you work for?"

"*Playboy,*" I said.

He laughed. "Well, goddam! What are you gonna take pictures of—nekkid horses? Haw! I guess you'll be workin' pretty hard when they run the Kentucky Oaks. That's a race just for fillies." He was laughing wildly. "Hell yes! And they'll all be nekkid too!"

I shook my head and said nothing; just stared at him for a moment, trying to look grim. "There's going to be trouble," I said. "My assignment is to take pictures of the riot."

"What riot?"

I hesitated, twirling the ice in my drink. "At the track. On Derby Day. The Black Panthers." I stared at him again. "Don't you read the newspapers?"

The grin on his face had collapsed. "What the *hell* are you talkin about?"

"Well . . . maybe I shouldn't be telling you . . ." I shrugged. "But hell, everybody else seems to know. The cops and the National Guard have been getting ready for six weeks. They have 20,000 troops on alert at Fort Knox. They've warned us—all the press and photographers—to wear helmets and special vests like flak jackets. We were told to expect shooting. . . ."

"No!" he shouted; his hands flew up and hovered momentarily between us, as if to ward off the words he was hearing. Then he whacked his fist on the bar. "Those sons of bitches! God Almighty! The Kentucky Derby!" He kept shaking his head. "No! *Jesus!* That's almost too bad to believe!" Now he seemed to be sagging on the stool, and when he looked up his eyes were misty. "Why? Why *here*? Don't they respect *anything*?"

I shrugged again. "It's not just the Panthers. The FBI says

busloads of white crazies are coming in from all over the country—to mix with the crowd and attack all at once, from every direction. They'll be dressed like everybody else. You know—coats and ties and all that. But when the trouble starts . . . well, that's why the cops are so worried."

He sat for a moment, looking hurt and confused and not quite able to digest all this terrible news. Then he cried out: "Oh . . . Jesus! What in the name of God is happening in this country? Where can you get *away* from it?"

"Not here," I said, picking up my bag. "Thanks for the drink . . . and good luck."

He grabbed my arm, urging me to have another, but I said I was overdue at the Press Club and hustled off to get my act together for the awful spectacle. At the airport newsstand I picked up a *Courier-Journal* and scanned the front page headlines: "Nixon Sends GI's into Cambodia to Hit Reds" . . . "B-52's Raid, then 2,000 GI's Advance 20 Miles" . . . "4,000 U.S. Troops Deployed Near Yale as Tension Grows Over Panther Protest." At the bottom of the page was a photo of Diane Crump, soon to become the first woman jockey ever to ride in the Kentucky Derby. The photographer had snapped her "stopping in the barn area to fondle her mount, Fathom." The rest of the paper was spotted with ugly war news and stories of "student unrest." There was no mention of any trouble brewing at a university in Ohio called Kent State.

I went to the Hertz desk to pick up my car, but the moon-faced young swinger in charge said they didn't have any. "You can't rent one anywhere," he assured me. "Our Derby reservations have been booked for six weeks." I explained that my agent had confirmed a white Chrylser convertible for me that very afternoon but he shook his head. "Maybe we'll have a cancellation. Where are you staying?"

I shrugged. "Where's the Texas crowd staying? I want to be with my people."

He sighed. "My friend, you're in trouble. This town is flat *full*. Always is, for the Derby."

I leaned closer to him, half-whispering: "Look, I'm from *Playboy*. How would you like a job?"

He backed off quickly. "What? Come on, now. What kind of a job?"

"Never mind," I said. "You just blew it." I swept my bag off the counter and went to find a cab. The bag is a valuable prop in this kind of work; mine has a lot of baggage tags on it—SF, LA, NY, Lima, Rome, Bangkok, that sort of thing—and the most prominent tag of all is a very official, plastic-coated thing that says "Photog. Playboy Mag." I bought it from a pimp in Vail, Colorado, and he told me how to use it. "Never mention *Playboy* until you're sure they've seen this thing first," he said. "Then, when you see them notice it, that's the time to strike. They'll go belly up every time. This thing is magic, I tell you. Pure magic."

Well . . . maybe so. I'd used it on the poor geek in the bar, and now, humming along in a Yellow Cab toward town, I felt a little guilty about jangling the poor bugger's brains with that evil fantasy. But what the hell? Anybody who wanders around the world saying, "Hell, yes, I'm from Texas," deserves whatever happens to him. And he had, after all, come here once again to make a nineteenth-century ass of himself in the midst of some jaded, atavistic freakout with nothing to recommend it except a very saleable "tradition." Early in our chat, Jimbo had told me that he hasn't missed a Derby since 1954. "The little lady won't come anymore," he said. "She just grits her teeth and turns me loose for this one. And when I say 'loose' I do mean *loose!* I toss ten-dollar bills around like they were goin' outa style! Horses, whiskey, women . . . shit, there's women in this town that'll do *anything* for money."

Why not? Money is a good thing to have in these twisted times. Even Richard Nixon is hungry for it. Only a few days before the Derby he said, "If I had any money I'd invest it in the stock market." And the market, meanwhile, continued its grim slide.

*   *   *

The next day was heavy. With only thirty hours until post time I had no press credentials and—according to the sports editor of the Louisville *Courier-Journal*—no hope at all of getting any. Worse, I needed *two* sets; one for myself and another for Ralph Steadman, the English illustrator who was coming from London to do some Derby drawings. All I knew about him was that this was his first visit to the United States. And the more I pondered that fact, the more it gave me the fear. How would he bear up under the heinous culture shock of being lifted out of London and plunged into a drunken mob scene at the Kentucky Derby? There was no way of knowing. Hopefully, he would arrive at least a day or so ahead, and give himself time to get acclimated. Maybe a few hours of peaceful sightseeing in the Bluegrass country around Lexington. My plan was to pick him up at the airport in the huge Pontiac Ballbuster I'd rented from a used-car salesman named Colonel Quick, then whisk him off to some peaceful setting that might remind him of England.

Colonel Quick had solved the car problem, and money (four times the normal rate) had bought two rooms in a scumbox on the outskirts of town. The only other kink was the task of convincing the moguls at Churchill Downs that *Scanlan's* was such a prestigious sporting journal that common sense compelled them to give us two sets of the best press tickets. This was not easily done. My first call to the publicity office resulted in total failure. The press handler was shocked at the idea that anyone would be stupid enough to apply for press credentials two days before the Derby. "Hell, you can't be serious," he said. "The deadline was two months ago. The press box is full; there's no more room . . . and what the hell is *Scanlan's Monthly* anyway?"

I uttered a painful groan. "Didn't the London office call you? They're flying an artist over to do the paintings. Steadman. He's Irish, I think. Very famous over there. Yes. I just got in from the Coast. The San Francisco office told me we were all set."

He seemed interested, and even sympathetic, but there was nothing he could do. I flattered him with more gibberish, and finally he offered a compromise: he could get us two passes to the clubhouse grounds but the clubhouse itself and especially the press box were out of the question.

"That sounds a little weird," I said. "It's unacceptable. We *must* have access to everything. *All* of it. The spectacle, the people, the pageantry and certainly the race. You don't think we came all this way to watch the damn thing on television, do you? One way or another we'll get inside. Maybe we'll have to bribe a guard—or even Mace somebody." (I had picked up a spray can of Mace in a downtown drugstore for $5.98 and suddenly, in the midst of that phone talk, I was struck by the hideous possibilities of using it out at the track. Macing ushers at the narrow gates to the clubhouse inner sanctum, then slipping quickly inside, firing a huge load of Mace into the governor's box, just as the race starts. Or Macing help-less drunks in the clubhouse restroom, for their own good . . .)

By noon on Friday I was still without credentials and still unable to locate Steadman. For all I knew he'd changed his mind and gone back to London. Finally, after giving up on Steadman and trying unsuccessfully to reach my man in the press office, I decided my only hope for credentials was to go out to the track and confront the man in person, with no warning—demanding only one pass now, instead of two, and talking very fast with a strange lilt in my voice, like a man try-ing hard to control some inner frenzy. On the way out, I stopped at the motel desk to cash a check. Then, as a useless afterthought, I asked if by any wild chance a Mr. Steadman had checked in.

The lady on the desk was about fifty years old and very pe-culiar-looking; when I mentioned Steadman's name she nod-ded, without looking up from whatever she was writing, and said in a low voice, "You bet he did." Then she favored me with a big smile. "Yes, indeed. Mr. Steadman just left for the racetrack. Is he a friend of yours?"

I shook my head. "I'm supposed to be working with him, but I don't even know what he looks like. Now, goddammit, I'll have to find him in that mob at the track."

She chuckled. "You won't have any trouble finding him. You could pick *that* man out of any crowd."

"Why?" I asked. "What's wrong with him? What does he look like?"

"Well . . ." she said, still grinning, "he's the funniest looking thing I've seen in a long time. He has this . . . ah . . . this *growth* all over his face. As a matter of fact it's all over his *head.*" She nodded. "You'll know him when you see him; don't worry about that."

Creeping Jesus, I thought. That screws the press credentials. I had a vision of some nerve-rattling geek all covered with matted hair and string-warts showing up in the press office and demanding *Scanlan's* press packet. Well . . . what the hell? We could always load up on acid and spend the day roaming around the clubhouse grounds with big sketch pads, laughing hysterically at the natives and swilling mint juleps so the cops wouldn't think we're abnormal. Perhaps even make the act pay: set up an easel with a big sign saying, "Let a Foreign Artist Paint Your Portrait, $10 Each. Do It NOW!"

I took the expressway out to the track, driving very fast and jumping the monster car back and forth between lanes, driving with a beer in one hand and my mind so muddled that I almost crushed a Volkswagen full of nuns when I swerved to catch the right exit. There was a slim chance, I thought, that I might be able to catch the ugly Britisher before he checked in.

But Steadman was already in the press box when I got there, a bearded young Englishman wearing a tweed coat and RAF sunglasses. There was nothing particularly odd about him. No facial veins or clumps of bristly warts. I told him about the motel woman's description and he seemed puzzled. "Don't let it bother you," I said. "Just keep in mind for the next few days that we're in Louisville, Kentucky. Not London. Not even New York. This is a weird place. You're lucky that mental defective at the motel didn't jerk a pistol out of the cash register and blow a big hole in you." I laughed, but he looked worried.

"Just pretend you're visiting a huge outdoor loony bin," I said. "If the inmates get out of control we'll soak them down with Mace." I showed him the can of "Chemical Billy," resisting the urge to fire it across the room at a rat-faced man typing diligently in the Associated Press section. We were standing at the bar, sipping the management's Scotch and congratulating each other on our sudden, unexplained luck in picking up two sets of fine press credentials. The lady at the desk had been very friendly to him, he said. "I just told her my name and she gave me the whole works."

By midafternoon we had everything under control. We had seats looking down on the finish line, color TV and a free bar in the press room, and a selection of passes that would take us anywhere from the clubhouse roof to the jockey room. The only thing we lacked was unlimited access to the clubhouse inner sanctum in sections "F&G" . . . and I felt we needed that, to see the whiskey gentry in action. The governor, a swinish neo-Nazi hack named Louie Nunn, would be in "G," along with Barry Goldwater and Colonel Sanders. I felt we'd be legal in a box in "G" where we could rest and sip juleps, soak up a bit of atmosphere and the Derby's special vibrations.

The bars and dining rooms are also in "F&G," and the clubhouse bars on Derby Day are a very special kind of scene. Along with the politicians, society belles and local captains of commerce, every half-mad dingbat who ever had any pretensions to anything at all within five hundred miles of Louisville will show up there to get strutting drunk and slap a lot of backs and generally make himself obvious. The Paddock bar is probably the best place in the track to sit and watch faces. Nobody minds being stared at; that's what they're in there for. Some people spend most of their time in the Paddock; they can hunker down at one of the many wooden tables, lean back in a comfortable chair and watch the ever-changing odds flash up and down on the big tote board outside the window. Black waiters in white serving jackets move through the crowd with trays of drinks, while the experts ponder their racing forms and the hunch bettors pick lucky numbers or scan the lineup for right-sounding names. There is a constant flow of traffic to and from the pari-mutuel windows outside in the wooden corridors. Then, as post time nears, the crowd thins out as people go back to their boxes.

Clearly, we were going to have to figure out some way to spend more time in the clubhouse tomorrow. But the "walk-around" press passes to F&G were only good for thirty minutes at a time, presumably to allow the newspaper types to rush in and out for photos or quick interviews, but to prevent drifters like Steadman and me from spending all day in the clubhouse, harassing the gentry and rifling the odd handbag or two while cruising around the boxes. Or Macing the governor. The time limit was no problem on Friday, but on Derby Day the walkaround passes would be in heavy demand. And since it took about ten minutes to get from the press box to the Paddock, and ten more minutes to get back, that didn't leave much time for serious people-watching. And unlike most of the others in the press box, we didn't give a hoot in hell what was happening on the track. We had come there to watch the *real* beasts perform.

Later Friday afternoon, we went out on the balcony of the press box and I tried to describe the difference between what we were seeing today and what would be happening tomorrow. This was the first time I'd been to a Derby in ten years, but before that, when I lived in Louisville, I used to go every year. Now, looking down from the press box, I pointed to the huge grassy meadow enclosed by the track. "That whole thing," I said, "will be jammed with people; fifty thousand or so, and most of them staggering drunk. It's a fantastic scene—thousands of people fainting, crying, copulating, trampling each other and fighting with broken whiskey bottles. We'll have to spend some time out there, but it's hard to move around, too many bodies."

"Is it safe out there? Will we *ever* come back?"

"Sure," I said. "We'll just have to be careful not to step on anybody's stomach and start a fight." I shrugged. "Hell, this clubhouse scene right below us will be almost as bad as the infield. Thousands of raving, stumbling drunks, getting angrier and angrier as they lose more and more money. By mid-afternoon they'll be guzzling mint juleps with both hands and vomiting on each other between races. The whole place will be jammed with bodies, shoulder to shoulder. It's hard to move around. The aisles will be slick with vomit; people falling down and grabbing at your legs to keep from being stomped. Drunks pissing on themselves in the betting lines. Dropping handfuls of money and fighting to stoop over and pick it up.''

He looked so nervous that I laughed. "I'm just kidding," I said. "Don't worry. At the first hint of trouble I'll start pumping this 'Chemical Billy' into the crowd."

He had done a few good sketches, but so far we hadn't seen that special kind of face that I felt we would need for the lead drawing. It was a face I'd seen a thousand times at every Derby I'd ever been to. I saw it, in my head, as the mask of the whiskey gentry—a pretentious mix of booze, failed dreams and a terminal identity crisis; the inevitable result of too much inbreeding in a closed and ignorant culture. One of the key genetic rules in breeding dogs, horses or any other kind of thoroughbred is that close inbreeding tends to magnify the weak points in a bloodline as well as the strong points. In horse breeding, for instance, there is a definite risk in breeding two fast horses who are both a little crazy. The offspring will likely be very fast and also very crazy. So the trick in breeding thoroughbreds is to retain the good traits and filter out the bad. But the breeding of humans is not so wisely supervised, particularly in a narrow Southern society where the closest kind of inbreeding is not only stylish and acceptable, but far more convenient—to the parents—than setting their offspring free to find their own mates, for their own reasons and in their own ways. ("Goddam, did you hear about Smitty's daughter? She went crazy in Boston last week and married a nigger!")

So the face I was trying to find in Churchill Downs that weekend was a symbol, in my own mind, of the whole doomed atavistic culture that makes the Kentucky Derby what it is.

On our way back to the motel after Friday's races I warned Steadman about some of the other problems we'd have to cope with. Neither of us had brought any strange illegal drugs, so we would have to get by on booze. "You should keep in mind," I said, "that almost everybody you talk to from now on will be drunk. People who seem very pleasant at first might suddenly swing at you for no reason at all." He nodded, staring straight ahead. He seemed to be getting a little numb and I tried to cheer him up by inviting him to dinner that night, with my brother.

Back at the motel we talked for a while about America, the South, England—just relaxing a bit before dinner. There was no way either of us could have known, at the time, that it would be the last normal conversation we would have. From that point on, the weekend became a vicious, drunken nightmare. We both went completely to pieces. The main problem was my prior attachment to Louisville, which naturally led to meetings with old friends, relatives, etc., many of whom were in the process of falling apart, going mad, plotting divorces, cracking up under the strain of terrible debts or recovering from bad accidents. Right in the middle of the whole frenzied Derby action, a member of my own family had to be institutionalized. This added a certain amount of strain to the situation, and since poor Steadman had no choice but to take whatever came his way, he was subjected to shock after shock.

Another problem was his habit of sketching people he met in the various social situations I dragged him into—then giving them the sketches. The results were always unfortunate. I warned him several times about letting the subjects see his foul renderings, but for some perverse reason he kept doing it. Consequently, he was regarded with fear and loathing by nearly everyone who'd seen or even heard about his work. He couldn't understand it. "It's sort of a joke," he kept saying. "Why, in England it's quite normal. People don't take offense. They understand that I'm just putting them on a bit."

"Fuck England," I said. "This is Middle America. These

people regard what you're doing to them as a brutal, bilious insult. Look what happened last night. I thought my brother was going to tear your head off.''

Steadman shook his head sadly. "But I liked him. He struck me as a very decent, straightforward sort.''

"Look, Ralph," I said. "Let's not kid ourselves. That was a very horrible drawing you gave him. It was the face of a monster. It got on his nerves very badly." I shrugged. "Why in hell do you think we left the restaurant so fast?''

"I thought it was because of the Mace," he said.

"What Mace?''

He grinned. "When you shot it at the headwaiter, don't you remember?''

"Hell, that was nothing," I said. "I missed him . . . and we were leaving, anyway.''

"But it got all over us," he said. "The room was full of that damn gas. Your brother was sneezing and his wife was crying. My eyes hurt for two hours. I couldn't see to draw when we got back to the motel.''

"That's right," I said. "The stuff got on her leg, didn't it?''

"She was angry," he said.

"Yeah . . . well, okay . . . Let's just figure we fucked up about equally on that one," I said. "But from now on let's try to be careful when we're around people I know. You won't sketch them and I won't Mace them. We'll just try to relax and get drunk.''

"Right," he said. "We'll go native.''

It was Saturday morning, the day of the Big Race, and we were having breakfast in a plastic hamburger palace called the Fish-Meat Village. Our rooms were just across the road in the Brown Suburban Hotel. They had a dining room, but the food was so bad that we couldn't handle it anymore. The waitresses seemed to be suffering from shin splints; they moved around very slowly, moaning and cursing the "darkies" in the kitchen.

Steadman liked the Fish-Meat place because it had fish and

chips. I preferred the "French toast," which was really pan-cake batter, fried to the proper thickness and then chopped out with a sort of cookie cutter to resemble pieces of toast.

Beyond drink and lack of sleep, our only real problem at that point was the question of access to the clubhouse. Finally we decided to go ahead and steal two passes, if necessary, rather than miss that part of the action. This was the last co-herent decision we were able to make for the next forty-eight hours. From that point on—almost from the very moment we started out to the track—we lost all control of events and spent the rest of the weekend churning around in a sea of drunken horrors. My notes and recollections from Derby Day are somewhat scrambled.

But now, looking at the big red notebook I carried all through that scene, I see more or less what happened. The book itself is somewhat mangled and bent; some of the pages are torn, others are shriveled and stained by what appears to be whiskey, but taken as a whole, with sporadic memory flashes, the notes seem to tell the story. To wit:

Rain all nite until dawn. No sleep. Christ, here we go, a nightmare of mud and madness . . . But no. By noon the sun burns through—perfect day, not even humid.

Steadman is now worried about fire. Somebody told him about the clubhouse catching on fire two years ago. Could it happen again? Horrible. Trapped in the press box. Holocaust. A hundred thousand people fighting to get out. Drunks screaming in the flames and the mud, crazed horses running wild. Blind in the smoke. Grandstand collapsing into the flames with us on the roof. Poor Ralph is about to crack. Drinking heavily, into the Haig & Haig.

Out to the track in a cab, avoid that terrible parking in peo-ple's front yards, $25 each, toothless old men on the street with big signs: PARK HERE, flagging cars in the yard. "That's fine, boy, never mind the tulips." Wild hair on his head, straight up like a clump of reeds.

Sidewalks full of people all moving in the same direction, towards Churchill Downs. Kids hauling coolers and blankets, teenyboppers in tight pink shorts, many blacks . . . black dudes in white felt hats with leopard-skin bands, cops waving traffic along.

The mob was thick for many blocks around the track; very slow going in the crowd, very hot. On the way to the press box elevator, just inside the clubhouse, we came on a row of soldiers all carrying long white riot sticks. About two platoons, with helmets. A man walking next to us said they were waiting for the governor and his party. Steadman eyed them nervously. "Why do they have those clubs?"

"Black Panthers," I said. Then I remembered good old "Jimbo" at the airport and I wondered what he was thinking right now. Probably very nervous; the place was teeming with cops and soldiers. We pressed on through the crowd, through many gates, past the paddock where the jockeys bring the horses out and parade around for a while before each race so the bettors can get a good look. Five million dollars will be bet today. Many winners, more losers. What the hell. The press gate was jammed up with people trying to get in, shouting at the guards, waving strange press badges: Chicago Sporting Times, Pittsburgh Police Athletic League . . . they were all turned away. "Move on, fella, make way for the working press." We shoved through the crowd and into the elevator, then quickly up to the free bar. Why not? Get it on. Very hot today, not feeling well, must be this rotten climate. The press box was cool and airy, plenty of room to walk around and balcony seats for watching the race or looking down at the crowd. We got a betting sheet and went outside.

Pink faces with a stylish Southern sag, old Ivy styles, seersucker coats and buttondown collars. "Mayblossom Senility" (Steadman's phrase) . . . burnt out early or maybe just not much to burn in the first place. Not much energy in these faces, not much *curiosity*. Suffering in silence, nowhere to go after thirty in this life, just hang on and humor the children. Let the young enjoy themselves while they can. Why not?

The grim reaper comes early in this league . . . banshees on the lawn at night, screaming out there beside that little iron nigger in jockey clothes. Maybe he's the one who's screaming. Bad DT's and too many snarls at the bridge club. Going down with the stock market. Oh Jesus, the kid has wrecked the new car, wrapped it around the big stone pillar at the bottom of the driveway. Broken leg? Twisted eye? Send him off to Yale, they can cure anything up there.

Yale? Did you see today's paper? New Haven is under siege. Yale is swarming with Black Panthers. . . . I tell you, Colonel, the world has gone mad, stone mad. Why, they tell me a goddam woman jockey might ride in the Derby today.

I left Steadman sketching in the Paddock bar and went off to place our bets on the fourth race. When I came back he was staring intently at a group of young men around a table not far away. "Jesus, look at the corruption in that face!" he whispered. "Look at the madness, the fear, the greed!" I looked, then quickly turned my back on the table he was sketching. The face he'd picked out to draw was the face of an old friend of mine, a prep school football star in the good old days with a sleek red Chevy convertible and a very quick hand, it was said, with the snaps of a 32 B brassiere. They called him "Cat Man."

But now, a dozen years later, I wouldn't have recognized him anywhere but here, where I should have expected to find him, in the Paddock bar on Derby Day . . . fat slanted eyes and a pimp's smile, blue silk suit and his friends looking like crooked bank tellers on a binge . . .

Steadman wanted to see some Kentucky Colonels, but he wasn't sure what they looked like. I told him to go back to the clubhouse men's rooms and look for men in white linen suits vomiting in the urinals. "They'll usually have large brown whiskey stains on the fronts of their suits," I said. "But watch the shoes, that's the tip-off. Most of them manage to avoid vomiting on their own clothes, but they never miss their shoes."

In a box not far from ours was Colonel Anna Friedman Goldman, *Chairman and Keeper of the Great Seal of the Honorable Order of Kentucky Colonels.* Not all the 76 million or so Kentucky Colonels could make it to the Derby this year, but many had kept the faith, and several days prior to the Derby they gathered for their annual dinner at the Seelbach Hotel.

The Derby, the actual race, was scheduled for late afternoon, and as the magic hour approached I suggested to Steadman that we should probably spend some time in the infield, that boiling sea of people across the track from the clubhouse. He seemed a little nervous about it, but since none of the awful things I'd warned him about had happened so far—no race riots, firestorms or savage drunken attacks—he shrugged and said, "Right, let's do it."

To get there we had to pass through many gates, each one a step down in status, then through a tunnel under the track. Emerging from the tunnel was such a culture shock that it took us a while to adjust. "God almighty!" Steadman muttered. "This is a . . . Jesus!" He plunged ahead with his tiny camera, stepping over bodies, and I followed, trying to take notes.

Total chaos, no way to see the race, not even the track . . . nobody cares. Big lines at the outdoor betting windows, then stand back to watch winning numbers flash on the big board, like a giant bingo game.

Old blacks arguing about bets; "Hold on there, I'll handle this" (waving pint of whiskey, fistful of dollar bills); girl riding piggyback, T-shirt says, "Stolen from Fort Lauderdale Jail." Thousands of teen-agers, group singing "Let the Sun Shine In," ten soldiers guarding the American flag and a huge fat drunk wearing a blue football jersey (No. 80) reeling around with quart of beer in hand.

No booze sold out here, too dangerous . . . no bathrooms either. Muscle Beach . . . Woodstock . . . many cops with riot sticks, but no sign of a riot. Far across the track the clubhouse looks like a postcard from the Kentucky Derby.

We went back to the clubhouse to watch the big race. When the crowd stood to face the flag and sing "My Old Kentucky Home," Steadman faced the crowd and sketched frantically. Somewhere up in the boxes a voice screeched, "Turn around, you hairy freak!" The race itself was only two minutes long, and even from our super-status seats and using 12-power glasses, there was no way to see what was really happening. Later, watching a TV rerun in the press box, we saw what happened to our horses. Holy Land, Ralph's choice, stumbled and lost his jockey in the final turn. Mine, Silent Screen, had the lead coming into the stretch, but faded to fifth at the finish. The winner was a 16—1 shot named Dust Commander.

Moments after the race was over, the crowd surged wildly for the exits, rushing for cabs and buses. The next day's *Courier* told of violence in the parking lot; people were punched and trampled, pockets were picked, children lost, bottles hurled. But we missed all this, having retired to the press box for a bit of post-race drinking. By this time we were both half-crazy from too much whiskey, sun fatigue, culture shock, lack of sleep and general dissolution. We hung around the press box long enough to watch a mass interview with the winning owner, a dapper little man named Lehmann who said he had just flown into Louisville that morning from Nepal, where he'd "bagged a record tiger." The sportswriters murmured their admiration and a waiter filled Lehmann's glass with Chivas Regal. He had just won $127,000 with a horse that cost him $6,500 two years ago. His occupation, he said, was "retired contractor." And then he added, with a big grin, "I just retired."

The rest of that day blurs into madness. The rest of that night too. And all the next day and night. Such horrible things occurred that I can't bring myself even to think about them now, much less put them down in print. Steadman was lucky to get out of Louisville without serious injuries, and I was lucky to get out at all. One of my clearest memories of that vicious time is Ralph being attacked by one of my old friends in the billiard room of the Pendennis Club in downtown Louisville on Saturday night. The man had ripped his own shirt open to the waist before deciding that Ralph was after his wife. No blows were struck, but the emotional effects were massive. Then, as a sort of final horror, Steadman put his fiendish pen to work and tried to patch things up by doing a little sketch of the girl he'd been accused of hustling. That finished us in the Pendennis.

Sometime around ten-thirty Monday morning I was awakened by a scratching sound at my door. I leaned out of bed and pulled the curtain back just far enough to see Steadman outside. "What the fuck do you want?" I shouted.

"What about having breakfast?" he said.

I lunged out of bed and tried to open the door, but it caught on the night-chain and banged shut again. I couldn't cope with the chain! The thing wouldn't come out of the track—so I ripped it out of the wall with a vicious jerk on the door. Ralph didn't blink. "Bad luck," he muttered.

I could barely see him. My eyes were swollen almost shut and the sudden burst of sunlight through the door left me stunned and helpless like a sick mole. Steadman was mumbling about sickness and terrible heat; I fell back on the bed and tried to focus on him as he moved around the room in a very distracted way for a few moments, then suddenly darted over to the beer bucket and seized a Colt .45. "Christ," I said. "You're getting out of control."

He nodded and ripped the cap off, taking a long drink. "You know, this is really awful," he said finally. "I *must* get out of this place . . ." he shook his head nervously. "The plane leaves at three-thirty, but I don't know if I'll make it."

I barely heard him. My eyes had finally opened enough for me to focus on the mirror across the room and I was stunned at the shock of recognition. For a confused instant I thought that Ralph had brought somebody with him—a model for that one special face we'd been looking for. There he was, by God—a puffy, drink-ravaged, disease-ridden caricature . . . like an awful cartoon version of an old snapshot in some once-proud mother's family photo album. It was the face we'd been looking for—and it was, of course, my own. Horrible, horrible. . . .

"Maybe I should sleep in a while longer," I said. "Why don't you go on over to the Fish-Meat place and eat some of those rotten fish and chips? Then come back and get me around noon. I feel too near death to hit the streets at this hour."

He shook his head. "No . . . no . . . I think I'll go back upstairs and work on those drawings for a while." He leaned down to fetch two more cans out of the beer bucket. "I tried to work earlier," he said, "but my hands keep trembling . . . It's teddible, teddible."

"You've got to stop this drinking," I said.

He nodded. "I know. This is no good, no good at all. But for some reason it makes me feel better . . ."

"Not for long," I said. "You'll probably collapse into some kind of hysterical DT's tonight—probably just about the time you get off the plane at Kennedy. They'll zip you up in a straitjacket and drag you down to the Tombs, then beat you on the kidneys with big sticks until you straighten out."

He shrugged and wandered out, pulling the door shut behind him. I went back to bed for another hour or so, and later—after the daily grapefruit juice run to the Nite Owl Food Mart—we had our last meal at Fish-Meat Village: a fine lunch of dough and butcher's offal, fried in heavy grease.

By this time Ralph wouldn't even order coffee; he kept asking for more water. "It's the only thing they have that's fit for human consumption," he explained. Then, with an hour or so to kill before he had to catch the plane, we spread his drawings out on the table and pondered them for a while, wondering if he'd caught the proper spirit of the thing . . . but we couldn't make up our minds. His hands were shaking so badly that he had trouble holding the paper, and my vision was so blurred that I could barely see what he'd drawn. "Shit," I said. "We both look worse than anything you've drawn here."

He smiled. "You know—I've been thinking about that," he said. "We came down here to see this teddible scene: people all pissed out of their minds and vomiting on themselves and all that . . . and now, you know what? It's us. . . ."

*   *   *

Huge Pontiac Ballbuster blowing through traffic on the expressway.

A radio news bulletin says the National Guard is massacring students at Kent State and Nixon is still bombing Cambodia. The journalist is driving, ignoring his passenger who is now nearly naked after taking off most of his clothing, which he holds out the window, trying to wind-wash the Mace out of it. His eyes are bright red and his face and chest are soaked with the beer he's been using to rinse the awful chemical off his flesh. The front of his woolen trousers is soaked with vomit; his body is racked with fits of coughing and wild choking sobs. The journalist rams the big car through traffic and into a spot in front of the terminal, then he reaches over to open the door on the passenger's side and shoves the Englishman out, snarling: "Bug off, your worthless faggot! You twisted pigfucker! [Crazed laughter.] If I weren't sick I'd kick your ass all the way to Bowling Green—you scumsucking foreign geek. Mace is too good for you . . . We can do without your kind in Kentucky."

BEST WITCHES FROM SLATS

Slats Grobnik never cared much for Halloween.

It made him angry that all the kids in the neighborhood went around soaping windows, tipping over garbage cans, and leaping out of gangways to scare old ladies.

That's the way he acted all year, and it was no fun when everybody else did it.

He didn't like going to parties, either. "All they do is tell stories about witches on brooms," he sneered. He said he would rather go to the tavern with his uncle, Beer Belly Frank Grobnik. "At least they tell stories about women on streets," he said.

He did attend one party, though, because his mother insisted he accept an invitation from a kid in the nice neighborhood two blocks away, where some people owned their own houses.

"I want to wear a costume so nobody will recognize me," Slats said.

"All you gotta do is wash your face for that," his father said.

His mother suggested he dress up like a bum, and Slats asked how bums dress. After she told him, he looked at his father and said: "You got anything that'll fit me?"

He went to the party but didn't have a good time. When it was time to duck for apples, Slats plunged his head into the tub. The water turned a muddy color and he was thrown out.

Slats didn't go trick-or-treating, either, which was surprising because his uncle Chester Grobnik had been the greatest trick-or-treater in the neighborhood. He was still at it when he was twenty-nine. That's when he walked into a place on Milwaukee Avenue wearing a mask, carrying a Molotov cocktail, and whispered to a cashier: "Trick or treat—fast!" It was a bank and he got three to five years.

Slats worked out a system that made walking the streets unnecessary. He stayed home while his parents went to the costume party at the VFW hall.

Slats would pull a nylon stocking over his head and face, turn out all the lights in the flat, and wait.

When there was a knock on the door, his little brother Fats would yank it open.

For a moment, the little kids outside would see nothing.

Then Slats would click on a flashlight held to his chin. In broad daylight, Slats had a face that made some old ladies cross themselves. And with the stocking and the flashlight in the dark, the effect was ghastly.

Most of the kids would scream, drop their bags of candy, and run.

Then Slats and Fats would gather up the bags, take them inside, close the door, and wait for the next bunch.

Slats justified this practice by saying: "You don't see the alderman going door-to-door to get his; so why should I?"

He stopped doing it, though, when his trick almost led to tragedy one year.

When the door was yanked open, and Slats turned on his flashlight, there were no trick-or-treat kids outside.

Instead, it was Mrs. Ruby Peak, the stout, balding little widow from Arkansas, who lived above the war surplus store.

She had come by to borrow a cup of bourbon from Mrs. Grobnik.

At the sight of the shapeless, glowing head, Mrs. Peak shrieked: "Billy Tom," and fell over in a faint, cracking her head on the bald spot.

Billy Tom was her late husband. He had died of a sudden stroke some years earlier while moving furniture. A night watchman in the furniture store had surprised him, and during the tussle he gave Billy Tom a terrific stroke on the brow with his club.

When Mrs. Peak came to, Slats kept his mouth shut about what he had done, and Mrs. Peak swore she had seen the ghost of her husband in the Grobnik flat. "I'd know that face anywhere," she said.

And in the long run, everything turned out for the best.

Mr. Kapusta, the landlord, agreed to pay for the stitches in Mrs. Peak's head, and threw in a cash settlement besides, if she would promise not to tell anyone what she had seen.

Mr. Kapusta, who wasn't a very democratic person, said: "If people hear I got a hillbilly—even a ghost of one—in my building, the property value will go down."

Mr. Grobnik was so upset about being haunted by the ghost of Ruby Peak's husband that he threatened to report Mr. Kapusta to the building department. So his rent was reduced by five dollars a month.

And Mr. Kapusta hired Aunt Wanda Grobnik, who had strange powers, such as reading the future in coffee grounds and pinochle cards, to drive Billy Tom's ghost away. "See if you can drive him the other side of the viaduct," Mr. Kapusta said. "Then maybe I can pick up a building there cheap."

She spread some garlic and dried cabbage leaves around the flat and was paid ten dollars when the ghost didn't reappear.

Everybody got something out of it except Slats. And for a long time he was bitter about it, saying: "People never appreciate what you do for them. Next Halloween, I'll set fire to a garage."

THE CAPTAIN OF "THE CAMEL"

This ship was named the *Camel*. In some ways she was an extraordinary vessel. She measured six hundred tons; but when she had taken in enough ballast to keep her from upsetting like a shot duck, and was provisioned for a three months' voyage, it was necessary to be mighty fastidious in the choice of freight and passengers. For illustration, as she was about to leave port a boat came alongside with two passengers, a man and his wife. They had booked the day before, but had remained ashore to get one more decent meal before committing themselves to the "briny cheap," as the man called the ship's fare. The woman came aboard, and the man was preparing to follow, when the captain leaned over the side and saw him.

"Well," said the captain, "what do *you* want?"

"What do *I* want?" said the man, laying hold of the ladder. "I'm a-going to embark in this here ship—that's what I want."

"Not with all that fat on you," roared the captain. "You don't weigh an ounce less than eighteen stone, and I've got to have in my anchor yet. You wouldn't have me leave the anchor, I suppose?"

The man said he did not care about the anchor—he was just as God had made him (he looked as if his cook had had something to do with it) and, sink or swim, he purposed embarking in that ship. A good deal of wrangling ensued, but one of the sailors finally threw the man a cork life-preserver, and the captain said that would lighten him and he might come aboard.

This was Captain Abersouth, formerly of the *Mudlark*—as good a seaman as ever sat on the taffrail reading a three-volume novel. Nothing could equal this man's passion for literature. For every voyage he laid in so many bales of novels that there was no stowage for the cargo. There were novels in the hold, and novels between-decks, and novels in the saloon, and in the passengers' beds.

The *Camel* had been designed and built by her owner, an architect in the City, and she looked about as much like a ship as Noah's Ark did. She had bay windows and a veranda; a cornice and doors at the waterline. These doors had knockers and servant's bells. There had been a futile attempt at an area. The passenger saloon was on the upper deck, and had a tile roof. To this humplike structure the ship owed her name. Her designer had erected several churches—that of St. Ignotus is still used as a brewery in Hotbath Meadows—and, possessed of the ecclesiastic idea, had given the *Camel* a transept; but, finding this impeded her passage through the water, he had it removed. This weakened the vessel amidships. The mainmast was something like a steeple. It had a weathercock. From this spire the eye commanded one of the finest views in England.

Such was the *Camel* when I joined her in 1864 for a voyage of discovery to the South Pole. The expedition was under the "auspices" of the Royal Society for the Promotion of Fair Play. At a meeting of this excellent association, it had been "resolved" that the partiality of science for the North Pole was an invidious distinction between two objects equally meritorious; that Nature had marked her disapproval of it in the case of Sir John Franklin and many of his imitators; that it served them very well right; that this enterprise should be undertaken as a protest against the spirit of undue bias; and, finally, that no part of the responsibility or expense should devolve upon the society in its corporate character, but any individual member might contribute to the fund if he were fool enough. It is only common justice to say that none of them was. The *Camel* merely parted her cable one day when I happened to be on board—drifted out of the harbor southward, followed by the execrations of all who knew her, and could not get back. In two months she had crossed the equator, and the heat began to grow insupportable.

Suddenly we were becalmed. There had been a fine breeze up to three o'clock in the afternoon and the ship had made as much as two knots an hour when without a word of warning the sails began to belly the wrong way, owing to the impetus that the ship had acquired; and then, as this expired, they hung as limp and lifeless as the skirts of a claw-hammer coat. The *Camel* not only stood stock still but moved a little backward toward England. Old Ben the boatswain said that he'd never knowed but one deader calm, and that, he explained, was when Preacher Jack, the reformed sailor, had got excited in a sermon in a seaman's chapel and shouted that the Archangel Michael would chuck the Dragon into the brig and give him a taste of the rope's-end, damn his eyes!

We lay in this woful state for the better part of a year, when, growing impatient, the crew deputed me to look up the captain and see if something could not be done about it. I found him in a remote cobwebby corner between-decks, with a book in his hand. On one side of him, the cords newly cut, were three bales of "Ouida"; on the other a mountain of Miss M. E. Braddon towered above his head. He had finished "Ouida" and was tackling Miss Braddon. He was greatly changed.

"Captain Abersouth," said I, rising on tiptoe so as to overlook the lower slopes of Mrs. Braddon, "will you be good enough to tell me how long this thing is going on?"

"Can't say, I'm sure," he replied, without pulling his eyes off the page. "They'll probably make up about the middle of the book. In the meantime old Pondronummus will foul his top-hamper and take out his papers for Looney Haven, and young Monshure de Boojower will come in for a million. Then if the proud and fair Angelica doesn't luff and come into his wake after pizening that sea lawyer, Thundermuzzle, I don't know nothing about the deeps and shallers of the human heart."

I could not take so hopeful a view of the situation, and went on deck, feeling very much discouraged. I had no sooner got my head out than I observed that the ship was moving at a high rate of speed!

We had on board a bullock and a Dutchman. The bullock was chained by the neck to the foremast, but the Dutchman was allowed a good deal of liberty, being shut up at night only. There was bad blood between the two—a feud of long standing, having its origin in the Dutchman's appetite for milk and the bullock's sense of personal dignity; the particular cause of offense it would be tedious to relate. Taking advantage of his enemy's afternoon *siesta,* the Dutchman had now managed to sneak by him, and had gone out on the bowsprit to fish. When the animal waked and saw the other creature enjoying himself he straddled his chain, leveled his horns, got his hind feet against the mast and laid a course for the offender. The chain was strong, the mast firm, and the ship, as Byron says, "walked the water like a thing of course."

After that we kept the Dutchman right where he was, night and day, the old *Camel* making better speed than she had ever done in the most favorable gale. We held due south.

We had now been a long time without sufficient food, particularly meat. We could spare neither the bullock nor the Dutchman; and the ship's carpenter, that traditional first aid to the famished, was a mere bag of bones. The fish would neither bite nor be bitten. Most of the running-tackle of the ship had been used for macaroni soup; all the leather work, our shoes included, had been devoured in omelettes; with oakum and tar we had made fairly supportable salad. After a brief experimental career as tripe the sails had departed this life forever. Only two courses remained from which to choose; we could eat one another, as is the etiquette of the sea, or partake of Captain Abersouth's novels. Dreadful alternative!—but a choice. And it is seldom, I think, that starving sailormen are offered a shipload of the best popular authors ready-roasted by the critics.

We ate that fiction. The works that the captain had thrown aside lasted six months, for most of them were by the best-selling authors and were pretty tough. After they were gone—of course some had to be given to the bullock and the Dutchman—we stood by the captain, taking the other books from his hands as he finished them. Sometimes, when we were apparently at our last gasp, he would skip a whole page of moralizing, or a bit of description; and always, as soon as he clearly foresaw the *dénoûment*—which he generally did at about the middle of the second volume—the work was handed over to us without a word of repining.

The effect of this diet was not unpleasant but remarkable. Physically, it sustained us; mentally, it exalted us; morally, it made us but a trifle worse than we were. We talked as no human beings ever talked before. Our wit was polished but without point. As in a stage broadsword combat, every cut has its parry, so in our conversation every remark suggested the reply, and this necessitated a certain rejoinder. The sequence once interrupted, the whole was bosh; when the thread was broken the beads were seen to be waxen and hollow.

We made love to one another, and plotted darkly in the deepest obscurity of the hold. Each set of conspirators had its proper listener at the hatch. These, leaning too far over would bump their heads together and fight. Occasionally there was confusion amongst them: two or more would assert a right to overhear the same plot. I remember at one time the cook, the carpenter, the second assistant-surgeon, and an able seaman contended with handspikes for the honor of betraying my confidence. Once there were three masked murderers of the second watch bending at the same instant over the sleeping form of a cabin-boy, who had been heard to mutter, a week previously, that he had "Gold! gold!" the accumulation of eighty—yes, eighty—years' piracy on the high seas, while sitting as M.P. for the borough of Zaccheus-cum-Down, and attending church regularly. I saw the captain of the foretop surrounded by suitors for his hand, while he was himself fingering the edge of a packing-case, and singing an amorous ditty to a lady-love shaving at a mirror.

Our diction consisted, in about equal parts, of classical allusion, quotation from the stable, simper from the scullery, cant from the clubs, and the technical slang of heraldry. We boasted much of ancestry, and admired the whiteness of our hands whenever the skin was visible through a fault in the grease and tar. Next to love, the vegetable kingdom, murder, arson, adultery and ritual, we talked most of art. The wooden figure-head of the *Camel,* representing a Guinea nigger detecting a bad smell, and the monochrome picture of two back-broken dolphins on the stern, acquired a new importance. The Dutchman had destroyed the nose of the one by kicking his toes against it, and the other was nearly obliterated by the slops of the cook; but each had its daily pilgrimage, and each constantly developed occult beauties of design and subtle excellences of execution. On the whole we were greatly altered; and if the supply of contemporary fiction had been equal to the demand, the *Camel,* I fear, would not have been strong enough to contain the moral and æsthetic forces fired by the maceration of the brains of authors in the gastric juices of sailors.

Having now got the ship's literature off his mind into ours, the captain went on deck for the first time since leaving port. We were still steering the same course, and, taking his first observation of the sun, the captain discovered that we were in latitude 83° south. The heat was insufferable; the air was like the breath of a furnace within a furnace. The sea steamed like a boiling cauldron, and in the vapor our bodies were temptingly parboiled—our ultimate meal was preparing. Warped by the sun, the ship held both ends high out of the water; the deck of the forecastle was an inclined plane, on which the bullock labored at a disadvantage; but the bowsprit was now vertical and the Dutchman's tenure precarious. A thermometer hung against the mainmast, and we grouped ourselves about it as the captain went up to examine the register.

"One hundred and ninety degrees Fahrenheit!" he muttered in evident astonishment. "Impossible!" Turning sharply about, he ran his eyes over us, and inquired in a peremptory tone, "who's been in command while I was run-nin' my eye over that book?".

"Well, captain," I replied, as respectfully as I knew how, "the fourth day out I had the unhappiness to be drawn into a dispute about a game of cards with your first and second officers. In the absence of those excellent seamen, sir, I thought it my duty to assume control of the ship."

"Killed 'em, hey?"

"Sir, they committed suicide by questioning the efficacy of four kings and an ace."

"Well, you lubber, what have you to say in defense of this extraordinary weather?"

"Sir, it is no fault of mine. We are far—very far south, and it is now the middle of July. The weather is uncomfortable, I admit; but considering the latitude and season, it is not, I protest, unseasonable."

"Latitude and season!" he shrieked, livid with rage—"latitude and season! Why, you junk-rigged, flat-bottomed, meadow lugger, don't you know any better than that? Didn't yer little baby brother ever tell ye that southern latitudes is colder than northern, and that July is the middle o' winter here? Go below, you son of a scullion, or I'll break your bones!"

"Oh! very well," I replied; "I'm not going to stay on deck and listen to such low language as that, I warn you. Have it your own way."

The words had no sooner left my lips, than a piercing cold wind caused me to cast my eye upon the thermometer. In the new régime of science the mercury was descending rapidly; but in a moment the instrument was obscured by a blinding fall of snow. Towering icebergs rose from the water on every side, hanging their jagged masses hundreds of feet above the masthead, and shutting us completely in. The ship twisted and writhed; her decks bulged upward, and every timber groaned and cracked like the report of a pistol. The *Camel* was frozen fast. The jerk of her sudden stopping snapped the bullock's chain, and sent both that animal and the Dutchman over the bows, to accomplish their warfare on the ice.

Elbowing my way forward to go below, as I had threatened, I saw the crew tumble to the deck on either hand like tenpins. They were frozen stiff. Passing the captain, I asked him sneeringly how he liked the weather under the new régime. He replied with a vacant stare. The chill had penetrated to the brain, and affected his mind. He murmured:

"In this delightful spot, happy in the world's esteem, and surrounded by all that makes existence dear, they passed the remainder of their lives. The End."

His jaw dropped. The captain of the *Camel* was dead.

THE FABLE OF PADUCAH'S FAVOURITE COMEDIANS AND THE MILDEWED STUNT

Once Upon a Time there was a Specialty Team doing Seventeen Minutes. The Props used in the Act included a Hatchet, a Brick, a Seltzer Bottle, two inflated Bladders and a Slap-Stick. The Name of the Team was Zoroaster and Zendavesta.

These two Troupers began their Professional Career with a Road Circus, working on Canvas in the Morning, and then doing a Refined Knockabout in the Grand Concert or After-piece taking place in the Main Arena immediately after the big Show is over.

When each of them could Kick Himself in the Eye and Slattery had pickled his Face so that Stebbins could walk on it, they decided that they were too good to show under a Round Top, so they became Artists. They wanted a Swell Name for the Team, so the Side-Show Announcer, who was something of a Kidder and had attended a Unitarian College, gave them Zoroaster and Zendavesta. They were Stuck on it, and had a Job Printer do some Cards for them.

By utilizing two of Pat Rooney's Songs and stealing a few Gags, they put together Seventeen Minutes and began to play Dates and Combinations.

Zoroaster bought a Cane with a Silver Dog's Head on it, and Zendavesta had a Watch Charm that pulled the Button-holes out of his Vest.

After every Show, as soon as they Washed Up, they went

and stood in front of the Theater, so as to give the Hired Girls a Treat, or else they stood around in the Sawdust and told their Fellow-Workers in the Realm of Dramatic Art how they killed 'em in Decatur and had 'em hollerin' in Lowell, Mass., and got every Hand in the House at St. Paul. Occasionally they would put a Card in the Clipper, saying that they were the Best in the Business, Bar None, and Good Dressers on and off the Stage. Regards to Leonzo Brothers. Charley Diamond please write.

They didn't have to study no New Gags or work up no more Business, becuz they had the Best Act on Earth to begin with. Lillian Russell was jealous of them and they used to know Francis Wilson when he done a Song and Dance.

They had a Scrap Book with a Clipping from a Paducah Paper, which said that they were better than Nat Goodwin. When some Critic who had been bought up by Rival Artists wrote that Zoroaster and Zendavesta ought to be on an Ice Wagon instead of on the Stage, they would get out the Scrap Book and read that Paducah Notice and be thankful that all Critics wasn't Cheap Knockers and that there was one Paper Guy in the United States that reckanized a Neat Turn when he seen it.

But Zoroaster and Zendavesta didn't know that the Dramatic Editor of the Paducah Paper went to a Burgoo Picnic the Day the Actors came to Town, and didn't get back until Midnight, so he wrote his Notice of the Night Owls' performance from a Programme brought to him by the Head Usher at the Opera House, who was also Galley Boy at the Office.

Zoroaster and Zendavesta played the same Sketch for Seventeen Years and made only two important Changes in all that Time. During the Seventh Season Zoroaster changed his Whiskers from Green to Blue. At the beginning of the Fourteenth Year of the Act they bought a new Slap-Stick and put a Card in the Clipper warning the Public to beware of Imitators.

All during the Seventeen Years Zoroaster and Zendavesta continued to walk Chesty and tell People how Good they were. They never could Understand why the Public stood for Mansfield when it could get Zoroaster and Zendavesta. The Property Man gave it as his Opinion that Mansfield conned the Critics. Zendavesta said there was only one Critic on the Square, and he was at Paducah.

When the Vodeville Craze came along Zoroaster and Zendavesta took their Paducah Scrap Book over to a Manager, and he Booked them. Zoroaster assured the Manager that Him and his Partner done a Refined Act, suitable for Women and Children, with a strong Finish, which had been the Talk of all Galveston. The Manager put them in between the Trained Ponies and a Legit with a Bad Cold. When a Legit loses his Voice he goes into Vodeville.

Zoroaster and Zendavesta came on very Cocky, and for the 7,800th Time Zoroaster asked Zendavesta:

"Who wuz it I seen you comin' up the Street with?"

Then, for the 7,800th Time, by way of Mirth-Provoking Rejoinder, Zendavesta kicked Zoroaster in the Stomach, after which the Slap-Stick was introduced as a Sub-Motive.

The Manager gave a Sign and the Stage Hands Closed in on the Best Team in the Business, Bar None.

Of course Zoroaster and Zendavesta were very sore at having their Act killed. They said it was no way to treat Artists. The Manager told them they were too Tart for words to tell it and to consider Themselves set back into the Supper Show. Then They saw through the whole Conspiracy. The Manager was Mansfield's Friend and Mansfield was out with his Hammer.

At Present they are doing Two Supper Turns to the Piano Player and a Day Watchman. They are still the Best in the Business, but are being used Dead Wrong. However, they derive some Comfort from reading the Paducah Notice.

MORAL: *A Dramatic Editor should never go to a Burgoo Picnic—especially in Kentucky.*

WHAT IS AND AIN'T GRAMMATICAL

I cannot overemphasize the importance of good grammar.

What a crock. I could easily overemphasize the importance of good grammar. For example, I could say: "Bad grammar is the leading cause of slow, painful death in North America," or "Without good grammar, the United States would have lost World War II."

The truth is that grammar is not the most important thing in the world. The Super Bowl is the most important thing in the world. But grammar is still important. For example, suppose you are being interviewed for a job as an airplane pilot, and your prospective employer asks you if you have any experience, and you answer: "Well, I ain't never actually flied no actual airplanes or nothing, but I got several pilot-style hats and several friends who I like to talk about airplanes with."

If you answer this way, the prospective employer will immediately realize that you have ended your sentence with a preposition. (What you should have said, of course, is "several friends with who I like to talk about airplanes.") So you will not get the job, because airline pilots have to use good grammar when they get on the intercom and explain to the passengers that, because of high winds, the plane is going to take off several hours late and land in Pierre, South Dakota, instead of Los Angeles.

We did not always have grammar. In medieval England, people said whatever they wanted, without regard to rules, and as a result they sounded like morons. Take the poet Geoffrey Chaucer, who couldn't even spell his first name right. He wrote a large poem called *Canterbury Tales,* in which people from various professions—knight, monk, miller, reever, riveter, eeler, diver, stevedore, spinnaker, etc.—drone on and on like this:

> *In a somer sesun whon softe was the sunne*
> *I kylled a younge birde ande I ate it on a bunne.*

When Chaucer's poem was published, everybody read it and said: "My God, we need some grammar around here." So they formed a Grammar Commission, which developed the parts of speech, the main ones being nouns, verbs, predicants, conjectures, particles, proverbs, adjoiners, coordinates, and rebuttals. Then the commission made up hundreds and hundreds of grammar rules, all of which were strictly enforced.

When the colonists came to America, they rebelled against British grammar. They openly used words like "ain't" and "finalize," and when they wrote the Declaration of Independence they deliberately misspelled many words. Thanks to their courage, today we Americans have only two rules of grammar:

Rule 1. THE WORD "ME" IS ALWAYS INCORRECT.

Most of us learn this rule as children, from our mothers. We say things like: "Mom, can Bobby and me roll the camping trailer over Mrs. Johnson's cat?" And our mothers say: "Remember your grammar, dear. You mean: 'Can Bobby and *I* roll the camping trailer over Mrs. Johnson's cat?' Of course you can, but be home by dinnertime."

The only exception to this rule is in formal business writing, where instead of "I" you must use "the undersigned." For example, this business letter is incorrect:

"Dear Hunky-Dory Canned Fruit Company: A couple of days ago my wife bought a can of your cling peaches and served them to my mother who has a weak heart and she damn near died when she bit into a live grub. If I ever find out where you live, I am gonna whomp you on the head with a ax handle."

This should be corrected as follows:

". . . If the undersigned ever finds out where you live, the undersigned is gonna whomp you on the head with a ax handle."

Rule 2. YOU'RE NOT ALLOWED TO SPLIT INFINITIVES

An infinitive is the word "to" and whatever comes right behind it, such as "to a tee," "to the best of my ability," "tomato," etc. Splitting an infinitive is putting something between the "to" and the other words. For example, this is incorrect:

"Hey, man, you got any, you know, spare change you could give to, like, me?"

The correct version is:

". . . spare change you could, like, give to me?"

The advantage of American English is that, because there are so few rules, practically anybody can learn to speak it in just a few minutes. The disadvantage is that Americans generally sound like jerks, whereas the British sound really smart, especially to Americans. That's why Americans are so fond of those British dramas they're always showing on public television, the ones introduced by Alistair Cooke. Americans *love* people who talk like Alistair Cooke. He could introduce old episodes of "Hawaii Five-O" and Americans would think they were extremely enlightening.

So the trick is to use American grammar, which is simple, but talk with a British accent, which is impressive. This technique is taught at all your really snotty private schools, where the kids learn to sound like Elliot Richardson. Remember Elliot? He sounded extremely British, and as a result he got to be Attorney General, Secretary of State, Chief Justice of the Supreme Court and Vice President *at the same time*.

You can do it, too. Practice in your home, then approach someone on the street and say: "Tally-ho, old chap. I would consider it a great honour if you would favour me with some spare change." You're bound to get quick results.

SOUP AS WHAT THE CHEF MADE

I have a small reputation as a gourmet. It is undeserved, as will appear, but at a time of a boom in cookbooks it has led to my receiving a fair number of requests for my favorite recipe, if possible accompanied by an anecdote. The requests come from people who say they are putting together books of recipes by celebrities that are guaranteed not to bring on gangrene or the pip, and who would like to have one from me.

The reputation led on one occasion to my being invited to address a luncheon at which awards were being given for the outstanding cookbooks of the year. I don't remember which books won, but among the entries that remained in the memory were *Mazel Tov Y'all,* a peculiarly graceful mingling of languages that sounded like the salutation of a southern politician seeking votes in the Catskills, and *The Pedernales Country Cookbook,* a book conceived of before President Johnson decided he would not run again but published afterward, by which time it had hardly more appeal than a study of the musicial tastes of Calvin Coolidge. There was also *The "I Married an Italian" Cookbook,* by Bette Scaloni, who must have been terribly chagrined when she realized what she had done. I hope that at least it was hard cover and profusely illustrated.

So far as my qualifications as a cook go, I, like a lot of other men, lean to complicated recipes. Our cookery is based on the theory that the more ingredients a dish has, the better it is likely to be, so that any dish with sour cream, wine, the outer leaves of a head of lettuce, lemon juice, onion juice (what a job that is!), green pepper, monosodium glutamate, flour, curry powder, and dry mustard added to almost anything must have a stirring effect on those who eat it. The longer it takes, the better. Recipes that call for cooking over a period of days—"Allow the stew to simmer on top of the stove for 48 hours, stirring frequently"—are ideal. All this is still more the case if you use a lot of herbs. Men have faith in herbs. When I see them floating at the top of the pot, or flecking a chop, I know that success will soon be mine. Men also tend to make a lot of spaghetti, more than anybody can eat, especially at the beginning of their cooking careers.

I had two friends in college who were too poor for spaghetti and who made a dish using barley. They had no idea how much to cook and wound up depositing the surplus in brown paper bags on the doorsteps of people they didn't like.

But about the requests for recipes: I obliged only once, with a recipe for steak topped with a latticework of anchovies hugging—that's a cookery word, hugging—slices of olives stuffed with pimientos, and herb butter made with three herbs for the necessary excess. Magnifique! I wish I could remember its name. The other requests I declined because the reputation was cheaply won. It came about when I found myself living in Britain during the period of austerity after the Second World War, when green-grocers put out signs saying "Plums for All" and newspapers ran scare headlines like "Threat to Your Christmas Fruit and Nuts." Those were days when anybody whose gastronomic horizons went beyond cabbage, brussels sprouts, and cod was called a gourmet.

Not that I regret that time. It was rich in experience. I remember asking the flavor of the ice cream listed on the menu and being told, "Why, no flavor, sir," which turned out to be correct. And the waitress who, when asked for oil to put on hors d'oeuvres, replied, "The only oil we have at the moment, sir, is the oil we cook the chips in, and it's already been used, so it wouldn't be good." Or the waiter who, recommending rice pilaf, generously explained, "It isn't an English dish, sir, but it is very good." Or the waiter on the train between London and Penzance who, when asked what kind of soup was available, did not say, as tradition required, either that it was thick or that it was thin. He replied instead, "Soup as what the chef made."

Things were pretty bad in those days, as you will appreciate from the fact that newspapers printed recipes for carrot and turnip pie and for a dish called fadge, which I will not go into further, and from the fact that a line of frozen food was sold under the catchy name "Frood." This naturally had its effect on the confidence of the British, and even the food advertisements sounded intimidated. I remember a green pea boasting that it was "first choice for second vegetable."

It has changed greatly now, of course. London is a good place for food and drink, and has been for years. This has much to do with the foreign influence. (I don't mean that Britain is entirely transformed. My daughter went into an English restaurant not long ago, and she and her companion asked whether they might have some wine. The proprietor looked at them with annoyance. "We don't do ween and all that tackle," he said.) It might be added also that the British unduly handicap themselves with the names they apply to some foods—bloaters, pilchards, scrag end, bubble-and-squeak, toad-in-the-hole, nosh, fry-up, faggots, rolypoly pudding, stodge, black pudding, spotted dog. These things would not be acceptable even if decked out in slavering American menu prose. I inserted three of them in a TWA menu encountered on a transatlantic flight:

BRAISED SCRAG END BOURGEOISE

A classic dish. The scrag end is slowly simmered in a rich stock of natural juices accentuated by a bouquet of fine herbes, small onions, and spices. Served with Château Potatoes and honey-glazed carrots.

GRILLED STODGE CUMBERLAND

From the broiler we present a generous portion of suc-
culent stodge topped with Hawaiian pineapple ring and
sprinkles of orange rind. Enhanced with a tangy red
currant Cumberland Sauce and accompanied by Duchess
Potatoes and a fluffy Broccoli Soufflé.

BLOATER SAINT HUBERT

This French creation was a favorite of Saint Hubert,
Patron of the Hunters. In preparing this dish, tender
young bloater is cooked slowly in a zesty tomato sauce
with white wine, shallots, and mushrooms. We serve it
with Parslied Potatoes and Mixed Vegetables.

We have foreign influence in the United States, too, as may
be seen from the free use of the word gourmet, which the dictionary defines as a connoisseur in eating and drinking, an
epicure. A noun, in other words, which is used more frequently, in the United States, as an adjective. For example,
foods that used to be known as delicacies, and which you
would get at the delicatessen or fancy grocery, are now known
as gourmet foods, and you get them at a gourmet store. Recently I saw a package of gourmet blintzes. I don't think that
the blintz sees itself in that way. Maybe it could team up with
knish lorraine. The two of them might go on the menu of an
Israeli hotel in Jerusalem where gefilte fish came out carpe
farçie traditionelle.

This use of the word gourmet is part of the increasing popularity of foreign words and phrases that are imperfectly understood, and you never know what you are going to run into
when you enter a restaurant these days. I have come upon
"restauranteurs" serving such exotic items as chicken soup a
la raine; eminced chicken tetrazzini; lobster frad dabolo;
o'grattan potatoes—made, one supposes, from an old Irish
recipe; filet de mignon, perhaps from the opera by Ambroise
Thomas; broiled filet of sole armandine, served, I imagine,
with thin slices of the nut called the armand; bristling sardines, which may have been angry at being packed in that

way; and for dessert, cake du jour. Some Americans think you can turn English words to French by adding an e, so that you have caramel custarde, and fruite, but cake needs stronger measures.

Similar to cake du jour in the way it weds two languages is the dish "eggs andalouse." A French restaurant on Forty-eighth Street in New York went that one better. It came out with eggs andalouise. I thought about this for a long time and concluded that the chef spoke with an Italian accent. One day a restaurant, or gourmet, correspondent asked him for the secret of this marvelous dish, and he replied that he got it from his Aunta Louise.

At another restaurant I was offered, salaud de tomates, canapé d'anchovies, and egg in gélée, and invited to choose wine from a charto de vino. It reminded me of the liquor store in New York that proclaimed that it was selling wine of a fabulose vintage. And the place that called itself a saloon de thé.

A French restaurant in New York, or at any rate a restaurant with a French name, posts a menu du dinner. Quite by chance, it is not far from L'Embassy Coiffure and a drugstore that lists among the perfumes it sells Rêve Gauche.

The Loggia of the Polo Lounge of the Beverly Hills Hotel in Los Angeles mentions coffee, tea, and milk under breuvages, which is ancient French and possibly survives only in Beverly Hills (Les Collines Beverly). But the Loggia comes unstuck over coconut with a cocoanut milk mousse, and serves lucious apple slices with its Dutch apple pancake.

A restaurant on the roof of a Los Angeles office building offers Chef's Specials du Jour, and another establishment lists Beef French Dip, thoughtfully giving us the recipe: "Choice thin sliced beef, dipped in au jus. Set on a French roll." And wheeled in on an a la carte.

Another New York restaurant says it has "a complete salad and antipasto table, where you can help yourself to as much as you'd like as a compliment to your meal." The night I was there I helped myself to only a little, because there was some question about whether my meal deserved a compliment, but I did send my supplements to the chef.

Language is so misused, English as well as foreign tongues, that I sometimes think of asking for my steak media rare. Perhaps those of us who are troubled by these developments would be better off staying at home. We would miss the complementary hors d'oeuvres but we could, after all, avoid menu misspellings by having our egg's benedict and bar-ba-qued chicken at home.

My job does not permit this. It calls for much travel. That is how it came about that a visit to Lincoln, Nebraska, produced a restaurant that offered Maderia wine and quoted Louis Pasteur to the effect that wine was the most healthful and hygenic of beverages. Not surprisingly the restaurant served, if it said so itself, Food Supérbo. Said food defied pronunciation, if not eating. Another establishment, a block away, listed on its menu the Italianoburger, which was a hamburger on an English Muffin with mozzarella cheese and pizza sauce. Why was the English muffin left out of the title?

As long as I'm complaining—and my friends say that as long as I am awake I am complaining, which isn't true because in November, 1963, I covered the first annual International Banana Festival in Fulton, Kentucky, banana rail-transshipment capital of the United States, and saw a one-ton banana pudding being made, in a plexiglass container, of bananas, custard, and ginger snaps, and did not say an untoward word—as long as I'm complaining, I will go on with my theory about how 98 percent of the members of the waiters' union became waiters. It was because they couldn't remember the jobs they originally wanted to get.

I say this in memory of the old, passé assumption that waiters in a restaurant would remember what the customers ordered. Waiters whose memories were unreliable wrote down the orders and did it in such a way that they connected the items in question with those who asked for them.

No more. The art of waiting has undergone a transformation, and its language has shrunk almost to nothing. If a waiter is new to this country, there is little for him to learn. He is taught to say, "Who gets the?" and then the names of the items on the menu after, or, if you prefer, subsequent to,

"Who gets the?" With that, he is qualified. Not long ago I was in a group of five in a well-known New York restaurant. One person in the group ordered dessert, only one, and there was conversation between this person and the waiter about what it was to be. Nobody else took part in the conversation. One minute and forty-five seconds later the waiter reappeared with the single dessert. "Who," he asked triumphantly, "gets the sherbet?"

I cannot say with assurance that American restaurant food would be better if the spelling on menus were better or the waiters more conversant with their calling. But it would give diners more confidence, it would lend novelty to restaurant-going, and it *might* improve the cooking.

I have never been invited to address a luncheon at which awards were being given for the outstanding sex manuals of the year, but the language is much the same. Sex manuals are described as gourmet guides to lovemaking; as with cookbooks, consumer satisfaction depends on following the instructions implicitly; and if *The Joy of Cooking* tells you how to be happy at mealtime, *The Joy of Sex* offers between-meals snacks. Sex books are now as explicit and detailed as cookbooks, and have photographs intended to lead to coition as surely as photographs of Enchaud de Porc à la Périgourdine and Daube de Veau à l'Estragon are intended to encourage gluttony.

A bedroom is now to be thought of as a sindrome. In these days of sophisticated contraception it need not be in a condominium, but it is not complete without an illuminated stand next to the bed. The sex manual is placed on the stand so that the instructions may be followed as the lovemakers work their way through the foreword, chapters, footnotes, appendices, and index.

Ingredients:
Man (according to taste)
Woman (according to taste)
Bed, king-sized if possible
Mirror on ceiling, and also on wall

Incense

Flying trapeze

Whip

Champagne and four-course meal to be served during intermission

Artillery fire and pealing of Moscow church bells in Tchaikowsky's 1812 Overture, cued to play at moment of climax

Tape recorder in form of phallic symbol into which participants may dictate their impressions as act proceeds

Sexual fulfillment is becoming as compulsory as the gustatory kind. Civilization demands it, though in dining, if not in sex, the pleasure promised by the language employed exceeds any that is realized in fact. This is also true of travel. It may be especially true of travel:

"There's nothing ordinary in it because there's nothing ordinary about India. The dark eyes of gracious people. The highest mountains in the world. 5000 years of history in art and architecture. Temples. A tomb dedicated to love. Places and things out of the ordinary because they're in India."

"This season, why go south again? Head east. To the Soviet Union. Warm. Friendly. Hospitable. Come and celebrate the gala holiday season with us."

". . . the impeccable service of all-Italian personnel dedicated to your well-being and comfort, uncompromising quality and attention to detail. With it all, a spirited atmosphere that only a zestful Italian flair can achieve."

"Once, just once in your life. A long ocean cruise with Holland America. We think you deserve it. So we give you everything the unforgettable is made of."

"Give that cold, shivering body of yours a break. Escape the wrath of winter and come to a warm tropical island. To a delightful Holiday Inn resort, where all the comfort, conveniences, activities and fun-facilities are ready for your sun-drenched island adventure."

"This is not a tourist's cruise, bound for the long-exploited, over-exposed harbors. This is an explorer's voyage through little-traveled waters into unfamiliar ports—each one affording a new, exotic experience. Vividly contrasting with the super civilized life aboard the *Renaissance,* so French in its cuisine, its solicitous French service, its gaiety aboard ship, its continuous round of diversions above and below decks."

"Elegant dining, elegant night clubs, elegant beaches, elegant opera, elegant ballet, elegant race track. Elegant people—the in-people, the beautiful people. This cornucopia of elegance is spilling out to all who take advantage of VIASA's incredible $220 minimum to Caracas—to the city in the country in the Caribbean. To the most exciting tropical resort that's always been there but is only now being discovered."

"Meet the spirited, hospital people in Golden PRAGUE. Wander through medieval settings beating with the pulse of modern life. Listen to the music of Anton Dvořák in his native land and stroll the footsteps of Franz Kafka through the cobblestoned streets of Josefov. Wine and dine in romantic BRATISLAVA on the blue Danube . . ."

It has long seemed to this cold and shivering body, dark-eyed, gracious, spirited, zestful, elegant, spirited and sun-drenched though it is, that tourism, even on cruises that are not tourist's cruises and are not bound for long-exploited, over-exposed harbors, is out of hand. Every spring and summer, all over the civilized world—which is to say those countries that are obliged to advertise themselves as tourist paradises because their own citizens can't bear them and insist on going abroad as soon as vacation time arrives—every spring and summer, millions of people prepare for the experience of a lifetime. The French go to Spain, the Spaniards go to France, the British go to Italy, the Italians to Britain, others cavort in Kafka's footsteps to the tune of a Slavonic dance; there is a vast amount of churning around, and there is enormous competition for going somewhere nobody you know has been. The way tourism is expanding, people will soon be paying for the privilege of a hike along the natural gas pipelines in the Algerian desert, or for exposing themselves to tropical diseases in the Mato Grosso.

The director-general of the Vatican museums recently wrote to the *Times* of London:

"We have installed 21 television cameras with centralized monitors to keep the traffic situation under control (we shall have 35 in a short time). We are using 18 'walkie-talkies' and highly trained attendants manning them, for securing prompt communications. Five spacious galleries have been equipped to keep visitors at a stand-by position until difficult situations clear up in front of them. A complete public address system is being installed to keep visitors informed and interested in the surroundings, with messages in five languages, while they have to wait. A busy control room is operating to secure the safe flow of our visitors and to decide exactly when and where it has to be slowed down or stopped and resumed."

It seems to me that this is a lot of trouble, and expensive, and for the tourist nations self-defeating, and that there should be some easier way to do it.

Luckily, such a way lies to hand. It is an invention called the travel simulator. Everybody knows about those training devices the airplane pilot gets into and which lead him to believe that he is flying when he has never left the ground. The travel simulator operates on the same principle.

The travel simulator is an area, preferably at an airport, so that tourists are not deprived of the actual pleasure of going *there*. It could also be at a town terminal or at a specially equipped center financed by travel agencies, airlines, luggage manufacturers, hotel chains, and others dependent on tourist revenue. Wherever it is, the tourist must first call the airline on which he is booked to inquire about the flight departure, and be thanked for calling that airline, as though, having booked on TWA, he would be calling Northwest.

As the tourist enters the simulation area, he is given a check list on which he indicates the travel experiences he would like to have. Late departure of plane? There is a waiting room where he can sit, which is overheated and where the background music cannot be turned off. Flight overbooked? Tourist bumped? That can be arranged, and he can stay in

the waiting room that much longer. If a sea voyage is preferred, it is a short step from motel beds that give you a mild
shaking ("restful massage") for a quarter to a bed that can
simulate rough seas and malfunctioning stabilizers. The sea-
going passenger may, of course, choose the equivalent of the
airliner passenger's overbooked flight—a strike in port.

Those who enjoy having their luggage lost have only to ask.
Then, after checking into the hotel in the simulation area,
they have no clothes to change into. That is, if they do check
into the hotel. The clerks may have no record of the booking,
and no rooms even if they do.

There are restaurants in the area. Tourists who like them
overpriced, with uncooperative waiters, where Americans are
made to feel unwelcome, have only to mark their forms ac-
cordingly. Women traveling alone can be turned away or,
grudgingly, seated by the swinging kitchen door. No extra
charge.

Hotels in the simulation area are either unfinished or getting a new wing, with construction work beginning outside
your window at seven in the morning. Travel fatigue can be
induced, as can digestive trouble—the makers of Entero-Vio-
forme may well be willing to underwrite the cost of this—and
difficulty with the customs can be arranged when you return.
("Just think! You can be searched for dope!") Thanks to the
magic of multi-media presentations, tourists can be taken on
all-day jaunts of which the high point is an hour-long visit to a
glass-blowing factory, where it is quickly made clear that you
are grinding the faces of the poor if you do not buy. That is in
the morning. In the afternoon there is a visit to a perfume factory, where those who do not buy are quickly marked out as
wanting to bring on the poverty and resentment from which
flow crime, war, and revolution. Unpleasant travel companions, specially trained and always on call, are thrown in as
part of the basic package, as are fluctuating and unfavorable
rates of exchange. A devaluation of the dollar and refusal to
accept dollar traveler's checks—it's only fair—are counted as
an optional extra.

In brief, the travel simulator gives the tourist all the thrills of travel without his ever leaving the airport. It does, nonetheless, take time, and in view of the demand for the service that is likely to arise, there are plans to provide a short course. In this the whole business would be telescoped, and tourists would be able to buy slides and journals of MY TRIP attesting to typical but exotic experiences according to the kind of conversation they want to have when they get home ("Really mind-stretching," "Wild," "What a gyp," "Was I ever glad to get home," "We had a ball," "There was this very nice hotel," "They told me to take my winter coat but I didn't need it," "I just went crazy," "The waiters came out with this very big tray," "We had seen that before," "I just have gone crazy here for a week," "I don't know how they live the way prices are there"). These and many more they could claim as their own, thus leaving them at no conversational disadvantage against those who have had the real thing, i.e., the full simulated trip.

Veterans in the field will be eager to supply such accounts for an appropriate fee. For example, in November, 1973, I spent a few days in Moscow. The door of my hotel room opened onto a flight of four steps, the top one of which had its center part gouged out; it was ideal for provoking a fall. The door opened inward, so that when you wanted to open it from the inside you had to climb the four steps, and then, as you opened the door, go back down. Just inside the door there was a light for a dressing alcove. To light the alcove it was necessary to climb the steps, then come back. The light was turned off the same way, of course. The alcove held two wooden cupboards for clothes. The drawers in the cupboards could not be used because the cupboard doors could not be opened because there was not enough room in the alcove. Properly embellished, an account of all this, punctuated by nearly uncontrolled laughter and expressions of disbelief, can go on almost indefinitely.

If shorter reminiscences of simpler discomforts are needed, there was the time in Warsaw that I cut and bruised my knee on the footboard of the bed while getting up from the desk (I fall to the floor, holding my sides, while telling this one), and the bed in Jerusalem that seemed to be made of locally quarried stone. The essential point about such reminiscences is that they should have no intrinsic interest. All the foregoing qualify.

The idea of the travel simulator was born when I happened to find in Rome a leaflet the United States Travel Service had put out. The leaflet said: "Discover a new world of gastronomy. Visit the United States." It said that it was not true that Americans lived on coffee for breakfast, martinis for lunch, and frozen foods for dinner. It also explained that while the pioneers had had to use what they could find and borrow dishes from the Indians, these concoctions had since been refined. Being an American leaflet, it naturally misspelled the Caesar in Caesar salad. But no matter.

The Travel Service identified eight cooking regions in the United States. They were Gli stati dell' Atlantico Centrale, the Middle Atlantic States; Il Centro Ovest, the Middle West; Il New England; La regione dei creoli, that being Louisiana; Le Hawaii; La Pennsylvania Dutch; Il Sud, the South; and L'Alaska. The Italians were also told about drug stores. They were told that drug stores had developed so that their original function of selling medicines had become secondary, and that it was possible to take meals in them in an ambience without pretense (un ambienta senza pretese), which was a gentle way of putting it.

I soon had a vision of a tourist going to I Stati Uniti, and specifically to Gli stati dell' Atlantico Centrale, and to its greatest city, New York. Suppose that he had resigned himself to having gallons of ice water and ice cream forced down his throat, while legions of strangers told him their life stories and gave him their philosophies, and to being clubbed on general principles by any member of New York's finest who happened to catch sight of him, and that in search of a gastronomic discovery he took a city bus as transport to a native eatery. New York City buses have signs in them asking for contributions to the Legal Aid Society, the Visiting Nurses Service, the Greater New York Fund, the Boys Club of America, the Catholic Youth Organization, the Young Men's

Christian Association, the Federation of Jewish Charities—and also give to the college of your choice. A visitor might get the impression that we are in pretty awful shape if he rode a charity bus. But suppose he took an illness bus, the kind in which the signs ask for help to fight cancer, heart disease, multiple sclerosis, cerebral palsy, hemophilia, tuberculosis, mental retardation, and mental illness, among others. Afraid? Sick? Lonely? one sign asks. Christian Science Can Help.

New York is a vast sanitarium. Some buses used to carry signs that said one New Yorker in ten is mentally ill and needs help. Taken literally, from a pocket Italian-English dictionary, that could have been interpreted to mean that there is one chance in ten that your driver is a mental case. Now there is a new one: Rape Report Line. 233-3000. A policewoman will help you. The tourist's appetite for a scoperto gastronomico is not likely to survive this. Still another sign may well convince him that *he* will not survive:

> There's so much beauty in the blooming Rose
> And through its life, Who knows where it goes?
> Some Roses will live over a season through
> While others will enjoy part of the dew.
>
> But even Roses with all their splendor and heart
> Will one day their beautiful petals fall apart.
> Man too, has his season like the Rose
> And then, one day, he also must repose.

The sign is placed by Unity Funeral Chapels, Inc., whose slogan is, We Understand.

The simulator is better.

COOPED UP

I go to the movies. Gary Cooper is in the next seat as usual, wearing his badge and Stetson. I am sick and tired of him. He grins and offers popcorn. "What are we going to see tonight?" he asks. *"The Sting,"* I say, "and this time stay out of it, Coop."

"Shucks," says Cooper. "You know me."

I know Gary Cooper all right. The previous week he embarrassed me at *Chinatown*. The unprincipled cop was just about to let John Huston get away with murder, on account of Huston's being a millionaire, when Coop threw his popcorn box on the floor, strode down the aisle and drew his six-shooter on Huston and the cop.

"Get off the screen," the audience yelled, but Gary Cooper paid them no heed. "I'm takin' you both down to the U.S. marshal's office," he said.

"You can't do this," Jack Nicholson objected. "The whole point of this picture is that good guys never win."

"You better get on your buckboard and get out of town fast, son," Cooper told him, "before I take you in for interfering with an arrest."

It was a long speech for Cooper, so without another word he marched Huston and the cop off the screen and the movie ended with Nicholson heading for Laramie.

"I hear this a real good one," Cooper says of *The Sting*.

"Just stay out of it, Coop," I say.

After a while he begins stirring unhappily. "These fellows are nothing but a bunch of crooks," he whispers.

"They happen to be Robert Redford and Paul Newman," I say. "Even if they are crooks, they're charming and lovable, and the audience loves them, so stay out of it."

It is too late. He is already striding down the aisle and is up on the screen with the drop on the whole roomful of swindlers, before Newman can get away with the loot.

"Get those hands up," he says. "We're all going to take a little walk down to the marshal's office."

The audience boos as Cooper rides them all off into the sunset, manacled aboard cayuses. I am fearful that someone will know Cooper was with me and beat me for being an accessory to the triumph of law.

My analyst is no comfort.

"You are merely hallucinating Cooper as an agent for fulfilling a childish desire for heroes who are honest," he says. He suggests staying away from movies in which criminality and corruption prevail until I become less infantile.

So I go to *Deep Throat.* Cooper is there. After ten minutes he says, "Whew."

"Stay out of it, Coop," I plead. Futilely, of course.

"Miss Lovelace," says Cooper, towering over her on the screen, "you need a little church training."

He throws her over his shoulder, covers her with his badge and says, "I'm taking you down to the schoolmarm so she can introduce you to the Ladies Aid Society."

The audience pelts the screen with comic books and dark glasses.

My analyst loves this report. He asks me to commit myself for study at the Institute of Incredible Sexual Repressions in Zurich. I run.

To the movies, of course. But this time it's *The Apprenticeship of Duddy Kravitz,* which I know in advance is merely about an ambitious young man.

Cooper is there. He even likes the movie. "This is okay," he grins as Duddy goes into the business of making home movies of bar mitzvahs. But what is this? Duddy is behaving rudely to grown-ups. Yes, very rudely. He is laughing at them and or-dering them off his land. Cooper is in the aisle before I can stop him. "Stay out of it, Coop."

It is useless. Up on the screen Cooper has Duddy under his gun arm and he is saying, "Young fellow, I'm taking you over to old Judge Hardy's book-lined den for a man-to-man talk about good manners." End of picture.

Quickly, I run to see *Going Places*, figuring Cooper will be tied up giving Andy Hardy some quick-draw tips, but he ar-rives in time to see the movie's two utterly charming heroes engage charmingly in burglary, kidnapping, car theft and ca-sual thuggery. "Those fellows are nothing but a pair of skunks," he says, striding down the aisle.

"Stay out of it, Coop!"

The audience is enraged to see him rescue a lovely mother from ravishment, but Cooper takes the charmers to the mar-shal's office anyhow.

My analyst says Gary Cooper is dead and I am too immature to accept reality. Cooper looks at the analyst without expres-sion. "I could take him down to the marshal's office for taking money for useless explanations," says Cooper.

"Stay out of it, Coop," I plead.

WANDA HICKEY'S NIGHT OF GOLDEN MEMORIES

"**P**uberty rites in the more primitive tribal societies are almost invariably painful and traumatic experiences."

I half dozed in front of my TV set as the speaker droned on in his high, nasal voice. One night a week, as a form of masochistic self-discipline, I sentence myself to a minimum of three hours viewing educational television. Like so many other things in life, educational TV is a great idea but a miserable reality: murky films of home life in Kurdistan, jowly English authors being interviewed by jowly English literary critics, pinched-faced ladies demonstrating Japanese brush techniques. But I watch all of it religiously—I suppose because it is there, like Mount Everest.

"A classic example is the Ugga Buggah tribe of lower Micronesia," the speaker continued, tapping a pointer on the map behind him.

A shot of an Ugga Buggah teenager appeared on the screen, eyes rolling in misery, face bathed in sweat. I leaned forward. His expression was strangely familiar.

"When an Ugga Buggah reaches puberty, the rites are rigorous and unvarying for both sexes. Difficult dances are performed and the candidate for adulthood must eat a sickening ritual meal during the postdance banquet. You will also notice that his costume is as uncomfortable as it is decorative."

Again the Ugga Buggah appeared, clothed in a garment that seemed to be made of feathers and chain mail, the top grasping his Adam's apple like an iron clamp, his tongue lolling out in pain.

"The adults attend these tribal rituals only as chaperones and observers, and look upon the ceremony with indulgence. Here we see the ritual dance in progress."

A heavy rumble of drums; then a moiling herd of sweating feather-clad dancers of both sexes appeared on screen amid a great cloud of dust.

"Of course, we in more sophisticated societies no longer observe these rites."

Somehow, the scene was too painful for me to continue watching. Something dark and lurking had been awakened in my breast.

"What the hell you mean we don't observe puberty rites?" I mumbled rhetorically as I got up and switched off the set. Reaching up to the top bookshelf, I took down a leatherette-covered volume. It was my high school class yearbook. I leafed through the pages of photographs: beaming biology teachers, pimply-faced students, lantern-jawed football coaches. Suddenly, there it was—a sharply etched photographic record of a true puberty rite among the primitive tribes of northern Indiana.

The caption read: "The Junior Prom was heartily enjoyed by one and all. The annual event was held this year at the Cherrywood Country Club. Mickey Eisley and his Magic Music Makers provided the romantic rhythms. All agreed that it was an unforgettable evening, the memory of which we will all cherish in the years to come."

True enough. In the gathering gloom of my Manhattan apartment, it all came back.

"You going to the prom?" asked Schwartz, as we chewed on our salami sandwiches under the stands of the football field, where we preferred for some reason to take lunch at that period of our lives.

"Yep, I guess so," I answered as coolly as I could.

"Who ya takin'?" Flick joined the discussion, sucking at a bottle of Nehi orange.

"I don't know. I was thinking of Daphne Bigelow." I had dropped the name of the most spectacular girl in the entire high school, if not the state of Indiana itself.

"No kidding!" Schwartz reacted in a tone of proper awe and respect, tinged with disbelief.

"Yeh. I figure I'd give her a break."

Flick snorted, the gassy orange pop going down the wrong pipe. He coughed and wheezed brokenly for several moments. I had once dated Daphne Bigelow and, although the occasion, as faithful readers will recall, was not a riotous success, I felt that I was still in the running. Several occasions in the past month had led me to believe that I was making a comeback with Daphne. Twice she had distinctly acknowledged my presence in the halls between classes, once actually speaking to me.

"Oh, hi there, Fred," she had said in that musical voice.

"Uh . . . hi, Daph," I had replied wittily. The fact that my name is not Fred is neither here nor there; she had *spoken* to me. She had remembered my face from somewhere.

"Ya gotta go formal," said Schwartz. "I read on the bulletin board where it said you wear a summer formal to the prom."

"No kidding?" Flick had finished off the orange and was now fully with us. "What's a summer formal?"

"That's where you wear one of those white coats," I explained. I was known as the resident expert in our group on all forms of high life. This was because my mother was a fanatical Fred Astaire fan.

"Ya gotta rent 'em," I said with the finality of an expert.

Two weeks later, each one of us received a prim white envelope containing an engraved invitation.

The Junior Class is proud to invite you to the Junior Prom, to be held at the Cherrywood County Club beginning eight P.M. *June fifth. Dance to the music of Mickey Eisley and his Magic Music Makers.*

Summer formal required.

The Committee

It was the first engraved invitation I had ever received. The puberty rites had begun. That night around the supper table, the talk was of nothing else.

"Who ya gonna take?" my old man asked, getting right to the heart of the issue. Who you were taking to the prom was considered a highly significant decision, possibly affecting your whole life, which, in some tragic cases, it did.

"Oh, I don't know. I was thinking of a couple of girls." I replied in an offhand manner, as though this slight detail didn't concern me at all. My kid brother, who was taking all this in with sardonic interest, sneered derisively and went back to shoveling in his red cabbage. He had not yet discovered girls. My mother paused while slicing the meat loaf.

"Why not take that nice Wanda Hickey?"

"Aw, come on, Ma. This is the prom. This is important. You don't take Wanda Hickey to the *prom.*"

Wanda Hickey was the only girl who I knew for an absolute fact liked me. Ever since we had been in third grade, Wanda had been hanging around the outskirts of my social circle. She laughed at my jokes and once, when we were 12, actually sent me a valentine. She was always loitering around the tennis courts, the ball diamonds, the alleys where on long summer nights we played Kick the Can or siphoned gas to keep Flick's Chevy running. In fact, there were times when I couldn't shake her.

"Nah, I haven't decided who I'm gonna take. I was kind of thinking of Daphne Bigelow."

The old man set his bottle of Pabst Blue Ribbon down carefully on the table. Daphne Bigelow was the daughter of one of the larger men in town. There was, in truth, a street named after her family.

"You're a real glutton for punishment, ain't you?" The old man flicked a spot of foam off the table. He was referring to an unforgettable evening I had once spent with Daphne in my callow youth. "Oh, well, you might as well learn your lesson once and for all."

He was in one of his philosophical moods. The White Sox had dropped nine straight, and a losing streak like that usually brought out his fatalistic side. He leaned back in his chair, blew some smoke toward the ceiling and went on: "Yep. Too many guys settle for the first skirt that shows up. And regret it the rest of their lives."

Ignoring the innuendo, my mother set the mashed potatoes down on the table and said, "Well, I think Wanda is a very nice girl. But then, what I think doesn't matter."

My mother had the practiced turn of phrase of the veteran martyr, whose role in life is to suffer as publicly as possible.

"I gotta rent a summer formal," I announced.

"Christ, you gonna wear one a' them monkey suits?" the old man chuckled. He had never, to my knowledge, worn anything more formal than a sports jacket in his entire life.

"I'm going down to that place on Hohman Avenue tomorrow with Schwartz and see about it."

"Oh, boy! Lah-di-dah," said my kid brother with characteristically eloquent understatement. Like father, like son.

The next day, after school, Schwartz and I went downtown to a place we both had passed countless times in our daily meanderings. Hanging out over the street was the cutout of a tall, creamfaced man dressed to the nines in high silk hat, stiff starched shirt, swallow-tailed coat, striped morning trousers and an ivory-headed walking stick held with an easy grace by his dove-gray gloved hand. In red, sputtering neon script underneath: AL'S SWANK FORMALWEAR. RENTED BY THE DAY OR HOUR. FREE FITTINGS.

We climbed the narrow, dark wooden steps to the second floor. Within a red arrow painted on the wall were the words SWANK FORMAL—TURN LEFT.

We went past a couple of dentists' offices and a door marked BAIL BONDSMAN—FREEDOM FOR *you* DAY OR NIGHT.

"I wonder if Fred Astaire ever comes here," Schwartz said.

"Oh, come on, Schwartz. This is serious!" I could feel excitement rising deep inside me. The prom, the engraved invitation, the summer formal; it was all starting to come together.

Al's Swank Formalwear turned out to be a small room with a yellow light bulb hanging from the ceiling, a couple of tall glass cases containing suits on hangers, a counter and couple of smudgy full-length mirrors. Schwartz opened negotiations with a swarthy, bald, hawk-eyed, shirt-sleeved man behind the counter. Around his neck hung a yellow measuring tape. He wore a worn vest with a half-dozen chalk pencils sticking out of the pocket.

"Uh . . . we'd like to . . . uh . . ." Schwartz began confidently.

"OK, boys. Ya wanna make it big at the prom, am I right? Ya come to the right place. Ya goin' to that hop out at Cherrywood, right?"

"Uh . . . yeah," I replied.

"And ya wanna summah fawmal, right?"

"HEY, MORTY!" he shouted out. "HERE'S TWO MORE FOR THAT BASH AT CHERRYWOOD. I'D SAY ONE THIRTY-SIX SHAWT, ONE FAWTY REGULAH." His practiced eye had immediately sized us correctly.

"COMIN' UP!" Morty's voice echoed from the bowels of the establishment.

Humming to himself, Al began to pile and unpile boxes like we weren't even there. I looked around the room at the posters of various smartly turned out men of the world. One in particular, wearing a summer formal, had a striking resemblance to Cesar Romero, his distinguished gray sideburns and bronze face contrasting nicely with the snowy whiteness of his jacket.

There was another picture, of Tony Martin, who was at that time at the peak of his movie career, usually portraying Arab princes who disguised themselves as beggars in order to make the scene at the market place. He was always falling in love with a slave girl who turned out to be a princess in disguise, played by Paulette Goddard. Tony's roguish grin, somewhat flyspecked, showed that he was about to break into *Desert Song*.

Schwartz was busily inspecting a collection of bow ties displayed under glass in one of the showcases.

"OK ON THE THIRTY-SIX SHAWT, AL, BUT I'M OUTA FAWTIES.

HOW 'BOUT THAT FAWTY-TWO REGULAH THAT JUST CAME BACK FROM THAT DAGO WEDDING?'' shouted Morty from the back room.

"CUT THE TALK AN' BRING THE GOODS!" Al shouted back, straightening up, his face flushed.

"THE FAWTY-TWO AIN'T BEEN CLEANED YET!" came from the back room.

"BRING IT OUT, AWREADY!" barked Al. He turned to me.

"This suit just come in from anotha job. Don't worry about how it looks. We'll clean it up an' take it in so's it'll fit good."

Morty emerged, a tall, thin, sad man in a gray smock, even balder than Al. He carried two suits on hangers, draped them over the counter, gave Al a dirty look and stalked back into the shadows.

"OK now, boys. First you." Al nodded to Schwartz. "Take this and try it on behind the curtain. It should fit good. It's maybe a little long at the cuffs, but we'll take them up."

Schwartz grabbed the hanger and scurried behind the green curtain. Al held up the other suit. In the middle of a dark reddish-brown stain that covered the entire right breast pocket was a neat little hole right through the jacket. Al turned the hanger around and stuck his finger through the hole.

"HEY, MORTY!" he shouted.

"WHAT NOW?"

"HOW 'BOUT THIS HOLE INNA FAWTY-TWO? CAN YA FIX IT BY TO-NIGHT?"

"WADDAYA WANT, MIRACLES?" Morty whined.

"Don't worry, kid. We can fix this up good as new. You'll never tell it ain't a new coat."

Schwarz emerged from the fitting room shrouded in what looked like a parachute with sleeves.

"Perfect! Couldn't be bettuh!" shouted Al exultantly, darting from behind the counter. He grabbed Schwartz by the shoulders, spun him around and, with a single movement, ran his hand up into Schwartz' crotch, measured the inseam, spun him around again, made two pencil marks on the sleeves—which came almost to his finger tips—yanked up the collar, punched him smartly in the kidney, all the while murmuring in a hoarse stage whisper:

"It's made for you. Just perfect. Couldn't be bettuh. Perfect. Like tailormade."

Schwartz smiled weakly throughout the ordeal.

"OK, kid, take it off. I'll have it ready for you next week."

Obediently, Schwartz disappeared into the fitting room. Al turned to me. "Here, slip on this coat." He held it out invitingly. I plunged my arms into its voluminous folds. I felt his iron grip on my shoulder blades as he yanked me upward and spun me around, his appraising eye darting everywhere.

"Just perfect. Couldn't be bettuh. Fits like a glove. Take it in a little here; pull in the bias here. . . ."

He took out his chalk and made a few marks on my back.

"OK. Slip outa it."

Al again thrust his finger through the hole.

"Reweave it like new. An' doan worry 'bout the stain; we'll get it out. Musta been some party. Here, try on these pants."

He tossed a pair of midnight-blue trousers over the counter at me. Inside the hot little cubicle, as I changed into the pants, I stroked the broad black-velvet stripe that lined the outer seam. I was really in the big time now. They were rumpled, of course, and they smelled strongly of some spilled beverage, but they were truly magnificent. The waist came to just a shade below my armpits, beautifully pleated. Tossing the curtain aside, I sashayed out like Cary Grant.

"Stand up straight, kid," Al breathed into my ear. An aromatic blast of pastrami and pickled herring made my head reel.

"Ah. Perfect. Just right. Put a little tuck in the waist, so." He grabbed several yards of the seat. "And a little in here." A sudden thrill of pain as he violently measured the inseam. Then it was all over.

"Now," he said, back behind his counter once again, "how do ya see the shirts? You want 'em straight or ruffled? Or pleated, maybe? Very smart." He indicated several shirts on display in his grimy glass case. "I would recommend our Monte Carlo model, a real spiffy numbah."

We both peered down at the shirts. The Monte Carlo number was, indeed, spiffy, its wide, stiff, V-cut collar arching over cascading ribbons of razor-sharp pleats.

"Boy, now that's a shirt!" Schwartz breathed excitedly.

"That what *I* want," I said aloud. No other shirt would do.

"Me, too," Schwartz seconded.

"OK now," Al continued briskly, "how 'bout studs? Ya got 'em?"

"Uh . . . what?"

He had caught me off guard. I had heard the word "stud" before, but never in a tailor shop.

"OK, I guess not. I'll throw 'em in. Because you're high-class customers. Now, I suppose ya wanna go first-class, right?"

Al directed this question at both of us, his face assuming a look of concerned forthrightness.

"Right?" he repeated.

"Yeah." Schwartz answered uncertainly for both of us.

"I knew that the minute you two walked in. Now, I'm gonna show you somepin that is exclusive with Al's Swank Formalwear."

With an air of surreptitious mystery, he bent over, slid open a drawer and placed atop the counter an object that unfocused my eyes with its sheer kaleidoscopic brilliance.

"No place else in town can supply you with a genuwine Hollywood paisley cummabund. It's our trademark."

I stared at the magnificent band of glowing, scintillating fabric, already seeing myself a total smash on the dance floor.

"It's only a buck extra. And worth five times the price. Adolphe Menjou always wears this model. How 'bout it, men?"

We both agreed in unison. After all, you only live once.

"Of course, included for half a dolla more is our fawmal bow tie and matchin' booteneer. I would suggest the maroon."

"Sounds great," I answered.

"Isn't that everything?" asked Schwartz with some concern.

"Is that all! You gotta be kiddin', sonny. How do you expect to trip the light fantastic without a pair a black patent-leatha dancin' pumps?"

"Dancin' what?" I asked.

"Shoes, shoes," he explained irritably. "And we throw in the socks for nuttin'. How 'bout it?"

"Well, uh. . . ."

"Fine! So that's it, boys. I'll have everything all ready the day before the Prom. You'll really knock 'em dead."

As we left, another loud argument broke out between Morty and Al. Their voices accompanied us down the long flight of narrow stairs and out into the street.

Step by step, in the ancient tradition, the tribal ritual was being acted out. The prom, which was now two weeks off, began to occupy our minds most of the waking day. The semester had just about played itself out; our junior year was almost over. The trees and flowers were in blossom, great white clouds drifted across deep-blue skies and baseball practice was in full swing—but somehow, this spring was different from the rest. The prom was something that we had heard about since our earliest days. A kind of golden aura hung over the word itself. Every couple of days, the P.A. at school announced that the prom committee was meeting or requesting something.

There was only one thing wrong. As each day ticked inexorably by toward that magic night at the Cherrywood Country Club, I still could not steel myself to actually seek out Daphne Bigelow and ask her the fatal question. Time and again, I spotted her in the halls, drifting by on gossamer wings, her radiant complexion casting a glow on all those around her, her brilliant smile lighting up the corners of 202 homeroom. But each time, I broke into a fevered sweat and chickened out at the last instant.

The weekend before the prom was sheer torture. Schwartz, always efficient and methodical, had already made all his plans. We sat on the back steps of my porch late Sunday afternoon, watching Lud Kissel next door struggle vainly to adjust the idling speed on his time-ravaged carburetor so that the family Nash didn't stall at 35 miles an hour. He had been drinking, of course, so it was quite a show.

"How ya' doin' with Daphne Bigelow?" asked Schwartz sardonically, knowing full well the answer.

"Oh, that. I haven't had time to ask her," I lied.

"Ya better get on the stick. There's only a week left."

"Who *you* got lined up?" I asked, tossing a pebble at old Lud, who was now asleep under his running board.

"Clara Mae Mattingly," Schwartz replied in a steady, expressionless voice.

I was surprised. Clara Mae was one of those shadowy, quiet girls who rarely were mentioned outside of honor rolls and stuff like that. She wore gold-rimmed glasses and still had pigtails.

"Yep," Schwartz added smugly, gratified by my reaction.

"Boy, she sure can spell." It was all I could think of to say that was good about her, other than the fact that she was female.

"Sure can," Schwartz agreed. He, too, had been quite a speller in our grade school days; and on more than one occasion, Clara Mae had demolished him with a brilliant display of virtuosity in a school-wide spelldown, a form of verbal Indian wrestling now almost extinct but which at one time was a Waterloo for many of us among the unlettered. Clara Mae had actually once gone to the state final and had lost out to a gangly farm girl from downstate who apparently had nothing else to do down there but read *Webster*'s through the long winter nights.

"You gonna send her a corsage?" I asked.

"Already ordered it. At the Cupid Florist." Schwartz' self-satisfaction was overflowing.

"An orchid?"

"Yep. Cost eight bucks."

"Holy God! Eight bucks!" I was truly impressed.

"That includes a gold pin for it."

Our conversation trailed off as Lud Kissel rose heavily to his knees and crawled off down the driveway on all fours, heading for the Bluebird Tavern, which was closed on Sundays. Lud always got restless in the spring.

A few hours later, after supper, I went out gloomily to water the lawn, a job that purportedly went toward earning my allowance, which had reached an all-time high that spring of three dollars a week. Fireflies played about the cottonwoods in the hazy twilight, but I was troubled. One week to go; less, now, because you couldn't count the day of the prom itself. In the drawer where I kept my socks and scout knife, buried deep in the back, were 24 one-dollar bills, which I had saved for the prom. Just as deep in my cowardly soul, I knew I could never ask Daphne Bigelow to be my date.

Refusing to admit it to myself, I whistled moodily as I sprayed the irises and watched a couple of low-flying bats as they skimmed over the lawn and up into the poplars. Mrs. Kissel, next door, creaked back and forth on her porch swing, a copy of *True Romances* open in her lap, as she waited for Lud's return with his usual snootful. My kid brother came out onto the porch and, from sheer habit, I quickly shot a stream of water over him, catching him in mid-air as he leaped high to avoid the stream. It was a superbly executed shot. I had led him just right. He caught it full in the chest, his yellow polo shirt clinging to his ribs wetly, like a second skin. Bawling at the top of his lungs, he disappeared into the house and slammed the screen door behind him. Ordinarily, this small triumph would have cheered me up for hours; but tonight, I tasted nothing but ashes. Suddenly, his face reappeared in the doorway.

"I'M GONNA TELL MA!" he yelled.

Instantly, like a cobra, I struck. Sweeping the stream quickly over the screen door, I got him again. Another scream of rage and he was gone. Again, I sank into my moody sea of reflection. Was I going to boot the prom?

Flick had asked Janie Hutchinson, a tall, funny girl who had been in our class since kindergarten. And Schwartz was lined up with Clara Mae; all he had talked about that week had been that crummy orchid and how good a dancer he was. Flick had stopped asking me about Daphne ever since the past Wednesday, when I had gotten mad because he'd been needling me. All week, I had been cleaning up my Ford for the big night. If there was one thing in my life that went all the way, my only true and total love, it was my Ford V8, a convertible that I had personally rebuilt at least 35 times. I knew every valve spring personally, had honed each valve, burnished every nut and bolt she carried. Tuesday, I had simonized her completely; Wednesday, I had repeated the job; and Thursday, I had polished the chrome until my knuckles ached and my back was stiff. I had spent the past two days minutely cleaning the interior, using a full can of saddle-soap on the worn leather. Everything was set to go, except for one thing—no girl.

A feeling of helpless rage settled over me as I continued spraying the lawn. I flushed out a poor, hapless caterpillar from under a bush, squirting him mercilessly full blast, until he washed down the sidewalk and disappeared into the weeds. I felt a twinge of evil satisfaction as he rolled over and over helplessly. It was getting dark. All that was left of the sun was a long purple-orange streak along the western horizon. The glow of the steel mills to the north and east began to light up the twilight sky. I had worked my way down to the edge of our weedy, pock-marked bed of sod when, out of the corner of my eye, I noticed something white approaching out of the gloom. I sprinkled on, not knowing that another piece was being fitted into the intricate mosaic of adolescence. I kicked absentmindedly at a passing toad as I soaked down the dandelions.

"What are you doing?"

So deeply was I involved in self-pity that at first my mind wouldn't focus. Startled, I swung my hose around, spraying the white figure on the sidewalk ten feet away.

"I'm sorry!" I blurted out, seeing at once that I had washed down a girl dressed in white tennis clothes.

"Oh, hi, Wanda. I didn't see you there."

She dried herself with a Kleenex.

"What are you doing?" she asked again.

"I'm sprinkling the lawn." The toad hopped past, going the other way now. I squirted him briefly, out of general principles.

"You been playing tennis?" Since she was wearing tennis clothes and was carrying a racket, it seemed the right thing to say.

"Me and Eileen Akers were playing. Down at the park," she answered.

Eileen Akers was a sharp-faced, bespectacled girl I had, inexplicably, been briefly in love with in the third grade. I had come to my senses by the time we got into 4-B. It was a narrow escape. By then, I had begun to dimly perceive that there was more to women than being able to play a good game of Run Sheep, Run.

"I'm sure glad school's almost over," she went on, when I couldn't think of anything to say. "I can hardly wait. I never thought I'd be a senior."

"Yeah," I said.

"I'm going to camp this summer. Are you?"

"Yeah," I lied. I had a job already lined up for the summer, working for a surveyor. The next camp I would see would be in the Ozarks, and I'd be carrying an M-1.

Wanda swung her tennis racket at a June bug that flapped by barely above stall speed. She missed. The bug soared angrily up and whirred off into the darkness.

"Are you going to college when you graduate next year?" she asked. For some reason, I didn't like the drift of the conversation.

"Yeah, I guess so, if I don't get drafted."

"My brother's in the Army. He's in the Artillery." Her brother, Bud Hickey, was a tall, laconic type four or five years older than both of us.

"Yeah, I heard. Does he like it?"

"Well, he doesn't write much," she said. "But he's gonna get a pass next September, before he goes overseas."

"How come he's in the Artillery?" I asked.

"I don't know. They just put him there. I guess because he's tall."

"What's that gotta do with it? Do they have to *throw* the shells, or something?"

"I don't know. They just did it."

Then it happened. Without thinking, without even a shadow of a suspicion of planning, I heard myself asking: "You going to the prom?"

For a long instant she said nothing, just swung her tennis racket at the air.

"I guess so," she finally answered, weakly.

"It's gonna be great," I said, trying to change the subject.

"Uh . . . who are you going with?" She said it as if she really didn't care one way or the other.

"Well, I haven't exactly made up my mind yet." I bent down unconcernedly and pulled a giant milkweed out by the roots.

"Neither have I," she said.

It was then that I realized there was no sense fighting it. Some guys are born to dance forever with the Daphne Bigelows on shining ballroom floors under endless starry skies. Others—well, they do the best they can. I didn't know that yet, but I was beginning to suspect something.

"Wanda?"

"Yes?"

"Wanda. Would you . . . well . . . I mean . . . would you, you see, I was thinking. . . ."

"Yes?"

Here I go, in over the horns: "Wanda, uh . . . how about . . . going to the prom with me?"

She stopped twitching her tennis racket. The crickets cheeped, the spring air was filled with the sound of singing froglets. A soft breeze carried with it the promise of a rich summer and the vibrant aromas of a nearby refinery.

She began softly, "Of course, I've had a lot of invitations, but I didn't say yes to any of them yet. I guess it would be fun to go with you," she ended gamely.

"Yeah, well, naturally, I've had four or five girls who wanted to go with me, but I figured that they were mostly jerks anyway, and . . . ah . . . I meant to ask you all along."

The die was cast. There was no turning back. It was an ironclad rule. Once a girl was asked to the prom, only a total crumb would even consider ducking out of it. There had been one or two cases in the past, but the perpetrators had become social pariahs, driven from the tribe to fend for themselves in the unfriendly woods.

Later that night, hunched over the kitchen table, still somewhat numbed by the unexpected turn of events, I chewed thoughtfully on a peanut-butter-and-jelly sandwich, while my mother, hanging over the sink in her rump-sprung Chinese-red chenille bathrobe, droned on monotonously: "You're just going to *have* to stop squirting Randy."

"Yeah," I answered, my mind three light-years away.

"You got his new Flash Gordon T-shirt all wet."

"Sorry," I said automatically. It was a phrase I used often in those days.

"It shrunk. And now he can't wear it."

"Why not?" I asked.

"It comes up around his chest now."

"Well, why can't he stretch it?"

"You just stop squirting him, that's all. You hear me?"

"It's a silly T-shirt, anyway," I said truculently.

"You heard what I said. No more squirting." That ended the conversation.

Later, in bed, I thought briefly of Daphne Bigelow, but was interrupted by a voice from the bed on the other side of the room.

"You rotten crumb. You squirted my T-shirt!"

"Ah, shaddup."

"You wait. I'm gonna get you!"

I laughed raucously. My kid brother wailed in rage.

"SHUT UP, YOU TWO! CUT OUT THE FIGHTING OR I'LL COME IN THERE AND DO SOME HEAD KNOCKING!"

The old man meant what he said and we knew it. I promptly fell asleep. It had been a long and tumultuous day.

I broke the news to Schwartz the next morning, after biology. We were hurrying through the halls between classes on our way to our lockers, which were side by side on the second floor.

"Hey, Schwartz, how about double-dating for the prom?" I asked. I knew he had no car and I needed moral support, anyway.

"Great! I'll help you clean up the car."

"I've already simonized her. She's all set."

"Are you gonna send Daphne an orchid, or what?"

"Well, no . . ." I said lamely, hoping he'd forget what he asked.

"What do you mean? Ya gotta send a corsage."

"Well, I *am* going to send a corsage."

"I thought you said you weren't."

I just couldn't shake him off. "I never said I wasn't gonna send a corsage."

"Are you nuts? You just said you weren't gonna."

"I'm not gonna send a corsage to Daphne Bigelow. You asked me if I was gonna send a corsage to Daphne. I'm not."

"She's gonna think you're a real cheap skate."

It was getting ridiculous. Schwartz was being even more of a numskull than usual.

"Schwartz, I have decided not to ask Daphne Bigelow to the prom."

He looked directly at me, which caused him to slam into two strolling freshman girls. Their books slid across the floor, where they were trampled underfoot by the thundering mob.

"Well, who *are* you taking?" he asked, oblivious to their shrieks of dismay.

"Wanda Hickey."

"Wanda Hickey!"

Schwartz was completely thrown by the bit of news. Wanda Hickey had never been what you could call a major star in our Milky Way. We walked on, saying nothing, until finally, as we opened our lockers, Schwartz said: "Well, she sure is good at algebra."

It was true. Wanda was an algebra shark in the same way

that Clara Mae was a spelling nut. Maybe we both got what we deserved.

Later that day, in the study hall, after I had polished off a history theme on some stupid thing like the Punic Wars, I got to thinking about Wanda. I could see her sitting way over on the other side of the room, a dusty sunbeam filtering through the window and lighting up her straw-colored hair. She was kind of cute. I'd never really noticed it before. Ever since second grade, Wanda had just been there, along with Eileen Akers, Helen Weathers and all the other girls who—along with me and Schwartz and Flick and Jossway and the rest— had moved together step by step up the creaky ladder of education. And here I was, at long last, taking Wanda Hickey— *Wanda Hickey*—to the prom, the only junior prom I would ever attend in my life.

As I chewed on the end of my fake-marble Wearever pen, I watched Wanda through half-closed eyes in the dusty sunbeam as she read *The Lady of the Lake*. Ahead of me, Schwartz dozed fitfully, as he always did in study hall, his forehead occasionally thumping the desk. Flick, to my right, struggled sullenly over his chemistry workbook. We both knew it was hopeless. Flick was the only one in our crowd who consistently flunked everything.

The prom was just five days away. This was the last week of school. Ahead our long summer in the sun stretched out like a lazy yellow road. For many of us, it was the last peaceful summer we were to know.

Mr. Wilson, the study-hall teacher, wandered aimlessly up and down the aisles, pretending he was interested in what we were pretending to be doing. From somewhere outside drifted the cries of a girls' volleyball game, while I drew pictures of my Ford on the inside cover of my three-ring notebook: front view, side view, rear view, outlining the drawings with ink.

That morning, on my way to school, I had gone down to the Cupid Florist Shop and ordered an orchid. My 24 dollars were shrinking fast. The eight-dollar bite for the orchid didn't help. Schwartz and I were going to split on the gas, which would come to maybe a buck apiece. After paying for the summer formal I'd have a fast ten dollars left for the night. As I sat in study hall, I calculated, writing the figures down, adding and subtracting. But it didn't come out to much, no matter how I figured it.

Schwartz passed a note back to me. I opened it: "How about the Red Rooster afterward?"

I wrote underneath, "Where else?" and passed it back. The Red Rooster was part of the tribal ritual. It was *the* place you went after a big date, if you could afford it.

I glanced over across the room at Wanda and caught her looking at me. She instantly buried her head in her book. Good old Wanda.

On the way home from school every day that week of course, all we talked about was the prom. Flick was double-dating with Jossway and we were all going to meet afterward at the Rooster and roister until dawn, drinking deeply of the sweet elixir of the good life. The only thing that nagged me now was financial. Ten bucks didn't look as big as it usually did. Ordinarily, ten bucks could have gotten me through a month of just fooling around, but the prom was the big time.

Friday night, as I sat in the kitchen before going to bed, knocking down a liverwurst on whole wheat and drinking a glass of chocolate milk, the back door slammed open and in breezed the old man, carrying his bowling bag. Friday night was his big night down at the PinBowl. He was a fanatical bowler, and a good one, too. He slid the bag across the floor, pretending to lay one down the groove, his right arm held out in a graceful follow-through, right leg trailing in the classic bowling stance.

"Right in the pocket," he said with satisfaction.

"How'd you do tonight?" I asked.

"Not bad. Had a two-oh-seven game. Damn near cracked six hundred."

He opened the refrigerator and fished around for a beer, then sat down heavily, took a deep drag from the bottle, burped loudly and said:

"Well, tomorrow's the big day, ain't it?"

"Yep," I answered. "Sure is."

"You takin' Daphne Bigelow?" he asked.

"Nah. Wanda Hickey."

"Oh, yeah? Well, you can't win 'em all. Wanda's old man is some kind of a foreman at the mill or something, ain't he?"

"I guess so."

"He drives a Studebaker Champion, don't he? The green two-door with the whitewalls."

The old man had a fine eye for cars. He judged all men by what they drove. Apparently a guy who drove a two-door Studebaker was not absolutely beyond the pale.

"Not a bad car. Except they burn oil after a while," he mused, omitting no aspects of the Studebaker.

"They used to have a weak front end. Bad kingpins." He shook his head critically, opening another beer and reaching for the rye bread.

I said nothing, lost in my own thoughts. My mother and kid brother had been in bed for an hour or so. We were, for all practical purposes, alone in the house. Next door, Mrs. Kissel threw out a pail of dishwater into the back yard with a swoosh. Her screen door slammed.

"How ya fixed for tomorrow night?" the old man asked suddenly, swirling his beer bottle around to raise the head.

"What do you mean?"

"I mean, how are ya *fixed*?"

My father never talked money to me. I got my allowance every Monday and that was that.

"Well, I've got about ten bucks."

"Hm." That was all he said.

After sitting in silence for a minute or so, he said, "You know, I always wished I coulda gone to a prom."

How can you answer something like that? He had barely gotten out of eighth grade when he had to go to work, and he never stopped for the rest of his life.

"Oh, well, what the hell." He finally answered himself.

He cut himself a slice of boiled ham and made a sandwich.

"I was really hot tonight. Got a string of six straight strikes in the second game. The old hook was movin', getting a lot of wood."

He reached into his hip pocket, took out his wallet and said: "Look, don't tell Ma." He handed me a $20 bill.

"I had a couple of bets going on the second game, and I'm a money bowler."

He was that. No doubt of it. In his early teens, he had scrounged out a living as a pool shark, and he had never lost the touch. I took the $20, glommed onto it the way the proverbial drowning man grabs at a straw. I was so astounded at this unprecedented gesture that it never occurred to me to say thanks. He would have been embarrassed if I had. A miracle had come to pass. There was no doubt about it—the prom was going to be an unqualified gas.

The next day dawned bright and sunny, as perfect as a June day can be—in a steel-mill town. Even the blast-furnace dust that drifted aimlessly through the soft air glowed with promise. I was out early, dusting off the car. It was going to be a top-down night. If there is anything more romantic than a convertible with the top down in June going to a prom, I'd like to hear about it. Cleopatra's barge couldn't have been much more seductive.

My kid brother, his diminutive Flash Gordon T-shirt showing a great expanse of knobby backbone and skinny belly, yapped around me as I toiled over the Ford.

"Look what you done to my T-shirt!" he whined, his runny nose atrickle. He was in the midst of his annual spring cold, which would be superseded by his summer cold, which lasted nicely to the whopper he got in the fall, which, of course, was only a prelude to his winter-long *monster* cold.

"Stay away from the fender. You're dripping on it!" I shouted angrily, shoving him away.

"Flash Gordon's only about an inch high now!"

I couldn't help laughing. It was true. Flash had shrunk, along with the shirt, which Randy had earned by doggedly eating three boxes of Wheaties, saving the boxtops and mailing them in with 25 cents that he had, by dint of ferocious self-denial, saved from his 30-cent weekly allowance.

"Look, I'll get you another Flash Gordon T-shirt."

"You can't. They're not givin' 'em away no more. They're

givin' away Donald Duck beanies with a propeller on top now."

"Well, then, stretch the one you got now, stupid."

"It won't stretch. It keeps getting littler."

He bounced up and down on a clothes pole, joggling the clothesline and my mother's wash. Within three seconds, she was out on the back porch.

"CUT IT OUT WITH THE CLOTHES POLE."

Sullenly, he slid off into the ground. I went back to work, until the Ford gleamed like some rare jewel. Then I went into the house to begin the even more laborious process of getting *myself* in shape for the evening ahead. Locking the bathroom door, I took two showers, wearing a brand-new bar of Lifebuoy down to a nub. I knew what happened to people who didn't use it; every week, little comic strips underneath *Moon Mullins* told endless tales of disastrous proms due to dreaded B.O. It would not happen to me.

I then shaved for the second time that week, using a new Gillette Blue Blade. As usual when an important shave was executed, I nicked myself nastily in several places.

"Son of a bitch," I muttered, plastering the wounds with little pieces of toilet paper.

Carefully, I went over every inch of my face, battling that age-old enemy, the blackhead, and polished off the job with a copious application of stinging Aqua Velva. Next I attacked my hair, combing and recombing, getting just the right insouciant pitch to my pride and joy, my d.a. cut. Tonight, I would be a truly magnificent specimen of lusty manhood.

Twilight was fast approaching when I emerged from the bathroom, redolent of rare aromas, pink and svelte. But the real battle had not yet begun. Laid out on my bed was my beautiful summer formal. Al was right: The elegant white coat truly gleamed in virginal splendor. Not a trace of the red stain nor the sinister hole could be detected. The coat was ready for another night of celebration, its lapels spotless, its sleeves smooth and uncreased.

Carefully, I undid the pins that festooned my pleated Monte Carlo shirt. It was the damnedest thing I had ever seen, once I got it straightened out: long, trailing gauzelike shirttails, a crinkly front that thrummed like sheet metal and a collar that seemed to be carved of white rock. I slipped it on. Panic! It had no buttons—just holes.

Rummaging around frantically in the box the suit came in, I found a cellophane envelope containing little round black things. Ripping the envelope open, I poured them out; there were five of them, two of which immediately darted under the bed. From the looks of the remaining three, they certainly weren't buttons; but they'd have to do. Although I didn't know it at the time, I had observed a classic maneuver executed by at least one stud out of every set rented with a tux. Down on my hands and knees, already beginning to lose my Lifebuoy sheen, sweat popping out here and there, I scrambled around for the missing culprits.

The ordeal was well under way. Seven o'clock was approaching with such rapidity as to be almost unbelievable. Schwartz, Clara Mae and Wanda would *already* be waiting for me, and here I was in my drawers, crawling around on my hands and knees. Finally, amid the dust and dead spiders under my bed, I found the two studs cowering together behind a hardball I'd lost three months earlier.

Back before the mirror again, I struggled to get them in place between the concrete slits. Sweat was beginning to show under my arms. I got two in over my breastbone and now I tried to get the one at the collar over my Adam's apple. It was impossible! I could feel from deep within me several sobs beginning to form. The more I struggled, the more hamfisted I became. Oh, no! Two blackish thumb smudges appeared on my snowwhite collar.

"MA!" I screamed, "LOOK AT MY SHIRT!"

She rushed in from the kitchen, carrying a paring knife and a pan of apples. "What's the matter?"

"Look!" I pointed at the telltale prints.

My kid brother cackled in delight when he saw the trouble I was in.

"Don't touch it," she barked, taking control immediately. Dirty collars were her métier. She had fought them all her life. She darted out of the room and returned instantly with an artgum eraser.

"Now, hold still."

I obeyed as she carefully worked the stud in place and then artistically erased the two monstrous thumbprints. Never in my life had I experienced a collar remotely like the one that now clamped its iron grasp around my windpipe. Hard and unyielding, it dug mercilessly into my throat—a mere sample of what was to come.

"Where's your tie?" she asked. I had forgotten about that detail.

"It . . . ack . . . must be . . . in the box," I managed to gasp out. The collar had almost paralyzed my voice box.

She rummaged around and came up with the bow tie. It was black and it had two metal clips. She snapped it onto the wing collar and stood back.

"Now, look at yourself in the mirror." I didn't recognize myself.

She picked up the midnight-blue trousers and held them open, so that I could slip into them without bending over.

True to his word, Al had, indeed, taken in the seat. The pants clamped me in a viselike grip that was to damn near emasculate me before the evening was out. I sucked in my stomach, buttoned the waistband tight, zippered up the fly and stood straight as a ramrod before the mirror. I had no other choice.

"Gimme your foot."

My mother was down on all fours, pulling the silky black socks onto my feet. Then, out of a box on the bed, she removed the gleaming pair of patent-leather dancing pumps, grabbed my right foot and shoved it into one of them, using her finger as a shoehorn. I tromped down. She squealed in pain.

"I can't get my finger out!"

I hobbled around, taking her finger with me.

"STAND STILL!" she screamed.

I stood like a crane, one foot in the air, with her finger jammed deep into the heel.

"RANDY! COME HERE!" she yelled.

My kid brother, who was sulking under the day bed, ran into the room.

"PULL HIS SHOE OFF, RANDY!" She was frantic.

"What for?" he asked sullenly.

"DON'T ASK STUPID QUESTIONS. JUST DO WHAT I SAY!"

I was getting an enormous cramp in my right buttock.

"STAND STILL!" she yelled. "YOU'RE BREAKING MY FINGER!" Randy looked on impassively, observing a scene that he was later to weave into a family legend, embroidering it more and more as the years went by—making himself the hero, of course.

"RANDY! *Take off his shoe!*" Her voice quavered with pain and exasperation.

"He squirted my T-shirt."

"If you don't take off his shoe this instant, you're gonna regret it." This time, her voice was low and menacing. We both knew the tone. It was the end of the line.

Randy bent over and tugged off the shoe. My mother toppled backward in relief, rubbing her index finger, which was already blue.

"Go back under the day bed," she snapped. He scurried out of the room. I straightened out my leg—the cramp subsiding like a volcano in the marrow of my bones—and the gleaming pumps were put in place without further incident. I stood encased as in armor.

"What's this thing?" she asked from behind me. I executed a careful 180-degree turn.

"Oh, that's my cummerbund."

Her face lit up like an Italian sunrise. "A cummerbund!" She had seen Fred Astaire in many a cummerbund while he spun down marble staircases with Ginger Rogers in his arms, but it was the first actual specimen she had ever been close to. She picked it up reverently, its paisley brilliance lighting up the room like an iridescent jewel.

"How does it work?" she asked, examining it closely.

Before I could answer, she said, "Oh, I see. It has clips on the back. Hold still."

Around my waist it went. She drew it tight. The snaps clicked into place. It rode snugly halfway up my chest.

She picked up the snowy coat and held it out. I lowered my arms into it and straightened up. She darted around to the front, closed the single button and there I stood—Adonis!

Posing before the full-length mirror on the bathroom door, I noted the rich accent of my velvet stripes, the gleam of my pumps, the magnificent dash and sparkle of my high-fashion cummerbund. What a sight! What a feeling! This is the way life should be. This is what it's all about.

I heard my mother call out from the next room: "Hey, what's this thing?" She came out holding a cellophane bag containing a maroon object.

"Oh, that's my boutonniere."

"Your what?"

"It's a thing for the lapel. Like a fake flower."

It was the work of an instant to install my elegant wool carnation. It was the crowning touch. I was so overwhelmed that I didn't care about the fact that it didn't match my black tie, as Al had promised. With the cummerbund I was wearing, no one would notice, anyway.

Taking my leave as Cary Grant would have done, I sauntered out the front door, turned to give my mother a jaunty wave—just in time for her to call me back to pick up Wanda's corsage, which I'd left on the front-hall table.

Slipping carefully into the front seat with the cellophane-topped box safely beside me, I leaned forward slightly, to avoid wrinkling the back of my coat, started the motor up and shoved off into the warm summer night. A soft June moon hung overhead. The Ford purred like a kitten. When I pulled up before Wanda's house, it was lit up from top to bottom. Even before my brakes had stopped squealing, she was out on the porch, her mother fluttering about her, her father lurking in the background, beaming.

With stately tread, I moved up the walk; my pants were so tight that if I'd taken one false step, God knows what would have happened. In my sweaty, Aqua Velva-scented palm, I clutched the ritual largess in its shiny box.

Wanda wore a long turquoise taffeta gown, her milky skin and golden hair radiating in the glow of the porch light. This was *not* the old Wanda. For one thing, she didn't have her glasses on, and her eyes were unnaturally large and liquid, the way the true myopia victim's always are.

"Gee, thanks for the orchid," she whispered. Her voice sounded strained. In accordance with the tribal custom, she, too, was being mercilessly clamped by straps and girdles.

Her mother, an almost exact copy of Wanda, only slightly puffy here and there, said, "You'll take care of her now, won't you?"

"Now, Emily, don't start yapping," her old man muttered in the darkness. "They're not kids anymore."

They stood in the door as we drove off through the soft night toward Schwartz' house, our conversation stilted, our excitement almost at the boiling point. Schwartz rushed out of his house, his white coat like a ghost in the blackness, his hair agleam with Brylcreem, and surrounded by a palpable aura of Lifebuoy.

Five minutes later, Clara Mae piled into the back seat beside him, carefully holding up her daffodil-yellow skirts, her long slender neck arched. She, too, wasn't wearing her glasses. I had never realized that a good speller could be so pretty. Schwartz, a good half head shorter, laughed nervously as we tooled on toward the Cherrywood Country Club. From all over town, other cars, polished and waxed, carried the rest of the junior class to their great trial by fire.

The club nestled amid the rolling hills, where the Sinclair oil aroma was only barely detectable. Parking the car in the lot, we threaded our way through the starched and crinolined crowd—the girls' girdles creaking in unison—to the grand ballroom. Japanese lanterns danced in the breeze through the open doors to the garden, bathing the dance floor in a fairytale glow.

I found myself saying things like, "Why, hello there, Albert, how are you?" And, "Yes, I believe the weather is perfect." Only Flick, the unregenerate Philistine, failed to rise to the occasion. Already rumpled in his summer formal, he made a few tasteless wisecracks as Mickey Eisley and his Magic Music Makers struck up the sultry sounds that had made them famous in every steel-mill town that ringed Lake Michigan. Dark and sensuous, the dance floor engulfed us all. I felt tall, slim and beautiful, not realizing at the time that everybody feels that way wearing a white coat and rented pants. I could see myself standing on a mysterious balcony, a lonely, elegant figure, looking out over the lights of some exotic city, a scene of sophisticated gaiety behind me.

There was a hushed moment when Mickey Eisley stood in the baby spot, his wavy hair shining, before a microphone shaped like a chromium bullet.

"All right, boys and girls." The metallic ring of feed-back framed his words in an echoing nimbus. "And now something really romantic. A request: *When the Swallows Come Back to Capistrano.* We're going to turn the lights down for this one."

Oh, wow! The lights faded even lower. Only the Japanese lanterns glowed dimly—red, green, yellow and blue—in the enchanted darkness. It was unquestionably the high point of my existence.

Wanda and I began to maneuver around the floor. My sole experience in dancing had been gained from reading Arthur Murray ads and practicing with a pillow for a partner behind the locked door of the bathroom. As we shuffled across the floor, I could see the black footprints before my eyes, marching on a white page: 1-2-3; then the white one that said, "Pause."

Back and forth, up and down, we moved metronomically. My box step was so square that I went in little right angles for weeks afterward. The wool carnation rode high up on my lapel and was beginning to scratch my cheek, and an insistent itch began to nag at my right shoulder. There was some kind of wire or horsehair or something in the shoulder pad that was beginning to bore its way into my flesh.

By now, my dashing concrete collar, far from having wilted, had set into the consistency of carborundum, and its incessant abrasive action had removed a wide strip of skin

encircling my neck. As for my voice—due to the manic stran-
gulation of the collar, it was now little more than a hoarse
croak.

"When the swallows ... retuuurrrrrn to Capis-
traaaaaaaano ..." mooed the drummer, who doubled as the
band's romantic vocalist.

I began to notice Wanda's orchid leering up at me from her
shoulder. It was the most repulsive flower I had ever seen. At
least 14 inches across, it looked like some kind of overgrown
Venus's-flytrap waiting for the right moment to strike. Deep
purple, with an obscene yellow tongue that stuck straight out
of it, and greenish knobs on the end, it clashed almost audibly
with her turquoise dress. It looked like it was breathing, and it
clung to her shoulder as if with claws.

As I glided back and forth in my graceful box step, my left
shoulder began to develop an itch that helped take my mind
off of the insane itch in my right shoulder, which was beginning to feel like an army of hungry soldier ants on the march.
The contortions I made to relieve the agony were camou-
flaged nicely by a short sneezing fit brought on by the orchid,
which was exhaling directly into my face. So was Wanda, with
a heady essence of Smith Brothers cough drops and sauerkraut.

"When the deeeep purpullllll falllllllls ... Over sleeeeepy
gaaaardennnn wallllls ..." warbled the vocalist into his microphone, with which he seemed to be dancing the tango. The
loudspeakers rattled in three-quarter time as Wanda started
to sweat through her taffeta. I felt it running down her back.
My own back was already so wet you could read the label on
my undershirt right through the dinner jacket.

Back and forth we trudged doggedly across the crowded
floor. Another Arthur Murray ad man, Schwartz was doing
exactly the same step with Clara Mae directly behind me. We
were all in a four-part lock step. As I hit the lower left-hand
footprint in my square—the one marked "Pause"—he was
hitting the upper right-hand corner of his square. Each time
we did that, our elbows dug smartly into each other's ribs.

The jungle fragrance of the orchid was getting riper by the

minute and the sweat, which had now saturated my jockey shorts, was pouring down my legs in rivulets. My soaked cummerbund turned two shades darker. So that she shouldn't notice, I pulled Wanda closer to me. Sighing, she hugged me back. Wanda was the vaguely chubby type of girl that was so popular at the time. Like Judy Garland, by whom she was heavily influenced, she strongly resembled a pink beach ball—but a *cute* beach ball, soft and rubbery. I felt bumpy things under her taffeta gown, with little hooks and knobs. Schwartz caught me a nasty shot in the rib cage just as I bent over to kiss her lightly on the bridge of her nose. It tasted salty. She looked up at me, her great liquid myopic eyes catching the reflection of the red and green lanterns overhead.

During a brief intermission, Schwartz and I carried paper cups dripping syrupy punch back to the girls, who had just spent some time in the ladies' room struggling unsuccessfully to repair the damage of the first half. As we were sipping, a face from my dim past floated by from out of nowhere— haughty, alabaster, green-eyed, dangerous.

"Hi, Daph," I muttered, spilling a little punch on my gleaming pumps, which had turned during the past hour into a pair of iron maidens.

"Oh, Howard." She spoke in the breathy, sexy way that such girls always have at proms. "I'd like you to meet Budge. Budge Cameron. He's at Princeton." A languid figure, probably born in a summer formal, loomed overhead.

"Budge, this is Howard."

"Hiya, fella." It was the first time I had heard the tight, nasal, swinging-jaw accent of the true Princetonian. It was not to be the last.

They were gone. Funny, I couldn't even remember actually dating her, I reflected, as the lights dimmed once again. We swung back into action. They opened with *Sleepy Lagoon*. 1-2-3-pause . . . 1-2-3-pause.

It was certain now. I had broken out in a raging rash. I felt it spreading like lava across my shoulder blades under the sweat. The horsehair, meanwhile, had penetrated my chest cavity and was working its way toward a vital organ. Trying manfully to ignore it, I stared fixedly at the tiny turquoise ribbon that held Wanda's golden ponytail in place. With troubles of her own, she looked with an equally level gaze at my maroon-wool carnation, which by this time had wilted into a clump of lint.

All of a sudden, it was all over. The band played *Good Night, Sweetheart* and we were out—into a driving rain. A violent cloudburst had begun just as we reached the door. My poor little car, the pride and joy of my life, was outside in the lot. With the top down.

None of us, of course, had an umbrella. We stood under the canopy as the roaring thunderstorm raged on. It wasn't going to stop.

"You guys stay here. I'll get the car," I said finally. After all, I was in charge.

Plunging into the downpour, I sloshed through the puddles and finally reached the Ford. She must have had at least a foot of water in her already. Hair streaming down over my eyes, soaked to the skin and muddied to the knees. I bailed it out with a coffee can from the trunk, slid behind the wheel and pressed the automatic-top lever. Smooth as silk, it began to lift—and stuck halfway up. As the rain poured down in sheets and the lightning flashed, I pounded on the relays, furiously switched the lever off and on. I could see the country club dimly through the downpour. Finally, the top groaned and flapped into place. I threw down the snaps, rolled up the windows and turned on the ignition; the battery was dead. The strain of hoisting that goddamn top had drained it dry. I yelled out the window at a passing car. It was Flick in his Chevy.

"GIMME A PUSH! MY BATTERY'S DEAD!"

This had never, to my knowledge, happened to Fred Astaire. And if it rained on Gene Kelly, he just sang.

Flick expertly swung his Chevy around and slammed into my trunk as I eased her into gear, and when she started to roll, the Ford shuddered and caught. Flick backed up and was gone, hollering out the window:

"SEE YOU AT THE ROOSTER."

Wanda, Schwartz and Clara Mae piled in on the damp, soggy seats and we took off. Do you know what happens to a maroon-wool carnation on a white-serge lapel in a heavy June downpour in the Midwest, where it rains not water but carbolic acid from the steel-mill fallout? I had a dark, wide, spreading maroon stripe that went all the way down to the bottom of my white coat. My French cuffs were covered with grease from fighting the top, and I had cracked a thumbnail, which was beginning to throb.

Undaunted, we slogged intrepidly through the rain toward the Red Rooster. Wedged against my side, Wanda looked up at me—oblivious to the elements—with luminous love eyes. She was truly an incurable romantic. Schwartz wisecracked in the back seat and Clara giggled from time to time. The savage tribal rite was nearing its final and most vicious phase.

We arrived at the Red Rooster, already crowded with other candidates for adulthood. A giant red neon rooster with a blue neon tail that flicked up and down in the rain set the tone for this glamorous establishment. An aura of undefined sin was always connected with the name Red Rooster. Sly winks, nudgings and adolescent cacklings about what purportedly went on at the Rooster made it the "in" spot for such a momentous revel. Its waiters were rumored really to be secret henchmen of the Mafia. But the only thing we knew for sure about the Rooster was that anybody on the far side of seven years old could procure any known drink without question.

The decor ran heavily to red-checkered-oilcloth table covers and plastic violets, and the musical background was provided by a legendary jukebox that stood a full seven feet high, featuring red and blue cascading waterfalls that gushed endlessly though its voluptuous façade. In full 200-watt operation, it could be *felt*, if not clearly heard, as far north as Gary and as far south as Kankakee. A triumph of American aesthetics.

Surging with anticipation, I guided Wanda through the uproarious throng of my peers. Schwartz and Clara Mae trailed behind, exchanging ribald remarks with the gang.

We occupied the only remaining table. Immediately, a beady-eyed waiter, hair glistening with Vaseline Hair Oil, sidled over and hovered like a vulture. Quickly distributing the famous Red Rooster Ala Carte Deluxe Menu, he stood back, smirking, and waited for us to impress our dates.

"Can I bring you anything to drink, gentlemen?" he said, heavily accenting the gentlemen.

My first impulse was to order my favorite drink of the period, a bottled chocolate concoction called Kayo, the Wonder Drink; but remembering that better things were expected of me on prom night, I said, in my deepest voice, "Uh . . . make mine . . . bourbon."

Schwartz grunted in admiration. Wanda ogled me with great, swimming, lovesick eyes. Bourbon was the only drink that I had actually heard of. My old man ordered it often down at the Bluebird Tavern. I had always wondered what it tasted like. I was soon to find out.

"How will you have it, sir?"

"Well, in a glass, I guess." I had failed to grasp the subtlety of his question, but the waiter snorted in appreciation of my humorous sally.

"Rocks?" he continued.

Rocks? I had heard about getting your rocks, but never in a restaurant. Oh, well, what the hell.

"Sure," I said. "Why not?"

All around me, the merrymaking throng was swinging into high gear. Carried away by it all, I added a phrase I had heard my old man use often: "And make it a triple." I had some vague idea that this was a brand or something.

"*A triple?* Yes, sir." His eyes snapped wide—in respect, I gathered. He knew he was in the presence of a serious drinker. The waiter turned his gaze in Schwartz' direction. "And you, sir?"

"Make it the same." Schwartz had never been a leader.

The die was cast. Pink ladies, at the waiter's suggestion, were ordered for the girls, and we then proceeded to scan the immense menu with feigned disinterest. When the waiter returned with our drinks, I ordered—for reasons that even today I am unable to explain—lamb chops, yellow turnips, mashed potatoes and gravy, a side dish of the famous Red Rooster Roquefort Italian Cole Slaw—and a strawberry short-cake. The others wisely decided to stick with their drinks.

Munching bread sticks, Wanda, Schwartz, Clara and I engaged in sophisticated postprom repartee. Moment by moment, I felt my strength and maturity, my dashing bonhomie, my clean-cut handsomeness enveloping my friends in its benevolent warmth. Schwartz, too, seemed to scintillate as never before. Clara giggled and Wanda sighed, overcome by the romance of it all. Even when Flick, sitting three tables away, clipped Schwartz behind the left ear with a poppyseed roll, our urbanity remained unruffled.

Before me reposed a sparkling tumbler of beautiful amber liquid, ice cubes bobbing merrily on its surface, a plastic swizzle stick sporting an enormous red rooster sticking out at a jaunty angle. Schwartz was similarly equipped. And the fluffy pink ladies looked lovely in the reflected light of the pulsating jukebox.

I had seen my old man deal with just this sort of situation. Raising my beaded glass, I looked around at my companions and said suavely, "Well, here's mud in yer eye." Clara giggled; Wanda sighed dreamily, now totally in love with this man of the world who sat across from her on this, our finest night.

"Yep," Schwartz parried wittily, hoisting his glass high and slopping a little bourbon on his pants as he did so.

Swiftly, I brought the bourbon to my lips, intending to down it in a single devil-may-care draught, the way Gary Cooper used to do in the Silver Dollar Saloon. I did, and Schwartz followed suit. Down it went—a screaming 90-proof rocket searing savagely down my gullet. For an instant, I sat stunned, unable to comprehend what had happened. Eyes watering copiously, I had a brief urge to sneeze, but my throat seemed to be paralyzed. Wanda and Clara Mae swam before my misted vision; and Schwartz seemed to have disappeared under the table. He popped up again—face beet-red, eyes bugging, jaw slack, tongue lolling.

"Isn't this romantic? Isn't this the most wonderful night in all our lives? I will forever treasure the memories of this wonderful night." From far off, echoing as from some subterranean tunnel, I heard Wanda speaking.

Deep down in the pit of my stomach, I felt crackling flames licking at my innards. I struggled to reply, to maintain my élan, my fabled *savoir-faire*. "Urk . . . urk. . . . yeah," I finally managed with superhuman effort.

Wanda swam hazily into focus. She was gazing across the table at me with adoring eyes.

"Another, gents?" The waiter was back, still smirking.

Schwartz nodded dumbly. I just sat there, afraid to move. An instant later, two more triple bourbons materialized in front of us.

Clara raised her pink lady high and said reverently, "Let's drink to the happiest night of our lives."

There was no turning back. Another screamer rocketed down the hatch. For an instant, it seemed as though this one wasn't going to be as lethal as the first, but the room suddenly tilted sideways. I felt torrents of cold sweat pouring from my forehead. Clinging to the edge of the table, I watched as Schwartz gagged across from me. Flick, I noticed, had just chugalugged his third rum and coke and was eating a cheeseburger with the works.

The conflagration deep inside me was now clearly out of control. My feet were smoking; my diaphragm heaved convulsively, jiggling my cummerbund; and Schwartz began to shrink, his face alternating between purple-red and chalk-white, his eyes black holes staring fixedly at the ketchup bottle. He sat stock-still. Wanda, meanwhile, cooed on ecstatically—but I was beyond understanding what she was saying. Faster and faster, in ever-widening circles, the room, the jukebox, the crowd swirled dizzily about me. In all the excitement of preparations for the prom, I realized that I hadn't eaten a single thing all day.

Out of the maelstrom, a plate mysteriously appeared before

me; paper-pantied lamb chops hissing in bubbling grease, piled yellow turnips, gray mashed potatoes awash in rich brown gravy. Maybe this would help, I thought incoherently. Grasping my knife and fork as firmly as I could, I poised to whack off a piece of meat. Suddenly, the landscape listed 45 degrees to starboard and the chop I was about to attack skidded off my plate—plowing a swath through the mashed potatoes—and right into the aisle.

Pretending not to notice, I addressed myself to the remaining chop, which slid around, eluding my grasp, until I managed to skewer it with my fork. Hacking off a chunk, I jammed it fiercely mouthward, missing my target completely. Still impaled on my fork, the chop slithered over my cheekbone, spraying gravy as it went, all over my white lapels. On the next try, I had better luck, and finally I managed to get the whole chop down.

To my surprise, I didn't feel any better. Maybe the turnips will help, I thought. Lowering my head to within an inch of the plate to prevent embarrassing mishaps, I shoveled them in—but the flames within only fanned higher and higher. I tried the potatoes and gravy. My legs began to turn cold. I wolfed down the Red Rooster Roquefort Italian Cole Slaw. My stomach began to rise like a helium balloon, bobbing slowly up the alimentary canal.

My nose low over the heaping dish of strawberry shortcake, piled high with whipped cream and running with juice, I knew at last for a dead certainty what I had to do before it happened right here in front of everybody. I struggled to my feet. A strange rubbery numbness had struck my extremities. I tottered from chair to chair, grasping for the wall. There was a buzzing in my ears.

Twenty seconds later, I was on my knees, gripping the bowl of the john like a life preserver in pitching seas. Schwartz, imitating me as usual, lay almost prostrate on the tiles beside me, his body racked with heaving sobs. Lamb chops, bourbon, turnips, mashed potatoes, cole slaw—all of it came rushing out of me in a great roaring torrent—out of my mouth, my nose, my ears, my very soul. Then Schwartz opened up, and we took turns retching and shuddering. A head thrust itself between us directly into the pot. It was Flick moaning wretchedly. Up came the cheeseburger, the rum and Cokes, pretzels, potato chips, punch, gumdrops, a corned-beef sandwich, a fingernail or two—everything he'd eaten for the last week. For long minutes, the three of us lay there limp and quivering, smelling to high heaven, too weak to get up. It was the absolute high point of the junior prom; the rest was anticlimax.

Finally, we returned to the table, ashen-faced and shaking. Schwartz, his coat stained and rumpled, sat Zombie-like across from me. The girls didn't say much. Pink ladies just aren't straight bourbon.

But our little group played the scene out bravely to the end. My dinner jacket was now even more redolent and disreputable than when I'd first seen it on the hanger at Al's. And my bow tie, which had hung for a while by one clip, had somehow disappeared completely, perhaps flushed into eternity with all the rest. But as time wore on, my hearing and eyesight began slowly to return; my legs began to lose their rubberiness and the room slowly resumed its even keel—at least even enough to consider getting up and leaving. The waiter seemed to know. He returned as if on cue, bearing a slip of paper.

"The damages, gentlemen."

Taking the old man's $20 out of my wallet, I handed it to him with as much of a flourish as I could muster. There wouldn't have been any point in looking over the check; I wouldn't have been able to read it, anyway. In one last attempt to recoup my cosmopolitan image, I said offhandedly, "Keep the change." Wanda beamed in unconcealed ecstasy.

The drive home in the damp car was not quite the same as the one that had begun the evening so many weeks earlier. Our rapidly fermenting coats made the enclosed air rich and gamy, and Schwartz, who had stopped belching, sat with head pulled low between his shoulder blades, staring straight ahead. Only the girls preserved the joyousness of the occasion. Women always survive.

In a daze, I dropped off Schwartz and Clara Mae and drove

WANDA HICKEY'S NIGHT OF GOLDEN MEMORIES

in silence toward Wanda's home, the faint light of dawn beginning to show in the east.

We stood on her porch for the last ritual encounter. A chill dawn wind rustled the lilac bushes.

"This was the most wonderful, wonderful night of my whole life. I always dreamed the prom would be like this," breathed Wanda, gazing passionately up into my watering eyes.

"Me, too," was all I could manage.

I knew what was expected of me now. Her eyes closed dreamily. Swaying slightly, I leaned forward—and the faint odor of sauerkraut from her parted lips coiled slowly up to my nostrils. This was not in the script. I knew I had better get off that porch fast, or else. Backpedaling desperately and down the stairs, I blurted, "Bye!" and—fighting down my rising gorge—clamped my mouth tight, leaped into the Ford, burned rubber and tore off into the dawn. Two blocks away, I squealed to a stop alongside a vacant lot containing only a huge Sherwin-Williams paint sign. WE COVER THE WORLD, it aptly read. In the blessed darkness behind the sign, concealed from prying eyes, I completed the final rite of the ceremony.

The sun was just rising as I swung the car up the driveway and eased myself quietly into the kitchen. The old man, who was going fishing that morning, sat at the enamel table sipping black coffee. He looked up as I came in. I was in no mood for idle chatter.

"You look like you had a hell of a prom," was all he said.

"I sure did."

The yellow kitchen light glared harshly on my muddy pants, my maroon-streaked, vomit-stained white coat, my cracked fingernail, my greasy shirt.

"You want anything to eat?" he asked sardonically.

At the word "eat," my stomach heaved convulsively. I shook my head numbly.

"That's what I thought," he said. "Get some sleep. You'll feel better in a couple of days, when your head stops banging."

He went back to reading his paper. I staggered into my bed-room, dropping bits of clothing as I went. My soggy Holly-wood paisley cummerbund, the veteran of another gala night, was flung beneath my dresser as I toppled into bed. My brother muttered in his sleep across the room. He was still a kid. But his time would come.

Al Sarrantonio, writer, editor and House Dad, is the author of the novels *The Worms, Campbell Wood, Totentanz* and the recently published *The Boy with Penny Eyes.* His forty short stories have appeared in such magazines as *Heavy Metal* and *Isaac Asimov's Science Fiction Magazine,* as well as in such anthologies as *Laughing Space, Great Ghost Stories* and *The Year's Best Horror Stories.* He is book reviewer for *Night Cry* magazine and is currently completing a mystery novel, *Cold Night.* Two horror novels, *Moonbane* and *House Haunted,* will be published in 1988. He lives in Putnam Valley, New York, with his wife and two sons.